OUT OF RUSHMORE'S SHADOW

THE LUIGI DEL BIANCO STORY

Praise for *Out of Rushmore's Shadow*

"*Out of Rushmore's Shadow* is an eye-opening and amazing story about Luigi Del Bianco, the true chisel-genius behind the carving of Mount Rushmore. This fascinating book turns orthodox history on its head. From now on I will look at the Black Hills of South Dakota with Del Bianco in mind. Highly recommended!"

— DOUGLAS BRINKLEY
Author of *Rightful Heritage: Franklin D. Roosevelt and the Land of America* and Professor of History at Rice University.

"With all of Italy's richness in culture and craftsmanship, Luigi Del Bianco serves as a prime example of what Italians have contributed to our great nation."

— DANIEL J. LONGO
National President,
Order Sons of Italy in America®

"Growing up, I always thought Gutzon Borglum, with help in later years from his son, Lincoln, were solely responsible for the creation of Mount Rushmore. Then I met Lou Del Bianco. And only AFTER pouring through pages upon pages of his undeniable evidence, mostly written in Borglum's hand, did I learn the critical and historic role Luigi Del Bianco played as Chief Carver. *Out of Rushmore's Shadow* is a compelling history that Lou Del Bianco was meant to write; a meticulous gathering of facts that moved the National Park Service to do the right thing."

— T. SEAN HERBERT
Executive Producer,
UnXpected Development

OUT OF RUSHMORE'S SHADOW

THE LUIGI DEL BIANCO STORY

An Italian Immigrant's Unsung Role as Chief Carver

LOU DEL BIANCO

NICHE CONTENT PRESS | NEW JERSEY

Out of Rushmore's Shadow: The Luigi Del Bianco Story

Published by Niche Content Press

Picture credits: All photos, documents, letters, telegrams or postcards in this book are either public domain, from the Library of Congress or the Del Bianco Family Collection, unless otherwise indicated. Some images have been cropped or adjusted for printing purposes, but have not been changed from the originals.

Image quality varies greatly due to the age and quality of the originals. Some will print better than others, and some may look great in the e-book but not as good in print. All were important in telling the story of Luigi Del Bianco and were therefore included.

Cover and Book Design by James Woosley (FreeAgentPress.com)

Edited by Dolores Alfieri

Editorial Consultant: Camille Linen (artofenglish.net)

To contact Lou Del Bianco:
www.luigimountrushmore.com
www.findlou.com

First printed in September 2017.

ISBN: 978-0-9989987-2-5 (paperback)
ISBN: 978-0-9989987-3-2 (e-book)
ISBN: 978-0-9989987-4-9 (hardcover)

VID: 20181125

I would like to dedicate this book to all those who remain in the shadows....

"America appreciates the many gifts you bring to its altars. You have brought your music, your poetry, your art, your culture ... All of these things will become part of America. You have also brought hands with which to work, minds with which to conceive, hearts filled with hope."

— Wolfe Cribari, 1941

"Immigrants, we get the job done."

— Lin Manuel Miranda, Hamilton, 2015

Contents

FOREWORD

BY ANTHONY FASANO

IMAGINE YOU ARE IN second grade and you find a pamphlet about the iconic Mount Rushmore National Memorial. You ask your mother what the pamphlet is about, and she explains that it was a special project that your grandfather worked on. She explains that he was the Chief Carver of the memorial.

You are excited as can be to share this amazing news with everyone you know, especially your fellow second-grade classmates. However, soon after, you start to read books about Mount Rushmore and do further research, and you don't find anything about your grandfather. It's like he wasn't even there.

What would you do next?

Well, Lou Del Bianco made it his life's mission to get his grandfather the credit he deserved for his critical role in shaping the face of America through his role as Chief Carver of Mount Rushmore.

I serve as the host of The Italian American Podcast and have authored my own book, *Forty Days in Italy Con La Mia Famiglia*, both of which are aimed at helping Italian Americans discover their family roots; so when I met Lou, there was an instant bond.

My co-host had told me that we were going to interview a gentleman whose grandfather was one of the carvers of Mount Rushmore. It sounded interesting, but once we spoke to Lou, I knew that this was a very special story that held significant meaning for all Americans.

The United States of America is a country of immigrants. All of our ancestors, just like Luigi Del Bianco, came from somewhere else. They came to the United States to create better, happier lives for themselves, and most importantly for their families.

While many of these immigrants achieved their goals and played very important roles in the development of the United States, like Luigi who led the carving of one of our most storied monuments, many of them were not given the credit they were due. And what's even worse is that their families either don't know about their accomplishments, or they have an idea, but neither the desire nor time to dig deeper into their past. In my opinion, this is what makes Lou Del Bianco's story so powerful and so important.

Today in America, immigrants are often looked down upon and protested against, yet many Americans often forget that without them, without people like Luigi Del Bianco who sacrificed so much to contribute to the building of our country, it wouldn't be what it is today. Furthermore, without people like Lou Del Bianco, Americans wouldn't understand where they came from.

Lou dedicated a good portion of more than 25 years of his life trying to get his grandfather the credit he truly deserved, and in the process, he discovered so much about his family roots and about the roots of our country. Lou's even tied his career as a performer into his search for the truth, as one of his performances casts himself as his Grandfather Luigi Del Bianco in an effort to bring his grandfather's story, the immigrant story, to Americans young and old. This is truly inspiring.

In the pages ahead, Lou takes you on his amazing roller coaster ride over the last 40-plus years since he first found that pamphlet displaying his grandfather's work.

You're going to think that this is a fictional story, even the script of a thrilling movie, but it's not. This is a true story, and one that our country needs told.

Immigrants did shape the United States of America, and in Luigi Del Bianco's case, he shaped the face of one of our most important symbols.

I hope you enjoy Lou's story as much as I did, and I hope it inspires you to understand where you came from and the impact that your family had on our great nation.

Let the journey begin....

Anthony Fasano
Co-Host of The Italian American Podcast
Author of *Forty Days in Italy Con La Mia Famiglia*

PART I:

Discovering Luigi is Missing

CHAPTER ONE:

"I AM LUIGI, YOU ARE LUIGI"

WHEN I WAS 5 years old, I used to visit my grandfather every Sunday. As I walked through the door of his second-story apartment, the first thing I saw was a strong, handsome, stone-face carved in white marble. I thought it was the most beautiful thing I had ever seen.

A self portrait by Luigi Del Bianco.

After staring at that youthful bust, I remember my mother leading me to a bedroom where an old man sat on the edge of his bed, awaiting my arrival. As the only male grandchild in the family, and my Italian Grandfather's namesake, my position was firmly established. I'd edge shyly toward the bed as long, sinewy arms with bony fingers stretched out, beckoning me to come closer.

"Luigi, give your grandpa a hug."

Before he pulled me to his embrace, I glanced quickly at his face. It was craggy and rough-hewn with the impressive features of a Sioux Indian chief. In spite of my shyness, in spite of my hesitation, I welcomed that hug. It felt like home, filled with that thing we all need: unconditional love.

Grandpa and I two years before he passed away.

On certain Sundays, I'd help my grandfather out of his bed. He would take me by the hand and lead me back to the front entrance of the apartment to visit his marble bust.

"I make this," my grandpa would say proudly as his weak, raspy voice labored to push the words out. Then he would take my 5-year-old fingers and make them trace that Roman profile. Other times, I stood on a chair and placed my grandfather's fedora on his own carved head.

Then my grandfather would bend down, take me by the shoulders and say, "I am Luigi...you are Luigi."

Call it what you like: a bond, a connection. It was surely strengthened during those Sunday morning visits. Even though my grandpa died when I was 6, I can still feel that hug and those large hands on my tiny shoulders.

Two years later, I am rummaging around in a kitchen junk drawer, and I find an old, yellowed booklet.

Mount Rushmore
NATIONAL MEMORIAL
SECOND BOOK

Photographs of the Lead Tablet buried in the hills at Fort Pierre, on the west bank of the Missouri River, by Verendrye, 1743, as reported to France on his return. Discovered February 16, 1913. Now in the Historical Museum, Pierre, South Dakota

PUBLISHED BY THE
COMMITTEE ON DESIGN AND PUBLICITY
MOUNT RUSHMORE NATIONAL MEMORIAL
COMMISSION

COPYRIGHT 1931
PRINTED IN THE U. S. A.

Mount Rushmore National Memorial Booklet, circa 1930.

"Ma, what's this?"

My mother tells me that Grandpa Del Bianco was the Chief Carver on Mount Rushmore, the man who carved Lincoln's eyes. What? Did I hear that right? I couldn't believe it. Then, all at once, the hug, the bust, those hands that I hadn't felt on my shoulders since Grandpa's passing came rushing through my senses in the most visceral way.

An excitement came over me that I still feel today.

"Can I show this to my class tomorrow?"

As the very quiet brother of six gregarious sisters, this was unusual behavior for me. It was as if my grandpa's spirit channeled through that booklet, giving me a confidence I never knew I had. I immediately ran to my room, lay on my bed and flipped through every page looking for my grandpa, hoping to find his image in one of those old photographs.

He wasn't there.

I can still recall standing in front of my second-grade class at Park Avenue School, clutching that booklet and proudly proclaiming, "I wanna tell you about my grandpa. My grandpa, Luigi Del Bianco, was the Chief Carver on Mount Rushmore..."

Still, there was a sense of frustration that I couldn't *see* him working on that mountain, carving those giant faces. When I got home, I ran back to my room and gave it another try; my little fingers followed the faces of the workers. *I think I see him there! No, he's too short. He's too skinny. Wait, that looks like the hat he used to wear! Nope, not Grandpa.*

In the end, I couldn't find him. And I've been looking for him ever since.

As time went by, my interest and enthusiasm for my grandpa was tempered by GI-Joes, clubhouses, snowmen and the usual childhood distractions. That show-and-tell moment from second grade foreshadowed my great desire to express myself in front of an audience. High school became an opportunity to fulfill a lifelong ambition to perform. Little did I know I would someday use my talent for the stage to bring my grandpa back to life. But I am getting ahead of myself!

CHAPTER TWO:

UNCLE AND "NEFOO"

WHAT CAN I SAY about my Uncle Caesar? He was a character. Everyone in town knew him. He was colorful, funny and difficult. Still, he was my uncle. As much as I was put off by his sometimes-blunt behavior, I was also drawn to his natural charisma and unique views on life. Caesar had many opinions, and he stuck to those opinions.

You don't understand was his slogan. Many times, when he felt his point wasn't understood, his diatribe escalated to either insult or accusation. One friend told me his wife literally kicked Caesar out of the house after a heated argument about the role women should play in society. And then there was the time, while eating at a restaurant, Caesar got into a disagreement with the owner about the correct spelling of the establishment's name. "C-a-e-s-a-r," not "C-e-a-s-e-r." It started with *You don't understand* and ended with the owner screaming, *Out!* Caesar was escorted by a burly bartender and told never to come again. To be fair to Caesar, he battled manic depression; something which, as I discuss in the narrative to come, would not only impact his life, but also, at times, our search for Luigi.

Caesar wrote the book on button pushing; he could provoke anger in the calmest individual. I can recall pulling my car over many times and showing Caesar the sidewalk. Whenever that happened, the guilty little boy would appear, full of contrition and anxiety from his impending "punishment." "No, no, no! He would shout, begging and pleading to stay in the car. My anger would melt. He always got to me. He got to his friends, too. You can only stay mad at Caesar for so long. Every time he pushed you away, he found a way to get you back. It could be with a funny story or a quirky philosophical observance. Most of all, he would thank you time and again for helping with his daily helplessness or temporarily calming one of his many neuroses.

When I became an adult, I got closer to my uncle. Much closer than when I was a kid. We had a lot in common. We both loved to sing and act and even performed on stage together in a couple of local productions. We also loved old movies and had many a discussion about those character actors you don't see anymore. He turned me onto Frank Sinatra. I will always be grateful to him for that. But it was Christmas Day in 1986 when we had our first discussion on a subject that would bond us more than any of our other common interests. It was about his father and Mount Rushmore. He told me about a very important book he had read. This book would reignite my fascination with my grandpa and take the two of us on a journey: to find Luigi.

CHAPTER THREE:

How Do You Not Mention Luigi?

In 1985, the most definitive book on Mount Rushmore was published. It was titled, *The Carving of Mount Rushmore* by Rex Alan Smith. No book since has told the story as well (or so we thought). On Christmas Day, 1986, after a marvelous meal of chicken parmigiana, the family sat down to chat. I can still see Caesar yelling at the air, flailing his arms and shouting, "The goddamn book doesn't mention my father once! That's like talking about the Yankees and not mentioning DiMaggio!"

Understand, I was at a point in my life, at the age of 23, where my priorities were the usual goals for a young adult: independence from family and carving out a career. But hearing my uncle speak with such emotion brought me back to that great curiosity about my grandfather and our special connection. I was immediately transported back in time to second grade, poring over that booklet, looking for Luigi and never finding him. Now I'd discovered that his own son had been looking for him, too. My uncle's passion reawakened my own.

My sisters listened intently as I shared my own childhood memories, and it surprised me that I was telling Caesar and my family these stories for the first time. It didn't matter. Caesar got it. We bonded that Christmas, both angered and appalled that the Chief Carver, the right-hand man of Mount Rushmore's designer Gutzon Borglum, had not been mentioned once in the most definitive book on the subject. We both vowed to find Luigi once and for all.

Before we did anything, we had to ask ourselves: If we couldn't find Luigi in such an important book, where was he hiding? More importantly, who was hiding him? I was learning in my young adulthood that written history does not always tell the whole story. So where was Luigi's story?

Caesar had already acquired some other books about Mount Rushmore to see if there was a pattern. Fortunately, there were some bright spots. In his book, *Mount Rushmore*, Gilbert Fite mentioned Luigi only once, but what he wrote carried weight:

> *"L. Del Bianco, a skilled carver, was employed. Bianco was one of the most competent men ever to work on the mountain."*

Judith St. George, in her book, *The Mount Rushmore Story*, wrote how Luigi repaired a dangerous crack in Jefferson's lip and also wrote of his importance as a carver:

> *"The crack now ran through Jefferson's right eye, past his nose and upper lip, and through the middle of his chin. Unlike the nose, the face had the bulk of the mountain behind it, so after the crack was sealed with a mixture of equal parts granite dust and white lead with enough linseed oil to make a paste there would be no chance of its breaking off. Luigi Del Bianco, one of the best stonecutters Rushmore ever had, patched the crack in Jefferson's lip with a foot-deep piece of granite held in place by pins—the only patch on the whole sculpture, and one that is hard to detect even close up...*
>
> *"Under pressure, Borglum reluctantly turned his attention back to the heads, personally taking charge of the work on Roosevelt and the final finishing on Washington and Jefferson. At least he now had enough funds to hire skilled carvers, a lack he had been bemoaning for years. But to his surprise, with the exception of Luigi Del Bianco, few of the carvers worked out. By the time a carver was highly skilled, he had usually reached middle age, and the prospect of working in a harness or a swinging cage on the windy mountain held so little appeal that if any of them even started, they soon quit. Even Del Bianco always worked in a cage, refusing from the start ever to be lowered over the mountain in a harness."*

Finally, Lincoln Borglum [Gutzon's son] acknowledged Luigi as a skilled carver in his book, *Mount Rushmore: The Story Behind the Scenery*:

> *"Among the skilled carvers who worked on the project were three who studied under my father in the East—Luigi Del Bianco, William S. Tallman and Hugo Villa—and Joseph Bruner, an experienced stonecutter from Indiana."*

My uncle and I were certainly encouraged by what we found. Still, there were other authors, like Rex Alan Smith, who didn't mention Luigi at all: Howard and Audrey Karl Shaff's, *Six Wars at a Time*; John Taliaferro's, *Great White Fathers*; and Mary Borglum's, *Give the Man Room*.

In addition to reading the Rushmore books, Caesar also started writing to Lincoln Borglum in May of 1985. Lincoln was Gutzon's loyal son who worked alongside his dad during the entire project from 1927 to 1941. Lincoln eventually took over the project when his father became too ill to continue. Here is Caesar and Lincoln's correspondence:

Mr. Caesar DelBianco
108 South Regent Street
Port Chester, New York 10573
May 15, 1985

Dear Mr. Borglum;

I am writing this letter seeking information about my father, Luigi DelBianco, who you know worked on Mt. Rushmore from 1933 to 1941. I have some questions to ask you and would appreciate it if you could give me some answers. If you don't know the information that I'm seeking, maybe you could refer me to other sources for the answers.

These are the questions:

(a) Was my father involved in the carving of all faces?

(b) You were chief pointer with a crew of 3 carvers. Was my father one of them?

(c) Were there any film documentaries made of Mt. Rushmore? Where can they be secured?

(d) Was my father ever chief carver or pointer on Mt. Rushmore? If yes, what did it entail?

(e) Where can I purchase your book, "Unfinished Dreams."

(f) How many men worked on Mt. Rushmore? How many carvers and drillers, engineers, etc., etc.

(g) Is there a book published of just photos of the men working on the mountain?

I would like to add on a personal note I have many childhood memories of my father working on Mt. Rushmore. The family was out there the summer of 1935. I'm pretty sure we lived in Keystone. I remember the general store, the mines, the school, and of course, the mountain. I'm sure my father introduced our family to your family. My father took me along to North Stamford once to your home and I remember your mother.

I hope this letter finds you in good health and am anxiously awaiting your reply.

Sincerely yours,

Caesar Del Bianco

Lincoln Borglum

P.O. Box 908 La Feria, Texas 78559 512-423-1888

Dear Mr.Bianco:

I am sorry about the long delay in this letter but my wife has just passed away from cancer and we have been in hospitals for months.

I will try and answer your questions in the order you have written them.

Yes

No

There have been some made and I would suggest that you contact the Superintendent of Rushmore at Keystone,he should know.

Your father was chief carver and it mainly entailed that he wasthe most skilled stone carver,when he had that title.

At the Rushmore-Borglum Museum, in Keystone South Dakota.

An average of about thirty,with about drillers and the rest pointers,call boys,blacksmiths hoist people ,mechanics.

I think you can get a book of photos from the Keystone place.

Sorry it has taken so long to answer your letter.

Sincerely

Lincoln Borglum

Sept.16

You can see from Caesar's first question, "Was my father involved in the carving of all the faces?" that Lincoln answered, "Yes." Lincoln also made it clear that Luigi was the most skilled carver on the work: Two big pluses here from a very reliable source.

Caesar also wrote to Superintendent James C. Riggs at Mount Rushmore to see what kind of information he had on Luigi. I couldn't find Caesar's letter, but here is Mr. Riggs response below:

United States Department of the Interior
NATIONAL PARK SERVICE
MOUNT RUSHMORE NATIONAL MEMORIAL
KEYSTONE, SOUTH DAKOTA 57751

IN REPLY REFER TO:

H-14

January 30, 1986

Mr. Caesar Del Bianco
108 South Regent Street
Port Chester, New York 10573

Dear Mr. Del Bianco:

Thank you for your letter concerning information about your father Luigi Del Bianco, Chief Carver at Mount Rushmore National Memorial. Gilbert Fite in his book Mount Rushmore gives high praise to your father's work on Mount Rushmore. He was a talented man of whom you must be very proud.

In response to your list of questions, some research and records show the following information:

1. Approximately 400 men worked on Mount Rushmore from 1927 through 1941. The information we have on each employee is limited. No records of actual work exist except for payment records and daily logs. We are currently preparing a complete list, but need more research. Most of the men skipped around and were not assigned to the same job each year. Many only worked a few months, a year, or two years and then left.

2. Daily logs did exist throughout the project. The National Park Service assumed control in 1936 and until that time records are limited. Enclosed are copies of two daily logs referring to your father—one dated 1933 and the other 1936.

3. Information related to actual positions assigned to people is again limited. Workmen often did many of the jobs depending on amount of workers the project could afford at the time. Included is a sample list of workers employed in November 1935; their salaries and positions.

4. Mount Rushmore had many film documentaries completed during the construction. Most notable is one narrated by Lowell Thomas. Unfortunately, the documentaries are not available except through a visit to Mount Rushmore.

Save Energy and You Serve America!

5. Enclosed is a bibliography available on Mount Rushmore. Borglum's Unfinished Dream, Mount Rushmore is available at Rushmore-Borglum Story in Keystone (closed in winter) or our concessioner, Mountain Co., Inc., Keystone, South Dakota 57751. In reference to question Number 6, an excellent book of construction photos is Stan Cohen's book Borglum's Mountain, also available from the Mountain Company.

6. Refer to question Number 5.

7. Gilbert Fite refers to your father being employed first in 1933 as Chief Carver. Our records show the following information:

1933 - Chief Carver; worked on Washington and Jefferson figures.

1934 - No record of Mr. Del Bianco working at Mount Rushmore.

1935 - Chief Carver; salary raised to $1.50 per hour. (See enclosed letter approving payroll changes)

1936 - Chief Carver; finishing work on Washington figure. (No details)

1937 - Chief Carver; finishing work on Washington and Jefferson figures. (No details)

Our records are not complete after 1937. However, our information does not show your father working on Mount Rushmore after 1937.

We hope this will provide you some information previously not known about your father's work on Mount Rushmore. Hopefully in the near future our records on all the workers will be more complete. Time requirements on our part and poor record keeping early in the project have limited us from researching much of this information.

If you have other information concerning your father's work on Mount Rushmore or a photograph you could spare for our files; they would be appreciated. For further information please contact Chief of Interpretation Jim Popovich, (605) 574-2523.

Sincerely,

James C. Riggs
Acting Superintendent

Enclosures

Other than daily logs, it appeared the records from Rushmore in 1986 were very limited. At this point, according to Riggs, Luigi was there working for four years. After 1937, Rushmore had no record of him. At the end of the letter, Mr. Riggs even asks Caesar if he has any documents he can share. Not a good sign. I guess it was up to Caesar and me to take the bull by the horns and start our own investigative research. At the least, we had to fill in the years 1938 to 1941. Was Grandpa there?

Caesar was very excited to show me these letters. When I asked if I could borrow them to make copies, his eyes flashed.

"No, no. I don't want these letters to fall into the wrong hands. I don't want anyone to steal my ideas."

What? I didn't get it. After pleading with Caesar to trust me, I hit a brick wall. Why wouldn't he allow me this? Why was he being so protective of the letters where I was concerned? Well, Caesar was Caesar, and I had to accept it.

My uncle and I had to work as a team, so I backed off. We both concluded that we were still left with more questions than answers. We knew Luigi was a skilled carver and that he also held the title of Chief Carver. Why, then, did some authors mention him while others didn't? Why was it so hard to get any records of Luigi at the mountain? Caesar was starting to worry that maybe his father wasn't as important as he thought.

"You know, my old man used to like to tell stories and exaggerate," he would say, agonizing over many a cup of coffee that maybe his father inflated his contribution to the iconic sculpture. Even though the people at Rushmore were apparently telling us all they knew, there was only one thing left to do. We would have to be more aggressive and go directly to the source.

CHAPTER FOUR:

YOU'RE GONNA HAVE TO GO WITHOUT ME

MY UNCLE CAESAR HAD many phobias: dogs, electricity, thunder and lightning, to name a few. He had a stack of books and a chair in his closet to occupy himself whenever it thundered. Caesar's friends knew this and loved to call him on the phone during the height of a storm. I used to imagine his empty apartment replete with thunder and lightning, the phone ringing and a disembodied voice shouting, *I know that's you, Nicky Ply, ya bastard!*

The fear that topped my uncle's list? That's an easy one—flying. He had never been on a plane, and just the thought of getting on one was too much for him to bear.

"You're gonna have to go without me," he said, his face lined with regret and frustration.

"What about a train?" I suggested, hoping he would be open to the idea.

"Let me think about it," was his response.

Now, whenever my uncle said that, he would give himself *way* too much time to mull and ponder all the possible outcomes. In the end, he would come back with a *no*. My feelings were mixed; disappointed that he couldn't share the experience with me, yet relieved that I would not have to deal with his high-maintenance personality.

When I told my wife Camille that I wanted to make a pilgrimage to Mount Rushmore, she suggested we combine it with an overall trip out West. Along with her mom, we could fly to Bozeman, Montana to visit her relatives, and then rent a car and drive east to the Black Hills. Camille and I love traveling together, and I could also tell she was curious about my grandfather. She wanted to support me in my quest to find him. We flew out West in August 1988.

I loved Montana and really enjoyed connecting with Camille's relatives. Her mother, Carola, also from New York, had spent many summers in Bozeman as a child and young adult. Carola's Grandfather, Julius Lehrkind, was a famous local brewer in Bozeman and some of his descendants were still living. The Lehrkind mansion is now a bed and breakfast, and the owners were thrilled to meet someone who actually lived there throughout the early part of the 20th century. I remember Carola embracing her cousin, "Harm," with misty eyes, knowing this might be the last time she would see him. Even though I wouldn't be visiting actual family in South Dakota, I related to Camille and her mom reuniting with loved ones from their family tree. I was also, yet in a different form, on a quest to reunite with family.

Camille and I saw Carola off as she boarded the plane back to New York. Then we rented a car and drove for several days east toward the Black Hills, stopping over in different towns along the way. For two New Yorkers, the West was another planet. Beautiful, wide open and sparsely populated. Camille was driving, so I took out my little tape recorder and narrated our trip. *Hey, check out the welcome sign for this little town. Population 75…75?*

When I was a very shy and anti-social adolescent, I started an audio diary called "Manji Manjos." Please don't ask me where I got the name. As John Lennon said, "It came to me in a dream." I would talk about my daily activities and imagined a studio audience captivated by my every word. *Hi, it's time for another Manji Manjo. At the tone the time will be…beep! Six o'clock.* I guess it was a way for me to discover my own voice. When Camille and I started traveling, I decided to bring my little gray tape recorder and document our trips. Poor Camille. Who wants to be interviewed at the end of a long day, or when you first wake up? What a patient woman.

When we crossed the border into South Dakota, we immediately started seeing signs. Not for Mount Rushmore, but for its ingenious designer, Gutzon Borglum. "Gutzon Borglum: The Rushmore Story" was plastered on the side of what looked like a big abandoned train car sitting off the side of the highway. Five miles later, we'd see the same thing, and then again five miles later, all the way across the state. Apparently, a millionaire philanthropist opened up a Gutzon Borglum museum in the town called Keystone right next to the mountain. He must have purchased a ton of old train cars to advertise the museum all across South Dakota, which is by no means a small state. At least we knew we were going in the right direction! The problem was, every time we saw another sign, it made us feel we were almost there. This was in the days before GPS, so we had no real sense of how many miles or minutes away we were from Mount Rushmore.

I recorded myself anticipating that each next turn up the road would be the one to reveal those four faces.

Oh, there it is! I think I see it! Nope, not it.

This went on for about an hour.

Ah! I think I see it! Noooo... There it is, there it is... Aw, come on!

I was screaming into the tape recorder. When I turned to Camille and noticed that familiar smirk on her face, I laughed. She knew me so well.

Then all of a sudden, there it was. Even though the faces were in the distance and partially obscured by trees, their majesty was undeniable. As long as I could remember, I had heard about Rushmore and my grandfather. I had seen the image over and over again in photographs and on film. Mount Rushmore had become an iconic and legendary part of my family heritage, part of who I was. Now I was finally face to face with it. I immediately imagined my grandfather high on a scaffold, waving to me from a distance, beckoning me to get closer, to learn more, to discover the story. His story. My God, what Caesar was missing.

Camille was driving, so she couldn't get the full effect, but I could tell she was impressed. We made our way into Keystone and settled in the Rushmore Manor Inn. I lay on the bed, took out my little tape recorder and pushed record. I had to make sure I kept my listening audience informed. *Hi, it's time for another Manji Manjo. At the tone, the time is...beep!* Camille was putting her clothes away. She loves me, quirks and all.

After exhaustingly long hours in our rented car, we took a stroll around Keystone to stretch our legs. The town looked like a more modern version of the westerns I watched as a kid. I loved the feel of it. We were definitely not in New York. We decided our first stop would be "The Borglum Story," the museum we saw advertised on the way to the mountain. I was certainly interested in Borglum by virtue of his connection to my grandfather, but as we wandered through the museum, with every corner I turned, my eyes strained to find a photo or even a mention of Luigi. Instinctually, whenever I came in contact with anything Rushmore related, I started looking for Grandpa. Again and again, he wasn't there. The only connection I could make was finding the original bust of Jesus Christ that Borglum had my grandfather make a marble copy of. The copy was sitting in my uncle's apartment. Well, that's something.

Borglum's talent was undeniable. I would come to learn that my grandfather worshipped the ground he walked on. Borglum's bust of Lincoln, the one that sits in the rotunda in Washington, DC, is a true testament to his genius. My uncle was convinced it was the best portrait of our 16th president because it truly captured the essence of the man. I couldn't take my eyes off the original in that little Borglum museum. Still, where was Grandpa?

At the end of the tour, I noticed a kindly old gentleman wearing a name badge and talking to some tourists. Someone was saying that he worked on Rushmore. I walked over and introduced myself. The gentleman was Ed Hayes, and he was employed on the mountain from 1932 to 1941 when the sculpture was considered finished. Ed operated the lift that transported equipment across a cable to the mountain. He remembered my grandfather, although I could see in his eyes that he was failing a little; what did he remember, and how accurately? Ed was so pleased to talk to me. I told him why I was there and that I was doing research. I asked if he could help me get in touch with other people who worked on the faces. Ed told me he would get me the names and addresses of other workers who were still living. What a nice guy. What a find. I told Ed I would come back to the museum tomorrow so he would have time to get me the information.

CHAPTER FIVE:

IT LOOKS WAY BIGGER ON TV!

THE NEXT DAY WAS our chance to go to Rushmore itself and get a closer view of the four faces. The entranceway to the mountain is a promenade lined by flags that take you to the visitor's center and then to the main observation deck. Camille and I were immediately struck by the enormous pile of rubble at the base of the sculpture. This was obviously the tons and tons of stone that were blasted and carved off the mountain. For some ridiculous reason, it was never carted away. I mean, I knew the rubble was there, but to see it in reality was another thing. Imagine the base of the Statue of Liberty surrounded by large scraps of copper sheeting. It made no sense.

After we went through the visitor's center, we reached the main observation deck. We stood at the edge and looked up at the faces. Silence. More silence. And a little more. I looked at Camille.

"I don't know. From this vantage point, doesn't it look a little...small?"

Camille's eyes widened. "I was thinking the same thing."

For one thing, the faces didn't fill the panorama the way I thought they would. They seemed much smaller at the peak of a 500-foot mountain that lowers into an obnoxious pile of rubble. Then it hit me. Throughout my whole life, I have seen images of the mountain in neatly cropped close-ups, without the rest of the mountain and rubble. The four faces always seemed *huge* to me. Then again, if my grandfather came back to life, I would probably expect to meet a seven-foot giant. The images in my mind, especially as a child, were so iconic, so mythic. Of course, the actual faces could never compete with that. What's more, the other tourists were blown away and vocal about it. I decided to get away and look at them later with fresh eyes. Camille agreed. Back we went into the visitor center. I needed to talk to some officials to see if they could provide me with any details about Luigi.

Caesar and I knew he was Chief Carver from the limited sources he found, but what exactly did that mean? How important was he? Were there other Chief Carvers?

Here I am for the first time posing in front of the faces. Big stuff!

My wife, Camille Cribari-Linen. She loves Luigi's story.

Before I could talk to Rushmore officials, I needed to swing by the Borglum Museum first and reconnect with Ed Hayes. The museum was back in Keystone, which meant I had to leave Rushmore. When I got back to the museum, there was Ed, waiting for me with papers in his hand. I love people who offer to help and then come through. Caesar had already written to some key people, including Lincoln Borglum, so when Ed gave me names and addresses of people Caesar had not been in touch with, I was really happy. We started to chat, and Ed said it was okay if I recorded the conversation. I'm glad I did, because it turned out everything Ed told me about my grandfather was the *opposite* of what my uncle and I already knew. Ed said Luigi was on the mountain from 1927 to 1931. (Luigi, in fact, was there from 1933 to 1937, and we later learned he was there again in 1940.) Ed said Luigi was a professional prizefighter whose giant fist was cast in plaster. (Luigi actually made a cast of boxer Primo Carnera's fist, his paesan from Italy.) This went back and forth for a while until Ed admitted he didn't know Luigi well. In his defense, he worked on Rushmore quite a long time ago and memories can easily get jumbled. In Ed's case, it did in spades. Before I left, Ed told me to talk to Howard Shaff who was curator of the Borglum Museum. The name rang a bell. Of course. He was one of the authors who wrote about Rushmore and did not mention my grandfather.

I thanked Ed for being such a gentleman and for his generosity. I literally ran to my car and sped back to the mountain, where I had other appointments.

My first was with Dan Wenk, the superintendent of Mount Rushmore. I don't remember meeting in his office. Instead, we were somewhere in the museum, where there was not a trace of Luigi anywhere. To be fair, at that time the workers' museum was "in the works," where the 400 or so men who helped bring the faces to life would be recognized. (In 1988, most of the information about Rushmore was centered around Borglum and his son Lincoln.) The conversation was cordial enough. Wenk was familiar with Luigi, but that was about it. I asked if Rushmore had any information about my grandfather, and Dan admitted that the records were "sparse." He directed me to Jim Papovitch, the Chief of Interpretation.

I was led into an office where a mustachioed gentleman in a wheelchair greeted me. After the usual cordial introductions, Jim gave me the same response Dan had given: He was familiar with Luigi Del Bianco. Like Dan, Jim conceded that Luigi was in fact Chief Carver, but the specific records about the details of his involvement on the work were spotty. To my surprise, he asked me if I could provide him with any photos or records. I thought, *This is exactly what James Riggs asked my Uncle Caesar in 1986.* Here I travel 1,800 miles, looking for primary sources, and *they* start asking *me* for information. I had to remind myself that there were no guarantees. After all, we were warned that records were limited. And Jim was being a gentleman. I was a gentleman. It was all very gentlemanly, but I wasn't getting anywhere. Finally, I asked once more if he could provide me with anything. Jim wheeled over to a filing cabinet, pulled a couple of old records and had his secretary make copies for me.

DAILY RECORD---Men-on-the-Granite Drilling and Carving

Mount Rushmore National Memorial

Daily---Reported to Gutzon Borglum, Sculptor Engineer

Name	Hours	Location	Progress / Approximate Feet Drilled	Completed and Shot	
Luigi del Bianco, CARVER	8	Left Wig	33'	33'	
O. E. Anderson, DRILLER	8	" "	52'	52'	
James Payne, DRILLER	8	" "	Pointing 18'	18'	
Alton Leach, DRILLER	10	Collar	88'	88'	
Elton Gordon, DRILLER	8	R. Collar	40'	40'	
Ray Grover, DRILLER	10	Jefferson	83'	83'	
Merle Peterson, DRILLER	10	Jefferson	Drilling & Plugging		
George Hesnard, DRILLER	8	R. Collar	40'	40'	
H. Peterson	10	Collar 2 hr	20'	20	
Alfred Berg, POWDER MAN	10		Drilled Areas Shot: 11 lines	Wired and Net Shot	
M. I. Cindel, BLACKSMITH		No. Drills Sharpened: 95	1788		

Reported and Signed J. A. Johnson, Foreman on Granite

Date Oct 10 1933 W. S. Tallman, Superintendent of Works

I wasn't sure if these were the same records that James Riggs sent Caesar two years earlier. I decided to be optimistic and assume that they weren't. I thanked Jim and turned to leave. He stopped me and said, "If you have some time, you can go downstairs to our archival room. A number of workers were interviewed a couple years ago and perhaps they mention your grandfather." Now we were getting somewhere. I was chomping at the bit to hear those tapes. I thanked Jim and before we parted he told me that a workers' museum was being planned. He said if I had any photos of my grandfather, he would try to get one of them put on display. A worker? What a weird way to refer to the Chief Carver. Even though I knew very little about my grandpa's importance on the mountain at the time, I knew he was much more than that.

A park ranger led me to the basement of the visitor's center and sat me down next to a case with cassette tapes labeled by the name of the worker. My eye immediately went to the one labeled "Lincoln Borglum." Gutzon's son. This tape I had to play first. Fortunately, the tape came with a transcript in case I couldn't understand everything said. It was an interview with an unknown interviewer and Lincoln Borglum. The sound quality was very homemade. Not good at all. Still, I happened upon some interesting tidbits from the designer's son:

Q: How much of a problem were the cracks and fissures you ran into?

A: The cracks?

Q: Yeah, on the mountain.

A: Ah, well, they're still a problem... but we had to twist the Jefferson head quite a little bit because there was a bad crack running down through its nose. 'Course we got away from that and the crack comes through the lip, right through here. And that's the only patch on Rushmore.

Q: A patch on Jefferson, and that was patched with...

A: ... a piece of granite, a piece of granite.

Q: A beautiful job, too.

A: Yes, Sal Bianco (Luigi Del Bianco) the Italian stone cutter, mason that was out there did that. It's about, Oh; I guess it's about that deep, something like that...

Q: ... about a foot...

A: ... it's about that wide...

Q: Ah, about a foot...

A: ... and about a foot deep. He cut it in there far enough so that it would be solid. Then he cut another piece...

Q: ... did they fit that in them, with pins inside them, or how did that happen...

A: ... yeah, pins. He was a real good stone cutter, he was slow but good. Great, big, Italian, name was Bianco, oh; he worked for Dad for years.

Q: I don't know how many times I went over that face and I never noticed that was a complete block.

A: Yeah, he did a good job of it. He worked there off and on, I don't know, three or four years he was, he came back from CT and NY, Port Chester, NY family back there. And ah, he's come out and work sometimes for 4 or 5 months and once he had, he was the only guy working on the mountain...

Q: You mentioned quite a few workers, any other workers that sort of stand out in your memory or come to mind, or who, or was there any one man who was the, really the best worker, you thought?

A: Well, I think it's about a toss-up, of course Bianco this Italian, was not in that same classification. He was a trained stone-cutter and could carve a statue or something of marble if you wanted him to.

Several things stood out to me in that short excerpt: "Not in that same classification" and "Only guy working on the mountain." Already I was getting the impression that my grandfather's work on Rushmore was not only important, but special; a notch above the rest. Hearing this from the designer's son gave it weight. How can they call him a "worker"? Lincoln Borglum couldn't bring himself to compare Luigi to the other men on the mountain because there was no comparison. "Chief Carver" was making more and more sense.

I went to the other cassette tapes. The sound quality on the rest of them was awful and none of them had transcripts. Tough luck if I couldn't understand what was being said. After an hour of popping cassettes in and out and straining to listen, I gave up. At least I got Lincoln, by far the most important voice, so I was happy. Actually, I was excited. I found something! I hoped Caesar would be excited, too—and proud of me.

I made my way back to the main floor of the visitor's center and met Camille to show her what I found. We basked in my little success and decided to canvas the center some more. After all, you never know what you might have missed. We then walked right into a large list of the 400 "workers" on Mount Rushmore. How could I have missed that?

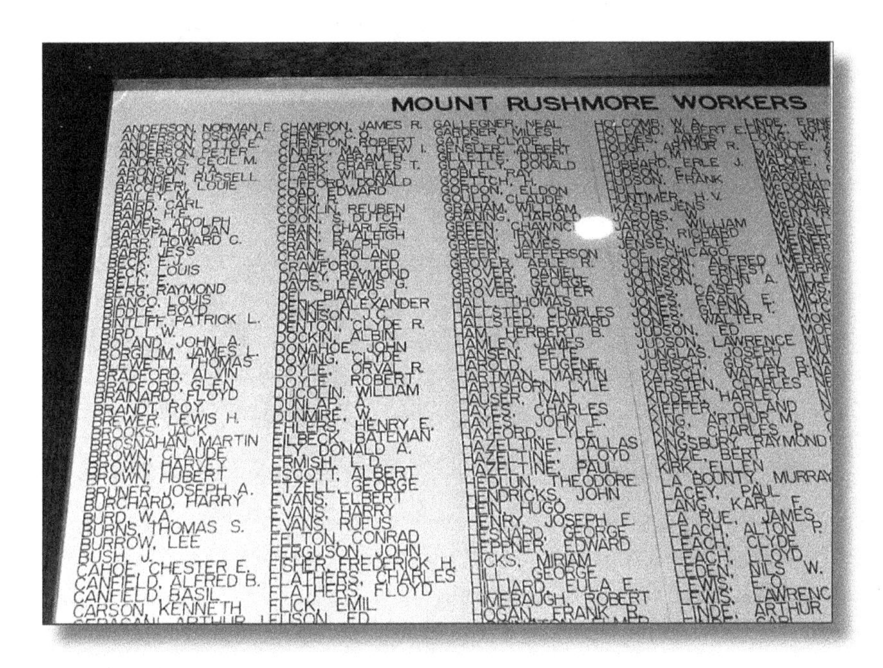

Original workers listing at the Mount Rushmore Visitors Center.

Ironically, my grandfather is listed twice as two separate people. Once as "Louis Bianco" and the other as "L. Del Bianco." Jim Papovitch told me the records at the Mountain were a little spotty and inconsistent. This was further proof of that.

We made our way over to the Sculptor's Studio. This is where Borglum made the models that he used to transfer the "points" to the much larger faces on the mountain. At this juncture, my knowledge of pointing, carving and the like was embryonic. There was so much I didn't know. My uncle was more knowledgeable on that front. Looking back, I realize my excitement during this trip of discovery was very childlike. I can see in the photos a little boy smiling in front of that model. I wasn't making light of the experience, but I do recall a playfulness about the whole thing. The emotional depth of my journey, and the story I would help my uncle unearth, still lay a couple years away.

This is me, standing before Borglum's model in the Sculptor's Studio.

Before I talked to more people, I wanted to go back to the observation deck and look at the mountain again with fresh eyes. This time I popped a quarter into the pay telescopes to get a closer look. When I did this, my whole perspective changed. The features on the presidents were breathtaking. The artistry was there. Chiaroscuro, the play of light and shadow, was also in full force, the way Borglum had intended it. Those faces had soul. Somewhere in those faces was my grandpa. I wished there was a second observation deck that brought you as close to the faces as this telescope did. I guess that's why the telescopes were there. I spent the next half hour and 20 quarters taking in the faces and realizing my initial reaction was a little unfair; my expectations too high. This was truly a work of genius with a power all its own. Sure, the pile of rubble stinks and the ways of viewing it could be improved. Still, I felt better. I also realized I had just enough time to zip back again to the Borglum Museum to talk to Howard Shaff.

CHAPTER SIX:

EVERY AUTHOR HAS A 'HOOK'

HOWARD WAS AN AUTHOR and historian who wrote a book with his wife about Borglum titled, *Six Wars at a Time*. We sat in his office and, like Ed Hayes, Howard was fine with me recording the conversation. To start, Howard's book was not focused solely on Mount Rushmore. It was a biography of Gutzon Borglum. I still wanted to know why Borglum's Chief Carver wasn't mentioned in his book. Howard's answer was this: His book was heavily researched over a seven-year period, and even though he came across documents pertaining to Luigi, they were not applicable to telling Borglum's life story the way Howard wanted it to be told. It was nothing against Luigi personally. I told Howard that I hoped he didn't think I was putting him in the hot seat; I was merely asking out of curiosity. Howard understood and wanted me to know that from his research, he knew that Borglum held Luigi in "high esteem" and would never have had a "studio artist" working for him if he didn't have exceptional talent.

He said that Luigi was a classic example of the immigrant who came to America not knowing how to assimilate and promote himself in the art world. If he was lucky, he got the privilege of working for a major sculptor like Gutzon Borglum, quietly taking his orders from "The Master" and doing the work. I also asked him why he thought the definitive book, *The Carving of Mount Rushmore*, also didn't mention Luigi. Again, Howard stated that Rex Alan Smith stuck mainly to the immediate area of Keystone, interviewed the miners who worked on the mountain and basically made them the focus of the book. Luigi Del Bianco just wasn't applicable to the story that Alan Smith wanted to tell. Okay, fair enough. I guess the lesson here is: If you are an immigrant artisan like Luigi, and not a savvy self-promoter, your story may never make it into the history books.

Howard ended by telling me that Borglum was not only a great sculptor, but a prolific writer. Maybe he wrote about grandpa, and why he held Luigi in high esteem? Before I left I asked where I could find writings by Borglum. Howard gave me the gold nugget that would change everything. He told me to go to the Library of Congress.

"The Borglum Papers" is a voluminous collection of daily correspondence by Borglum with all the players in the Rushmore story. Not to mention the countless directives and memoranda relating to the carving. Howard said a trip to Washington was vital if I were to find out anything substantive about my grandfather's work. I thanked Howard for taking the time to share his knowledge with me. I was still disappointed that he hadn't mentioned Luigi in his book, but he gave me his reasons, and I respected him for that. To quote my father, Howard was a "stand-up guy" who went out of his way to help me. All in all, it was a very productive day.

Now that my research work was done, Camille and I spent the remainder of the trip riding horses, eating good food and frequenting the local Keystone tourist spots. We also visited the old part of Keystone, where my grandfather boarded when he was working at Rushmore. At one point, my grandmother, father and uncles lived there for a year. I have heard many interesting stories from that time. Stay tuned.

Before we left for New York, I needed to visit the mountain one more time. I had become pretty attached to it by now; sort of like a legendary family member you've heard about your whole life, and when you finally get to meet him, it's hard to say good-bye. I switched between the telescope and the natural view, comparing the two, soaking it all in, when I heard a park ranger giving a tour nearby. I decided to attach myself to the group of tourists listening. The ranger was talking to a captive audience.

"Now, there was a crack that developed on the lip of Jefferson, and it had to be fixed right away. One of the workers did a very good job repairing the crack and the patchwork is hard to detect, even close-up. It is the only repair ever done on the faces at Rushmore."

In a flash, I recalled Judith St. George's book and what Lincoln Borglum said. Luigi fixed that lip. That was him. *Say something*, I thought! I am by nature a shy person, but I couldn't contain myself. I shouted, "My grandpa did that!" Forty heads turned. The park ranger craned his neck.

"Excuse me?" he asked.

Emboldened, I walked right up to the ranger and said, "My grandfather patched the lip."

Now, you'd think the ranger would be impressed, curious, but instead, he literally stared over me and said politely, "Thank you for sharing that" and went right on with his talk. Forty heads turned obediently back to him. It was the weirdest thing. It's as if the exciting information I shared with everyone never happened.

I walked away in a daze. With all the progress I'd made, this little episode was a stark reminder: Nobody at Rushmore, including the people who work here, know anything about Luigi. Even though I was happy that a workers' museum was being planned, I knew now that my family would have to fight very hard to make sure my grandpa was an important part of it.

Even with this one bizarre moment, the trip to Rushmore had so many positive discoveries on so many levels. I could go back to New York confident that I had made a good start. Still, unless I could somehow work both priorities into my life, I knew my priority was in building my career as a children's performer. I was only 25 and just starting out. My uncle was in a different part of his life. He would have to take the lead. But I had to try to help him as much as I could.

CHAPTER SEVEN:

THE BIGGEST LIBRARY IN THE WORLD

"GOOD JOB, NEFOO," MY uncle said as he leafed through the daily records and Lincoln Borglum transcript. Then Caesar looked away and pronounced, "I want the originals."

"Can't I have copies for myself?" I asked. After all, I found them. I could sense tension in the air.

"Let me think about it," Caesar countered.

Oh, that's never good. My uncle's "territorial imperative" was kicking in. I decided to back off again and be the dutiful nephew despite my uncle's strange behavior. I should be used to him by now, right? I tried to ignore the pit in my stomach and focus on the much more important task at hand. I handed Caesar the list of contacts Ed Hayes and Howard Shaff had given me. Caesar could continue his letter writing campaign. What about the Library of Congress? That seemed to be the next obvious step.

"You have to take me to Washington," Caesar said, never one to mince words.

Even though I was busy trying to establish myself as a storyteller, I had to be part of this. To be honest, the thought of one of Caesar's friends taking him instead of me sparked a little jealousy. Even though my uncle could be difficult, the idea of the son and grandson going through those important papers felt right. It was settled. We would go in October when I had a few days free. In the meantime, Caesar would contact the people from the list Ed Hayes had given me when I was at Rushmore.

Over the next few days, I also shared those same documents with my sisters. They were thrilled to see grandpa's name on the daily record, and the praise that came from the Lincoln Borglum transcript. Still, there was something unspoken between us; that I was the grandchild meant to take the lead, and my sisters would be more than happy to support me along the way. With everyone cheering from the sidelines, my trip to Washington with my uncle couldn't come fast enough.

When September rolled around, I was excited to make plans for the big excursion to our nation's capital. I called Caesar.

"I can't go. I'm too tired. I'm too depressed," he murmured.

After 20 minutes of trying to bolster Caesar's spirits, I realized it was futile. After all, my uncle's eccentricities went much deeper than just being a "character." Caesar suffered from manic depression. When he was "manic" or feeling energetic, he wrote letters, read materials and stopped strangers on the street. *Do you know what my old man did? Do you have any idea?* People were always fascinated by my grandfather's story and my uncle's passionate charm. Unfortunately, the high only lasted so long. The doubts would creep in. *Maybe my father wasn't that important. You know there were other guys who worked on it, too. We can't forget them.* Eventually, Caesar would refuse to leave his apartment, and he would sleep the days away. He couldn't get anything done. I knew this was one of those down times in the endless cycle. Poor guy. What could I do? I couldn't go without him. It would break his heart and he would never forgive me. We would have to wait until April of the next year when the weather was warmer, and I had a week off from my school schedule.

CHAPTER EIGHT:

Washington, Here We Come

*H**I, IT'S TIME FOR** another Manji Manjo. At the tone, the time will be…beep! 6:37 a.m. on April 17, 1989. It's the morning we've been waiting for! Well, the moment that Uncle Caesar and I have been waiting for. We're going to Washington! Ta dah!*

I was jumping out of my skin. When I picked up Caesar, we sat in the car and I turned on my little gray tape recorder and asked him to address the "studio audience." Other people would have pushed the recorder away, but Caesar wasn't fazed a bit. A natural ham, he was more than a willing participant. Caesar started with a message to his sister-in-law, my mother, Angie.

"What do I wanna say? I hope I didn't forget anything upstairs. I think everything is okay, Ang. You know, your mother told me not to worry about anything last night so Angie, everything is fine. We are going to do research in the land of Borglum and Bianco!"

My uncle and I were like two little kids going on a great adventure. Because we had so much in common, the drive went pretty quickly with talks about Sinatra, movies, baseball stats and other cultural subjects. And there was always time for a "Manji Manjo" update.

Caesar fell in love with that little recorder. My only regret was that it wasn't a video camera.

After five hours of driving and mounting excitement, we decided our first priority was getting a room for the night. This was the day before the instant gratification of GPS and all those handy apps that would have found us a hotel in two seconds. This was 1989, and we had to rough it. After spying a Best Western off the highway, we thought we had lucked out. Two and 1/2 hours later, we were still looking for it. (My sense of direction leaves something to be desired.) Caesar, who didn't drive, turned on the tape recorder.

"Well, ladies and gentlemen, we are still looking for a f-***-g room. It looks like we are in the sewers of Paris on a dead-end street. We literally saw a Best Western right off the thruway and somehow couldn't get to it. Three separate people who gave us directions made us even *more* lost."

Caesar continued, "People are going to ask us what we did on our first day. Well, we looked for a f-***-g room."

At least we were laughing about it. Sort of.

A half hour later we ran right into the very Best Western we saw right off the highway. Don't ask me how we found it. It was luck and not my sense of direction. We unpacked, grateful to finally be somewhere. Caesar did little or no traveling in his life, so being in a hotel was quite eventful for him. You'd think we were in the Carlisle.

"Ladies and gentlemen, we are in a beautiful room. Quite a spread here. TV, nice little phone, beds, pictures on the wall, bathroom, the whole works. I look tremendous, even without a tooth."

Let me be clear about my uncle. He was a little *curioso*. He was also very intelligent, cultured and well-read. But he was, for lack of a better term, "out there." The moment after that jubilant photo was taken, I was told to "take that TV off the stand because—Look! It's going to fall!" The TV wasn't going anywhere, but Caesar had a phobia about "things falling off of things," so I accommodated him. We ended the night watching a TV that was on the floor. Later on, the TV was joined on the floor by an alarm clock. And a lamp.

The next day found us bright eyed and ready to go. After a hardy breakfast at the Best Western, we hopped into my little Chrysler Sundance and crossed the Potomac River into Washington. (The land of "Borglum and Bianco," as my uncle liked to put it.) The plan was for me to drop Caesar off at the Library of Congress, park my car and walk back to help him research. After parking the car, I made my way on foot to the Library. It was a beautiful sunny day, and I couldn't help but be struck by how beautifully pristine the buildings were. They were absolutely gorgeous, and in such contrast to what we saw yesterday when we were lost and drove through some of the most depressed and poverty-stricken parts of D.C. I wondered if foreign heads of state were kept from seeing that part of Washington.

When I arrived at the Library of Congress, an employee had already provided Caesar with numerous cartons of documents from the Borglum papers. Caesar was itching to get started. I was, too. I walked over to Caesar and asked him for a carton for me to go through. He froze for a moment, and then put his head down in frustration. Instead of handing me an entire carton, he gave me one file and said, "Make sure you go through this very carefully!" Of course, I was going to be careful. I've been waiting to find my grandpa since I found that pamphlet back in second grade. And now we were in the very place that could answer so many questions. Of course, I would go through every paper with a fine toothcomb! Didn't my uncle trust me? As I looked at him reading and researching, I could feel an invisible wall between us.

That's how it felt the next half hour or so. Tension. Impatience. Distrust. Every so often Caesar would move past me like I was in his way, cursing under his breath. When I finished with the file he gave me, I told him there was nothing in there of interest. Caesar shot me a look, grabbed the file out of my hand, sat down and said, "Are you sure? Jesus Christ, you couldn't find anything? This is making me very nervous. Now I gotta go through this file to make sure you didn't miss anything!" We argued back and forth. I assured him there was nothing in there. He didn't buy it. Both our voices rose in volume and anger as heads started to turn in the library. I felt like I was an intruder invading my uncle's space. Didn't I have the right to find grandpa, too? Why was my uncle shutting me out? At this point, we wouldn't get anything done. Caesar would micro manage my every move, which also took away from his own progress. Looking back, I realize my initial handling of the situation could have been better. Someone had to take the high road; if either one of us was going to take it, it would have to be me.

"Uncle Caesar, would you like me to leave?"

Caesar stood up straight and replied, "Yes, I would like you to leave."

And that was that. Obviously, Caesar wanted to do the research by himself, without me. Ouch. As hurt as I felt, I wished him luck and told him I would come back at lunchtime. He looked grateful and relieved. I felt anything but.

I hated this side of my uncle, this "territorial imperative." Resentment started to build. What if *he* was the one who was careless and missed important documents? Worse, what if his depression kicked in, and he got nothing done and wanted to go back to Port Chester? He had a history of that kind of behavior. I was so angry, I made a promise to myself; if my uncle finds nothing at the end of the day, or exhibits any kind of self-sabotaging behavior, I am going to insist that I help. No discussion. This is as important to me as it is to him. I want to find my grandpa, too.

Caesar proudly posing in front of Borglum's bust of Lincoln.

I decided to distract myself and take advantage of all the museums and art galleries that D.C. had to offer. After an eventful visit to the National Gallery, I left feeling better. It was great to go off on my own. As I neared the Library of Congress, my step wasn't as light and my stomach started to knot. What if my worries about Caesar came to be? Then I would have to deal with *that* situation. I anticipated seeing Caesar depressed or agitated or arguing with an employee about something.

When I got to the research room, the first thing I saw was my uncle showing papers to the security guard.

"Do you have any idea how thrilling this is for me? Look at this! It's all about my old man!"

He was waving his hands, his eyes bright, his smile wide with excitement. The security guard was totally taken with Caesar's charm and enthusiasm. When my uncle saw me, he shouted, "Louis, get over here, I found gold!" I had never seen my uncle like this before. He was on fire in the best way: The way you feel when a fantastic discovery breaks through a deep sense of frustration.

"I have just scratched the surface, Nefoo! I'm going to come back to Washington another three or four times to get done what I need to get done."

His satisfaction was absolutely contagious, and I could feel people smiling at Caesar as he started instructing me to copy all of the papers he found. I had never seen him so focused, so directed, so *happy*. And then it occurred to me that as much as I wanted to be here doing the research, it was my uncle who was supposed to be doing it, not me. This was the only way Caesar was capable of working; alone, like a monk in a monastery. Who cared who found the documents, as long as they were *found*. Caesar was finding them with a passion and energy that I had to admire, in spite of myself. The resentment started to melt. Caesar was meant to do this, by himself. I was meant to *assist* him.

Yours truly with 80's hair in front of the Capitol.

The rest of the trip yielded the same wonderful results, as did subsequent trips. Not only did I accompany Caesar in 1990 and 1991, but his dear friends Jimmy and Judy Sapione took him to D.C., as did his other friend Peter Sgroi. Jimmy Sapione and I still laugh about what it was like to travel with Caesar and how many times we had to change rooms because the AC "didn't feel right" or "there's a hum in the room that's bothering me." Best of all was Jimmy's anecdote about the Library of Congress not letting Caesar in because he didn't have the proper identification. Because my uncle had been there so many times, he shouted, "But you know me, I'm Caesar!" Every neurotic incident was always countered with a new discovery of a letter, memo or work log as my uncle studied and explored the empirical proof of his papa's vital importance on Mount Rushmore. I look back on those trips with great pride knowing I was able to overcome my own emotional agenda and help Caesar to fulfill his own dream. As I tell my grandfather's story on Mount Rushmore, the telling will be reinforced and nurtured with these important documents. Documents found by a loving son who wanted his papa to have his rightful place in history.

PART II:
FINDING LUIGI

CHAPTER NINE:

THE CURIOUS LITTLE ONE

ON MAY 9, 1892, aboard a ship sailing off the coast of La Havre, France, Luigi Del Bianco was born. His parents Vincenzo and Osvalda were coming back from a failed attempt to start a new life in America. Just miles from home, Osvalda went into labor. My family has no idea how much time newborn Luigi spent on that ship. We only know the family returned home to Italy, specifically the region of Friuli Venezia Giulia and the province of Pordenone. Friuli is located in the northeast of Italy bordering Austria to the north and modern-day Slovenia to the east.

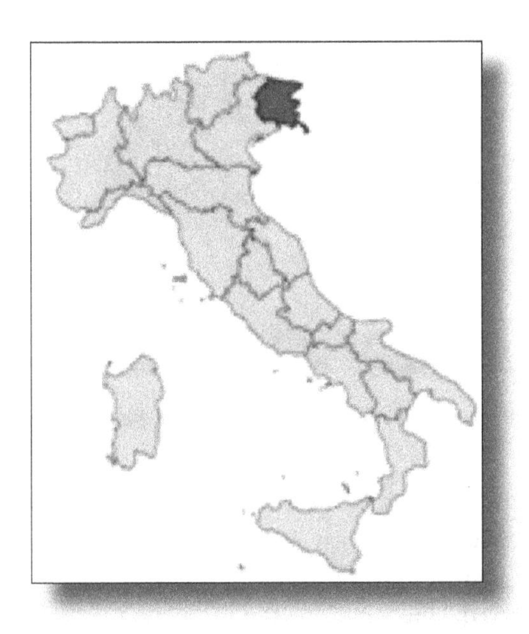

Friuli, Luigi's ancestral home, located at Italy's northeast tip.

Friuli has an interesting history of Roman occupation mixed in with the Germanic Lombard and Frankish cultures who invaded Northern Italy in the sixth to eighth centuries A.D. As a result, the Friulan language was born, unique to the Italians of that region. This is the language my grandfather probably spoke at home as a child. He also probably hunted deer, rabbit and played in the fields and forests of the Italian Alps in a small Borgo or "Burge," literally called "Del Bianco." This tiny cluster of families, all related to each other, is nestled just north of the nearest village, Meduno. It still exists today.

Luigi was the baby of the family. He had three older siblings, Silvio, Maria and Osvaldo.

Not much is known about the Del Bianco family at the turn of the 20th century. My grandfather's family was by no means poor. It would be safe to say that most of the inhabitants of that area were working class farmers and craftsmen.

Luigi's father, Vincenzo Del Bianco, who lived to be just shy of 100 years old.

We do know that Luigi's father, Vincenzo, came from a long line of wood carvers. According to my grandfather, when he was 11 years old, he was hanging outside his father's wood shop. Luigi loved to watch the men as they carved. "How curious the little one is!" they would say. With that, Luigi picked up a scrap of wood and after studying its texture and shape, proceeded to carve a small dog. Vincenzo immediately recognized his son's gift and decided to send him to Austria to study under a master stone carver.

Luigi, likely around 13 or 14 years old, as a stone carving student in Austria. He is to the right of the woman in the photo.

Why Luigi chose to carve stone instead of wood is not known. According to a diploma from Austria, Luigi attended stone carving school from 1905 to 1908. He also studied there privately under a master stone carver.

In 1908, Luigi studied for two more years in Venice. On July 23, 1910, at the age of 18, Luigi boarded the SS *La Touraine* out of Le Havre, France and made his first voyage to America. According to records, when Luigi arrived at Ellis Island, he was denied entry because he did not have the required fifty dollars. As a result, Luigi was detained for three days until his cousin and sponsor, Pietro Del Bianco, came with the additional twenty-five dollars needed. From there, Pietro took Luigi to Concord, New Hampshire, where a new life awaited this talented artist seeking his destiny in the new world.

CHAPTER TEN:

LUIGI IN THE GRANITE CAPITOL

TO BE HONEST, WE don't know how long Luigi stayed in Concord, New Hampshire. We are not even sure what he did there; it probably was related to stone carving. What we do know is that he eventually made a home for himself in Barre, Vermont, famously known as the "Granite Capitol" of America. When Luigi arrived in Barre, he must have felt at home; the mountainous topography and lush forests felt just like Meduno.

Luigi and the first selfie, 1910!

Barre has a rich history in stone. The quarries there are filled with gray granite, a stone Luigi was probably familiar with. Most of the artists in Barre were memorial stone carvers, and my grandfather certainly had the ability to carve headstones with the training he had acquired in Italy. Luigi called Barre home for about six or seven years. Little is known about his life there, other than the fact that he lived on 565 North Main Street and worked for the World Granite Company.

From left, Luigi looking dapper in Barre, VT; one of Luigi's Headstone in Barre, VT (just look at the artistry.)

CHAPTER ELEVEN:

WORLD WAR I AND ITALY BECKONS

WHEN ITALY ENTERED WORLD War I in 1915, Luigi returned to his native land to fight for his country. My maternal grandfather, Giovanni Bruni, was in America at the same time and also returned to fight. Even though these immigrants had been living in the States for some time, they still had an allegiance to their birthplace. Luigi joined the Italian Army and quickly attained the rank of Master Sergeant. I can recall sitting in the living room as a child and hearing my father Vincent recount the war stories he heard from his father.

Luigi (far left) dining with fellow officers.

"Grandpa went over the line 13 times and got shot every time. He got shot everywhere, even in his giggy [corrupt dialect for butt.] My old man couldn't sit for a week. He used to trick German soldiers into thinking he was German because he could speak the language. Then he would shoot them on the spot, or kill them with his bare hands."

It's important to note that both my grandfather and father were prone to exaggeration. Still, a family story is a family story. As a young boy, I ate it up.

When the war was over in 1918, Luigi spent two more years in Italy. The family isn't sure what he did during this time. It is possible he studied his art further or perhaps worked as a stone carver. On September 25, 1920, at the age of 28, Luigi boarded the SS *Dante Alighieri* out of Naples to take that month long boat ride back to America. He returned to Barre, VT and met a fellow stone carver who would change his life forever.

CHAPTER TWELVE:

YOU MUST MEET BORGLUM!

ALFONSO SCAFA WAS A good natured and friendly fellow who was immediately taken with my grandfather's charm, charisma and big personality. When he saw Luigi's ability as a stone carver, Alfonso suggested my grandfather take a trip with him to Stamford, Connecticut. *I work for the world-famous sculptor Gutzon Borglum*, Alfonso said. *You have talent. He will have work for you*. Luigi seized the opportunity.

Gutzon Borglum: sculptor, genius, and designer of Mount Rushmore.

The next day, the two carvers drove to Stamford to meet the irascible and supremely gifted Gutzon Borglum. People always ask what the first meeting was like and why Borglum immediately hired my grandfather to carve for him. I really don't know. Maybe Luigi had a 1920's version of an artist's portfolio to show Borglum. Perhaps Alfonso Scafa's recommendation was enough. What we do know is that this first meeting was the start of a 21-year relationship that ended when Borglum passed away in 1941. We also know that even though Borglum was a true renaissance man who excelled in every art form, he relied on Luigi's expertise as a classically trained stone carver and granite expert. For Luigi, Borglum became "The Master," who took my grandfather's already established abilities and developed them to the level of stone carver.

Also around this time Luigi began his path to citizenship, starting with his Declaration of Intention in 1920.

Fifteen minutes south of Stamford, just over the state line, sat Port Chester, New York. Alfonso bought Luigi there to meet his family, and he stayed on as a guest. My grandfather got to know the entire Scafa family, but was especially taken with Alfonso's sister-in-law, Nicoletta Cardarelli. Nicoletta was a petite 4'11" beauty. Luigi and Nicoletta obviously had eyes for each other.

My grandmother Nicoletta in Port Chester, NY, circa 1917.

It is amazing what life changing effects Alfonso Scafa had on my grandfather. He would not only introduce Luigi to the future designer of Mount Rushmore, but also to his future wife, my grandmother. According to my Aunt Gloria, her mother didn't like her father at first because she thought his Roman nose was "too big." That was not enough of a deterrent. After several more trips back and forth from Barre and a long courtship, they married on December 31, 1922 at Our Lady of the Rosary in Port Chester.

Luigi and Nicoletta's wedding photo. Luciano Cardarelli was the best man and Anna Dianni was the maid of honor.

After they were married, Luigi Left Barre, Vermont for good. Since he and Borglum had established such a good relationship, Borglum offered to let the newlyweds live in a cottage on his Stamford estate known as "Borgland." Borglum had his studio on the grounds of the estate, so Luigi could be close by. It was the beginning of a long relationship between a great carver and a great sculptor.

CHAPTER THIRTEEN:

BIANCO AND "THE MASTER"

Wars of America Memorial in Newark, New Jersey.

AT THE TIME WHEN Luigi and Nicoletta moved in, Borglum was working on his "Wars of America" sculpture, so my grandfather was put to work alongside another talented Italian, Hugo Villa. Villa would eventually assist Borglum in the design and pointing aspects of Mount Rushmore (pointing is the transference of measurements from the model to the sculpture.) Since this was a sculpture and not a carving, I would venture to guess that my grandfather and Villa laid a lot of clay for the model and assisted in the pointing aspects for the final piece. Luigi's powerful physique (particularly his legs) appealed to Borglum's artistic eye. As a result, about 20 of the figures on the "Wars of America" sculpture, especially Washington in the front, were physically modeled after my grandfather. Borglum and his wife, Mary, and son, Lincoln, were also memorialized in the piece. The sculpture itself is an impressive display of 42 figures and two horses relating to all the major wars our country had engaged in up to that time. It was dedicated in 1926 and today is still considered a masterpiece. I'm so glad my grandfather was part of such an ambitious project; the largest bronze sculpture in America up to that point.

Luigi's self-portrait, circa 1921. Photo: Del Bianco Family Collection.

Eventually, Luigi and Nicoletta left Borglum's estate and settled in Port Chester. Their first child, Teresa, was born in 1923 and was the apple of my grandfather's eye.

Luigi would come home from work every day to find little Teresa waiting in the foyer ready to jump into his arms. Silvio, the oldest son, came along in 1925.

Luigi and his daughter Teresa. Photo: Del Bianco Family Collection.

Just as Luigi and Nicoletta started to settle in with their growing family, Luigi received an important call from Borglum to help him carve something that had never been carved before: a sculpture on the side of a mountain. No, it wasn't Mount Rushmore. Before the four granite presidents were ever conceived, there was a previous attempt at carving colossal stone figures. It was Stone Mountain in Georgia. The United Daughters of the Confederacy commissioned Borglum to carve a bas-relief of the South's Civil War leaders, Jefferson Davis, Robert E. Lee and Stonewall Jackson. Actually, Borglum had been involved with the planning of the sculpture as far back as 1915, but now, in the early 1920's, work was ready to commence. Nothing of this magnitude had ever been tried before. Borglum would need "Bianco," his best carver, to aide him in achieving this monumental task.

Stone Mountain in Georgia. Photo: Public Domain.

The job would involve months away from Nicoletta and baby Teresa. As the patriarch of the family, I imagine Luigi decided to go with terribly mixed feelings, having just become a father. His time down in Georgia must have been lonely, as evidenced by the postcard below.

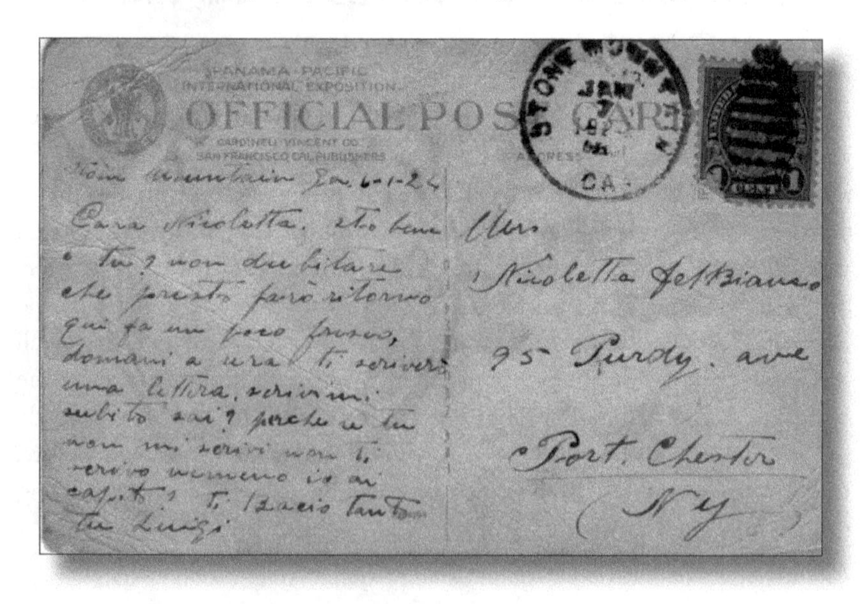

PANAMA-PACIFIC INTERNATIONAL EXPOSITION
OFFICIAL POS[T] CAR[D]
CARDINELL VINCENT CO. SAN FRANCISCO CAL. PUBLISHERS

STONE MOUNTAIN JAN 7 GA.

Stone Mountain Ga. 6-1-24
Cara Nicoletta, sto bene
e tu? non dubitare
che presto farò ritorno
qui fa un poco freddo,
domani a sera ti scriverò
una lettera, scrivimi
subito sai? perche se tu
non mi scrivi non ti
scrivo nemmeno io ai
capito? ti bacio tanto
tuo Luigi

Mrs
Nicoletta Delbianco
95 Purdy. ave
Port. Chester
(N.Y.)

Stone Mountain Jan. 6, 1924

Dear Nicoletta,

I am well, and you? Do not doubt that soon I will return. Here it's getting a little cool. Tomorrow night I will write you a letter. Write to me right now because if you do not write to me, I'm not going to write to you. Do you understand? I give you lots of Kisses.

Your Luigi.

As tough as my grandfather appeared to be, he must have had a tender side. (Although, here it is mixed in with an ultimatum.) I love the sentiment at the end: "Your Luigi."

Once Luigi arrived in Georgia, Borglum put him to work right away finishing the face of Robert E. Lee. This had to be done in time for the dedication. Here is a photo of Luigi with hammer and chisel. He is the good-looking guy wearing glasses.

Photo from Stone Mountain Magazine.

Unfortunately, Borglum's relationship with the United Daughters of the Confederacy was fraught with disagreements. He eventually abandoned Stone Mountain. You can call it a blessing in disguise. Soon after, Doane Robinson, the Historian for South Dakota, contacted Borglum about his own vision for a giant granite carving. Luigi would return home to Port Chester to be reunited with Nicoletta and Teresa. He would also go back to assisting Borglum with his Wars of America sculpture.

CHAPTER FOURTEEN:

TRIUMPH AND TRAGEDY

IN 1927, MY GRANDFATHER continued on his path to citizenship. Later that same year, Luigi submitted a Petition for Naturalization. Finally, in 1928, Luigi's path was complete when he took the Oath of Allegiance to become a citizen of the United States of America.

That same year, Nicoletta was pregnant with their third child, my father Vincent, when tragedy struck. Teresa, only 5 years old, became gravely ill with spinal meningitis. I don't know what treatments were available to save little Teresa. I only know that she died soon afterward. I can't begin to imagine what that must have been like for my grandparents. They must have been devastated. How do you bury your 5-year-old child and not be scarred for life? My poor grandmother, pregnant with her third child, poised for a new life, mourning the sudden death of her first born. Unimaginable. When the family asked to help Luigi and Nicoletta with all the necessary arrangements, my grandfather insisted on carving the headstone for Teresa himself. Every time I heard this story as a child, I imagined my grandfather in his little studio, wiping away tears while carving his daughter's name into the stone. The fact that he could do this must have been both a terrible burden and a great gift. Now when Luigi would come home from work, there was no one there waiting to jump into his arms. It was too much for him to bear. They would have to move. And they did, to another part of Washington Park, one of the two large Italian sections in Port Chester.

When my Dad, Vincent, was born, he must have come into the world shrouded by bittersweet emotions: the joy of new life, and the pain of its loss.

Form 2204—L
U. S. DEPARTMENT OF LABOR
NATURALIZATION SERVICE

13685
ORIGINAL

No. 13685

UNITED STATES OF AMERICA

PETITION FOR NATURALIZATION

To the Honorable the Supreme *Court of* County of Westchester, *at* White Plains, N.Y.

The petition of LUIGI DEL BIANCO *hereby filed, respectfully showeth:*

First. My place of residence is 107 Purdy Avenue, Port Chester, NY (Give number, street, city or town, and State.)

Second. My occupation is granite cutter

Third. I was born on the 9 *day of* May *anno Domini 1*892 *at* Meduno, Italy

Fourth. I emigrated to the United States from Naples, Italy *on or about the* 4 *day of* Sept. *anno Domini 1*920, *and arrived in the United States, at the port of* New York *on the* 9 *day of* Oct. *anno Domini 1*920 *on the vessel* Dante Alighieri (If the alien arrived otherwise than by vessel, the character of conveyance or name of transportation company should be given.)

Fifth. I declared my intention to become a citizen of the United States on the 21 *day of* June *anno Domini 1*921 *at* Barre, Vt. *in the* U.S.District *Court of* Dist. of Vermont, Barre, Vt.

Sixth. I am married. *My* wife's *name is* Nicoletta; she *was born on the* 6 *day of* Dec. *anno Domini 1*902 *at* Port Chester, N.Y. *and now resides at* with me (Give number, street, city or town, and State.)

I have two *children, and the name, date, and place of birth, and place of residence of each of said children is as follows:*

Teresa born 25 day of Jan. 1923 at Port Chester, N.Y. resides with me
Silvio " 15 " " Dec. 1925 " " " " " "

Seventh. I am not a disbeliever in or opposed to organized government or a member of or affiliated with any organization or body of persons teaching disbelief in or opposed to organized government. I am not a polygamist nor a believer in the practice of polygamy. I am attached to the principles of the Constitution of the United States, and it is my intention to become a citizen of the United States and to renounce absolutely and forever all allegiance and fidelity to any foreign prince, potentate, state, or sovereignty, and particularly to Victor Emmanuel III, King of Italy *of whom at this time I am a subject, and it is my intention to reside permanently in the United States.*

Eighth. I am able to speak the English language.

Ninth. I have resided continuously in the United States of America for the term of five years at least immediately preceding the date of this petition, to wit, since the 9 *day of* October *anno Domini 1*920, *and in the State of* New York *continuously next preceding the date of this petition, since the* 1 *day of* January *anno Domini 1*925, *being a residence within this State of at least one year next preceding the date of this petition.*

Tenth. I have not heretofore made petition for citizenship to any court. XXXXXXXXXXXXXXXXXXXX *Court of* ______ *at* ______ *on the* ______ *day of* ______ *anno Domini 1*______, *and the said petition was denied by the said Court for the following reasons and causes, to wit* ______ *and the cause of such denial has since been cured or removed.)*

Attached hereto and made a part of this petition are my declaration of intention to become a citizen of the United States and the certificate from the Department of Labor, together with my affidavit and the affidavits of the two verifying witnesses thereto, required by law. Wherefore your petitioner prays that he may be admitted a citizen of the United States of America.

Luigi Del Bianco
(Complete and true signature of petitioner.)

Declaration of Intention No. 5204 *and Certificate of Arrival from Department of Labor filed this* ______ *day of* SEP 27 1927, 19__.

Note to Clerk of Court.—If petitioner arrived in the United States on or before June 29, 1906, strike out the words reading "and Certificate of Arrival from Department of Labor."

AFFIDAVITS OF PETITIONER AND WITNESSES

State of New York
County of Westchester } ss:

The aforesaid petitioner being duly sworn, deposes and says that he is the petitioner in the above-entitled proceedings; that he has read the foregoing petition and knows the contents thereof; that the said petition is signed with his full, true name; that the same is true of his own knowledge, except as to matters therein stated to be alleged upon information and belief, and that as to those matters he believes it to be true.

Luigi Del Bianco
(Complete and true signature of petitioner.)

Peter Pappalardo, *occupation* Plasterer, *residing at* Port Chester, NY
and Frank Masilotti, *occupation* Agent, *residing at* " "
each being severally, duly, and respectively sworn, deposes and says that he is a citizen of the United States of America; that he has personally known LUIGI DEL BIANCO, *the petitioner above mentioned, to have resided in the United States continuously immediately preceding the date of filing his petition, since the* 1 *day of* June *anno Domini 1*922, *and in the State in which the above-entitled petition is made continuously since the* 1 *day of* January *anno Domini 1*925, *and that he has personal knowledge that the said petitioner is a person of good moral character, attached to the principles of the Constitution of the United States, and that the petitioner is in every way qualified, in his opinion, to be admitted a citizen of the United States.*

Peter Pappalardo
(Signature of witness.)
Frank Masilotti
(Signature of witness.)

No. 101079

Subscribed and sworn to before me by the above-named petitioner and witnesses in the office of the Clerk of said Court this ______ *day of* SEP 27 1927, *anno Domini 19*__. [Seal]

Chas J. F. Decker, *Clerk.*
By Jas B Reap, Special *Deputy Clerk.*

[OVER]

CHAPTER FIFTEEN:

LIFE GOES ON

AS THIS POINT, IN 1928, we know Luigi was working for Borglum, but we also know he started his own memorial stone-carving business in Port Chester in 1927. My Uncle Caesar talked about my grandfather doing business on Purdy Avenue with his brother-in-law Alfonso Scafa and another Port Chester stone-cutter, Saverio Terenzi. The three men were *cumpari*. They loved to sit on the porch after a long day's work drinking homemade wine and trading stories. My mother and father used to love telling us how Purdy Avenue was a bustling street filled with small family businesses and a plethora of meat, fruit and vegetable markets. If you wanted chicken for dinner, you didn't go to the supermarket; you went to Purdy Avenue and bought a live one from Vitti's Poultry market. When you got home, you had to kill it yourself, as well as pluck and gut it for cooking. Many families raised their own chickens at home. There was also the ice man, the bread man, a man that sharpened your knives or sold rags and second-hand goods for the house. They would walk the streets of Port Chester's Italian neighborhoods where everyone knew everyone. These were the people my parents told me about when I asked them of their own childhoods. This is the life I imagined for Luigi, Nicoletta and their children in Port Chester at the dawn of The Depression.

In 1931, the Del Bianco's fourth child was born. My grandfather named him Cesare Julio (using the Italian spelling), or Caesar Julius. What a name. My uncle had a lot to live up to!

The Del Bianco boys were an interesting trio with their own distinct personalities. Silvio, the oldest, had some of my grandfather's talent and was a sensitive and thoughtful boy whom everyone liked. Vincent, my father, was an unpredictable yet charming little hothead who loved pushing the envelope. My father also had a serious stutter; probably the symptom of an equally sensitive boy desperately trying to cover up his own fears and insecurities. Caesar was the actor and clown of the family, a chatterbox who used his natural charisma and sense of humor to win over anyone he met. He also had the ability to irritate, particularly my father, which was usually a recipe for disaster. Caesar would bother Vincent, Vincent would bully Caesar, and so on. Silvio probably spent a lot of time playing peacemaker. I'm sure there was never a dull moment.

The Del Bianco Family, circa 1930.
From left, Silvio, Luigi, Vincent and Nicoletta.

CHAPTER SIXTEEN:

"THE MASTER" CALLS

IN SOUTH DAKOTA, WORK was slowly progressing on the Mount Rushmore National Memorial for several years. The designer of the project was none other than "The Master" Gutzon Borglum. The first hint of Luigi's involvement comes in 1932. The photo below was taken by my grandfather at Mount Rushmore. (Washington was the only face being carved in 1932.) Was my grandfather working at the mountain, or did Borglum simply invite him to South Dakota to show him the project? Perhaps he wasn't out there at all and the photos were simply mailed to him.

Washington's profile. Photo: Del Bianco Family Collection.

Here is a really interesting photo of the mountain in 1932. My grandfather took it. You'll notice Jefferson is being carved on the opposite side of where it is today. Apparently, Borglum's original design had Jefferson in that position. His assistant at that time was Hugo Villa, a talented sculptor who my grandfather worked with under Borglum for many years. According to Rex Alan Smiths' book, *The Carving of Mount Rushmore*, Borglum and Villa were arguing back and forth about whether the face of Jefferson was being carved correctly or not. In the end, the face had to be abandoned and Villa was fired. It remains to be seen who was at fault for the failure of the first Jefferson face, Borglum or Villa. Rex Alan Smith sides with Villa, since Borglum was away from the mountain and not involved enough. This makes sense since Borglum and Villa rekindled their friendship years later. Regarding Luigi and 1932, there is no evidence of his being on the payroll that year. Still, these photos are an indication of the beginning of Luigi's relationship with Rushmore.

The original Jefferson head just to the left of Washington. Photo: Del Bianco Family Collection.

Did Borglum show Luigi the issues on the mountain and offer him the job of Chief Carver in 1932? After all, Villa was a talented sculptor, but Luigi was a talented stone carver. This was a work in stone. Eventually, the first Jefferson face was blasted off.

In 1933, Luigi did in fact get the call from Borglum to be Rushmore's only Chief Carver. As I said, George Washington was the only face completed at this point, although it wasn't in anyway considered complete. The Jefferson head had to be started again. The project was beset with several problems. One was the fact that the granite was ridden with pegmatite stone filled with mica and quartz, which made the carving extremely precarious. Any granite filled with these crystals would fall apart when a chisel or drill hit the stone. (Pegmatite stone was one of the reasons the first Jefferson face failed.) Borglum's design was changed nine times because of this problem, and the faces had to be constantly shifted and in one case moved to avoid the faulty rock. This caused the project to fall behind in time and money.

Money was certainly a problem. Because the mountain was being carved during The Depression, funds allocated from the federal government were not always released. Workers weren't always paid on time or sometimes not at all. As a result, the project would come to a halt. Borglum was constantly traveling to Washington, DC to get the money for the project released so work could continue. It was a vicious cycle that plagued Rushmore for years. Rushmore was supposed to take only five years to complete, but instead it took 14.

Finally, and most importantly, there remained a lack of truly skilled carvers. The vast majority of the men who worked on Rushmore were local silver miners who had lost their jobs when The Depression hit. They had to be trained on the job by Borglum and talented assistants like Hugo Villa, Bill Tallman, Ivan Houser and Walter Long. It was amazing to both my Uncle Caesar and me that, without any formal training, these men learned so quickly to become pointers and carvers. The transference of "points' or measurements from a model to the mountain and the precise removal of granite to create those remarkable 60-foot-high faces by amateurs will always be considered a remarkable feat. That said, by 1933, Borglum must have looked at the unfinished face of Washington and realized that these men, as good and as dedicated as they were, could only take the carving so far. The fact was that none of them were classically trained stone carvers who could give the faces the "refinement of expression" they desperately needed. Only an artist could achieve that. The talented men I mentioned above (Villa, Tallman, Houser and Long) all had impressive resumes in sculpture and design, but none of them were schooled in the art of stone carving. Borglum was a trained carver and could do it, but he was already 66 years old in 1933, and his age and physical limitations prevented him from the grueling task of refining the faces 500 feet in the air. He needed a trained carver and granite expert to finish the faces, to give them expression, to give them soul. He needed my grandpa.

Luigi got the call from "The Master." The two artists already had a 12-year working relationship, and my grandfather had become an even better carver from working under a man of Borglum's great genius. It was a perfect match. But there was a downside: Mount Rushmore was in South Dakota, and a season of carving was anywhere from six to eight months long. Luigi would have to be separated from his family for very long stretches of time. His sons were ages 8, 5 and 2. I wonder what those conversations were like for my grandparents at the kitchen table in 1933. I'm sure my grandmother got some help from extended family and friends, but the fact was she would be a single mother raising three boys during The Depression. It's very easy to focus on my grandfather's struggles and successes on Rushmore and just as easy to take for granted the great sacrifices and pressures my grandmother must have endured during those years. Not to mention three little boys without a father figure. Still, both parents must have recognized that this was The Depression and a once in a lifetime opportunity lay within my grandfather's reach—refining the faces on the world's most iconic memorial. How could he turn it down? He couldn't. It would turn out to be the greatest privilege, and the greatest artistic achievement of his life.

I imagine my grandfather hugging his little boys, holding on tight to Nicoletta and then getting into his green Chevy to drive the 1,800 miles to the Black Hills of South Dakota. Because there was no Italian food in South Dakota, Luigi made sure to load the backseat with plenty of soppresata, capicola and Parmesan cheese. I love this letter my uncle found from Borglum's wife, Mary, who gave Luigi directions and "travel tips" on the best way to navigate the roads and limited highways of 1933.

I love how detailed Mary Borglum was about how much gas Luigi would need and the estimated cost of driving 1,800 miles. I also looked up what "tourist camps" were like in the 1930's. It varied. My grandfather could have rented a small cabin, pitched a tent, or simply parked his car and slept in it. There obviously wasn't modern plumbing in any of these camps. Travel on the road wasn't very pretty. The fact that Borglum was in Washington further supports the fact that he was likely there to lobby for funding. This explains why Mary makes it very clear that Luigi won't get paid right away. She also asks him to "borrow money to get out with." Clearly, there were no funds to provide Luigi with any travel expenses.

THE MENGER
SAN ANTONIO
TEXAS

April 23,1933.

Dear Bianco:-

Mr. Borglum would like you to go out to the Black Hills now as soon as you can. The work has started. He is going to Washington on Tuesday and from there to South Dakota. Lincoln and I are going straight north from here and will meet you in Dakota. The best way to go is through Philadelphia, where you strike the Lincoln Highway. Stay on the Lincoln Highway until you reach Dennison, Iowa. From Dennison go to Sioux City, Iowa, from there to Yankton, South Dakota and from there to Rapid City, South Dakota. When you get to Rapid City telephone Mr. John Boland, who will tell you what to do. Can you possibly borrow money to get out with. If you go by car it will cost about $75. It is two thousand miles. I don't know how many miles you get to a gallon with your car, but I thought gas and oil ought not to cost more than $40.00, and there are tourist camps along the road, where you can stop for a couple of dollars a night. Mr. Borglum cannot send you money for ten days or more and he would like to have you start right away. If you go by train get your ticket to Rapid City, South Dakota, by the Chicago and Northwestern from Chicago and telephone Mr. Boland when you get there. Our place is thirty miles in the country, but Mr. Boland will tell you where we are and what to do. You will be on the payroll as soon as you get there. I shall be away from here by Thursday and after Sunday can be reached at Hermosa, South Dakota. Mr. Borglum will be at the Metropolitan Club, Washington, D.C. Friday.

Sincerely yours,

M

My grandfather eventually made it to Rapid City and then to Keystone, which is the closest town to Mount Rushmore. I'm not sure whether he lived alone or had to bunk with other men, but there was no running water and no modern plumbing of any kind. The way to relieve yourself was in the ol' outhouse.

Keystone itself looked like a town right out of a John Wayne western, and it still does. Most of the residents were rough-and-tumble miners who came from Irish or various Scandinavian stock. These were hard men who worked all day in the mine and played cards, drank and brawled in the many saloons at night. These were the people Luigi came in contact with. I'm sure an Italian from Italy who spoke with an accent was not the type of person Keystone natives were used to. I'm sure to many, my grandfather was an old-world fascination; maybe even a novelty. In a way, you couldn't blame them. With the exception of the tourists that frequent Mount Rushmore, South Dakota residents are still very much isolated from most other ethnicities. Luigi Del Bianco was not what they were used to. That said, I know my grandfather got along well with the residents of Keystone. We can only speculate on what my grandfather might have encountered in the way of prejudice and bigotry in South Dakota all those years ago

Luigi got right to work. He was to be Chief Carver, charged with carving the "refinement of expression" in the faces. On May 4, my grandfather's arrival was important enough to make the press. Here is a news clipping from the *Aberdeen Daily News*:

Borglum Aide Arrives to Assist in Rushmore Work

RAPID CIT. May 4.—(AP)—L. Del Bianco, Port Chester, N. Y., sculptor, arrived in Rapid City this morning and will be an assistant to Gutzon Borglum, sculptor of the Mount Rushmore memorial. Mr. Borglum who has been in San Antonio, Texas, for the winter, and later in Washington, D. C., on business, is expected to arrive here this week-end to resume work on the monument, according to John A. Boland, member of the national commission.

Work on the monument has been under way for several weeks, under the direction of W. S. Tallman, superintendent.

Assistant to Gutzon Borglum; clearly Luigi was to work side by side with The Master. You'll see that reinforced more and more as you read on. Now, an interesting side note: Two months later, on June 29, the *Aberdeen Daily News* came back to interview Luigi, but it had nothing to do with Mount Rushmore. There was to be a boxing match between champion Jack Sharkey and a 6' 6" challenger, the Italian Primo Carnera. It just so happened that Carnera and my grandfather were paesans, and somehow the press found out and wanted to talk to Luigi about it.

Hills Sculptor Knew Carnera As Youth in Italy

RAPID CITY, June 29—(AP)—L. Del Bianco, Port Chester, N. Y., an Italian sculptor working on the Mount Rushmore Memorial in the Black Hills, under Gutzon Borglum, is particularly interested in tonight's fight between Jack Sharkey and Primo Carnera, giant Italian.

Del Bianco and Carnera were friends in Italy before either of them came to America, and when the fighter arrived in this coountry, Del Bianco was one of the first persons to greet him.

At the Rushmore Memorial Del Bianco has a lifesize cast that he once made of the doubled fist of Carnera. He has had to explain to many curious visitors that it is a fist of Carnera, and not a sledge hammer.

Primo defeated Jack Sharkey and became the first Italian heavyweight champion of the world. And that giant fist? My grandfather made many copies and gave them to his friends as gifts.

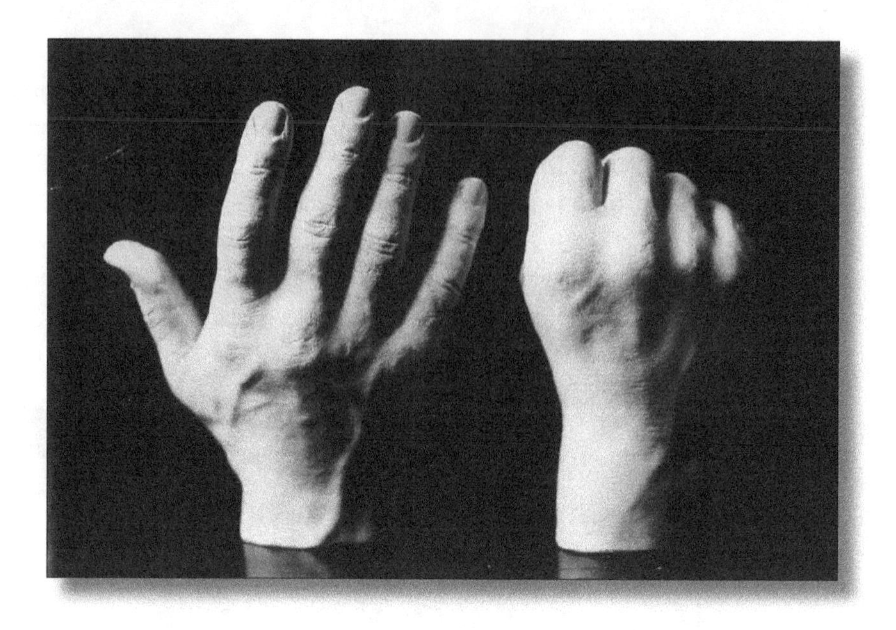

The open hand and fist of Primo Carnera, created by Luigi.

Luigi and Primo's families lived very close to each other in Pordenone, so the connection continued in America. It was an event when Primo Carnera, the heavyweight champion of the world, came to visit my grandfather's adopted hometown. Port Chester in 1933 had a very large Italian population, so Primo's visits were big news. My father remembers having to share a bed with the giant boxer; throughout the night Primo would turn over and constantly knock my father out of the bed. My father would then feel a giant hand grab his shoulder and a deep voice would bellow, "Vincenzo, vieni qui." Vincent would be hoisted back into the bed like a little doll.

When I was 6 or 7 years old, I discovered a torn photo stowed away in the cabinet above the kitchen sink. For years I always thought Primo was my grandfather. The mystery was solved one Thanksgiving when my Uncle Silvio told the family to gather around our 13-inch black and white TV to watch "Cousin Primo" in the movie "Mighty Joe Young." Primo was in a big nightclub scene where he and nine other strong men engaged in a tug of war with the giant ape. Thanksgiving and Primo on TV became a yearly tradition.

Luigi, left, and Primo, with copies of his giant fist.

But, I digress. Yes, Luigi comes to Rushmore to assist Borglum in finishing the faces. The memo below is the first evidence of my grandfather's role on the mountain. Borglum not only addresses Luigi as Chief Carver, he also outlines the work he needs him to do. (Keep in mind Luigi began work in April 1933. The chronology is solid, but not perfect.)

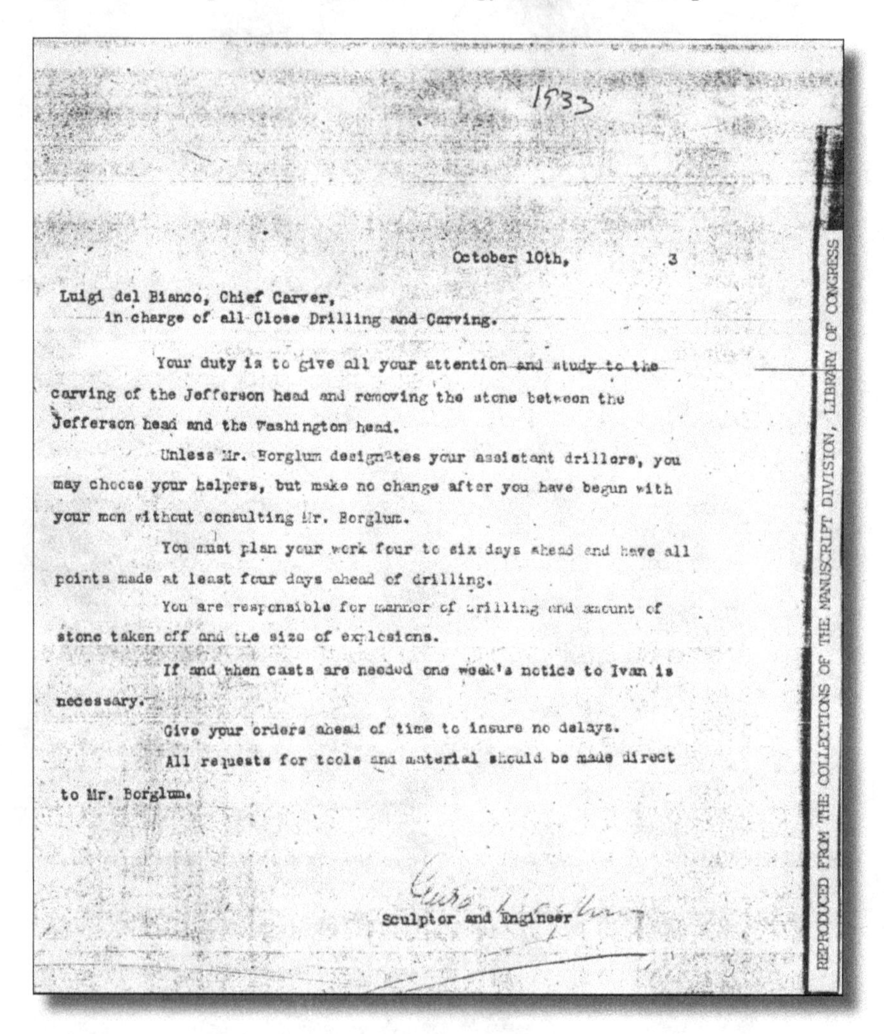

1933

October 10th, 3

Luigi del Bianco, Chief Carver,
in charge of all Close Drilling and Carving.

Your duty is to give all your attention ~~and study to the~~ carving of the Jefferson head and removing the stone between the Jefferson head and the Washington head.

Unless Mr. Borglum designates your assistant drillers, you may choose your helpers, but make no change after you have begun with your men without consulting Mr. Borglum.

You must plan your work four to six days ahead and have all points made at least four days ahead of drilling.

You are responsible for manner of drilling and amount of stone taken off and the size of explosions.

If and when casts are needed one week's notice to Ivan is necessary.

Give your orders ahead of time to insure no delays.

All requests for tools and material should be made direct to Mr. Borglum.

Sculptor and Engineer

You'll notice from this memo that Luigi was not only performing as Chief Carver, but also given the responsibility of directing precise removal of stone from drilling and dynamiting. (Not to mention the men working under him.)

Here is a daily record I found during my trip to Mount Rushmore in 1988. You'll see Luigi is listed as a carver, while all the other men are listed as drillers.

DAILY RECORD---Men-on-the-Granite Drilling and Carving

Mount Rushmore National Memorial

Daily---Reported to Gutzon Borglum, Sculptor Engineer

Name	Location	Progress / Approximate Feet Drilled	Completed and Shot	
Luigi del Bianco, CARVER 8	Jeff Wig	33'	33'	
O. E. Anderson, DRILLER 8	" "	52'	52'	
James Payne, DRILLER 8	" "	Pointing 18'	18'	
Alton Leach, DRILLER 10	Collar	88'	88'	
Elton Gordon, DRILLER 8	R. Collar	40'	40'	
Ray Grover DRILLER 10	Jefferson	83'	83'	
Merle Peterson, DRILLER 10	Jefferson	Drilling & Plugging		
George Hesnard, DRILLER 8	R. Collar	40'	40'	
H. Peterson 10	Collar 2 hrs	20'	20	
Alfred Berg, POWDER MAN 10		Drilled Areas Shot: 11 lines	Wired and Not Shot	
M. I. Cindel, BLACKSMITH	No. Drills Sharpened: 95	17 SD		

Reported and Signed J. A. Johnson, Foreman on Granite

Date Oct 10 1933

W. S. Tallman, Superintendent of Works

CHAPTER SEVENTEEN:

THE PROBLEMS BEGIN

IT IS IMPORTANT TO note that my grandfather was the only person to hold the title of Chief Carver on Mount Rushmore. Though it was only his first week on the project, it didn't take long for the other shoe to drop. Perhaps this important role, this great American privilege granted to an Italian immigrant, was too good to be true. From the start, Luigi's presence was met with resistance from those who Borglum described as "people in the Rapid City office."

One of the most compelling documents my Uncle Caesar discovered outlines the "petty dickering over wages" that forced my grandfather to threaten to quit. How can you blame him? It was The Depression. Luigi left his family for months at a time and wasn't being paid the money he needed to wire back to his family. But Borglum had my grandfather's back; he makes it very clear how vitally important my grandfather was and that without him, work on finishing the faces would have to stop.

In 1933 I notified Tallman and my son, Lincoln, who was here pointing, that I was bringing with me as assistant, a semi-sculptor who had been with me off and on in the east for twelve years, a powerful, capable granite man, whom I had converted into an efficient marble cutter. I was immediately notified that his presence here was objected to and that the Rapid City office did not want him. I ignored this and put him immediately in charge of the work and workmen on Washington's head, meaning the face and wig.

He complained to me within a week of the treatment he was being accorded from the Rapid City office,

9.

rudeness, insolence and petty dickering about wages. He remained here on my orders and my account, but, he will never come again. He will, however, form one of my head men at Stone Mountain. He is worth any three men I could find in America, for this particular type of work, here and now, but Mount Rushmore is not managed that way and doesn't want that kind of service. He entirely out-classed everyone on the hill, and his knowledge was an embarrassment to their amateur efforts and lack of knowledge, lack of experience and lack of judgment. He is the only man besides myself who has been on the work who knows the problems and how to instantly solve them. His absence is a great loss to this work this year.

Because of these conditions, I have left the head of Washington unfinished. It will remain unfinished in the vital points until interference with the executive work of the sculptor on the Mountain is stopped. The eyes, the nose, the mouth and chin, where the hair touches the face, will not be touched until men capable of handling such work are welcomed to the work. I intend to protect all the rest of the fine work on the Mountain in precisely the same way, and shall risk none of it until I have competent men to do it.

The loss of Bianco will probably prevent the finishing of the Washington and Jefferson heads this year.

I can remember like it was yesterday, when my Uncle Caesar read the statement—"He is worth more than any three men in America for this particular type of work." I can still see him there, practically shouting the quote, his hands shaking with excitement as he clutched the paper he had found. "The loss of Bianco will probably prevent the finishing of the Washington and Jefferson heads this year."

It doesn't get better than that. It was obvious from this primary source document, straight from the mouth of Gutzon Borglum, that Luigi Del Bianco was not just the only carver capable of refining the features of the faces, but that his quitting would leave those features untouched. I sincerely doubt that if any of the other 400 people who worked on the project quit, it would have had the same effect.

So, Luigi quits and Borglum is without his one and only Chief Carver. The memo below shows how Borglum will go to any length to keep his granite expert. (I added the text below the document because the handwriting is too difficult to read.)

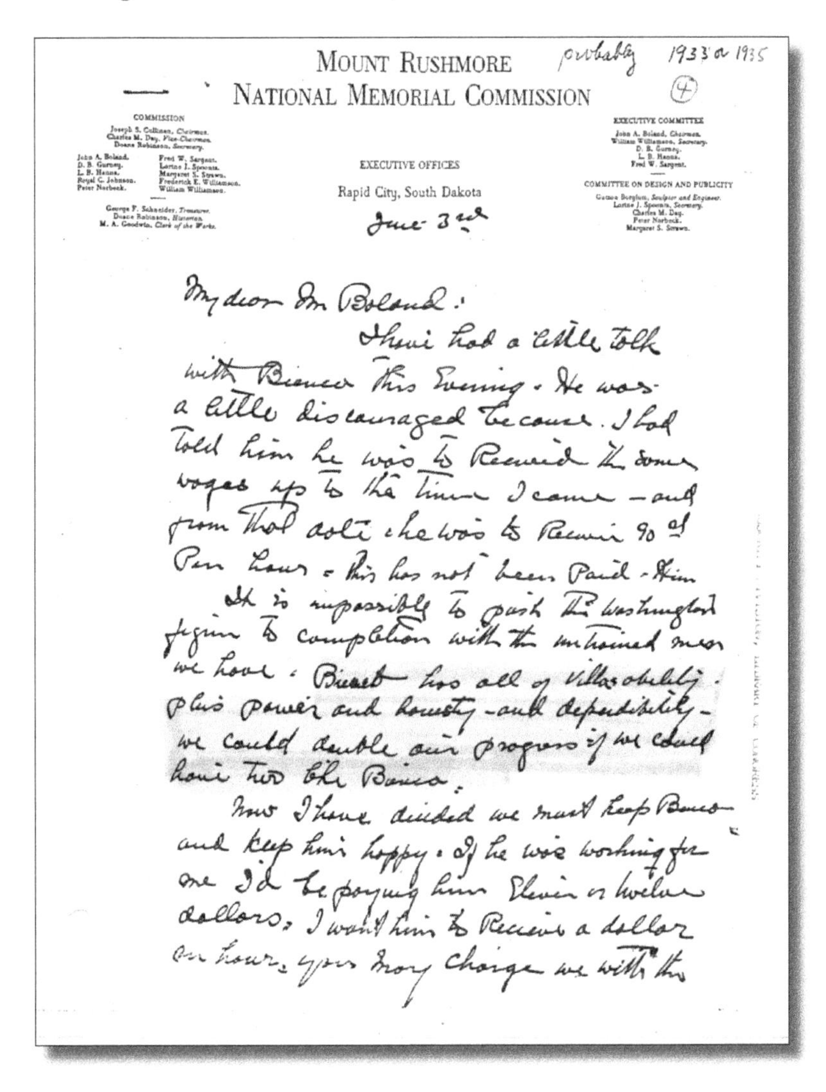

MOUNT RUSHMORE
NATIONAL MEMORIAL COMMISSION

probably 1933 or 1935 (4)

COMMISSION
Joseph S. Cullinan, Chairman.
Charles M. Day, Vice-Chairman.
Doane Robinson, Secretary.
John A. Boland. D. B. Gurney. L. B. Hanna. Royal C. Johnson. Peter Norbeck.
Fred W. Sargent. Lorine J. Spoonts. Margaret S. Strawn. Frederick E. Williamson. William Williamson.
George F. Schneider, Treasurer.
Doane Robinson, Historian.
M. A. Goodwin, Clerk of the Works.

EXECUTIVE OFFICES
Rapid City, South Dakota

EXECUTIVE COMMITTEE
John A. Boland, Chairman.
William Williamson, Secretary.
D. B. Gurney.
L. B. Hanna.
Fred W. Sargent.

COMMITTEE ON DESIGN AND PUBLICITY
Gutzon Borglum, Sculptor and Engineer.
Lorine J. Spoonts, Secretary.
Charles M. Day.
Peter Norbeck.
Margaret S. Strawn.

June 3rd

My dear Mr Boland:

I have had a little talk with Bianco this evening. He was a little discouraged because I had told him he was to receive the same wages up to the time I came — and from that date he was to receive 90 cts per hour — this has not been paid him.

It is impossible to push the Washington figure to completion with the untrained men we have. Bianco has all of Villa's ability plus power and honesty — and dependability — we could double our progress if we could have two like Bianco.

Now I have decided we must keep Bianco and keep him happy. If he was working for me I'd be paying him eleven or twelve dollars. I want him to receive a dollar an hour. You may charge me with the

the difference - the help he is, the ability to
understand is worth much more to the
work - I shall take him to Stone Mountain
with me next winter - which only means
he knows this kind of work - and there
are no trained men in this work except
such as I have trained.
Please give him this allowance
from the date of our talk - and as
I say charge the difference to me

Very Sincerely
Gutzon Borglum

Hon John A Boland
Rapid City
S. D.
Chairman Executive
Committee

P.S. -
Every thing is in shape in Chicago and [illegible] is
on the way Back.

June 3

My Dear Mr. Boland,

I had a little talk with Bianco this evening. He was a little discouraged because I had told him he was to receive the same wages up to the time I came—and from that date he was to receive 90 cents an hour. This has not been paid him.

It is impossible to push the Washington figure to completion with the untrained men we have. Bianco has all of Villa's ability plus power and honesty. We could double our progress if we had two like Bianco.

Now I have decided we must keep Bianco and keep him happy. If he was working for me, I'd be paying him eleven or twelve dollars. I want him to receive a dollar an hour. You may charge me with the difference. The help he is, the ability to understand, is worth much more to this work.

I will take him to Stone Mountain with me next winter—which means he knows this type of work—and there are no trained men in this work such is I have trained.

Please give him this allowance from the date of our talk—and as I say charge the difference to me.

Very Sincerely,

Gutzon Borglum

It is clear from this memo that Borglum is at his wit's end. If you are paying part of someone's salary that person must be very important to you. I won't belabor the point, except to say that Borglum's writing speaks for itself. In 1933, right after he is hired and then threatening to quit, Luigi decides to stay. I know this because the daily record I found and posted earlier shows the date of October 10, 1933, which was considered very late in the season. Luigi obviously worked on Rushmore for at least seven months; or in other words, most of the 1933 season.

As my Uncle Caesar uncovered more information in document after document, it became increasingly clear to us both that Borglum and Bianco had a special relationship. Mutual admiration existed between the two artists. Borglum trusted no one but Luigi to carve the most detailed part of the faces.

Luigi working on Washington's forehead.
Photo: Del Bianco Family Collection.

CHAPTER EIGHTEEN:

THE PULL OF *LA FAMIGLIA*

EVEN THOUGH LUIGI AGREED to stay on the project, something else was tugging at his heart. In Port Chester, NY, 1,800 miles away, lived his loving wife and three young sons, all under the age of 10. To be separated for many months had to have been a terrible emotional strain on a father and his family. In July of 1933, my grandfather sent this tender postcard to Silvio and Vincent. (Caesar was only 2 years old.)

POST CARD

23-7-1933.

Mr Vincent Del Bianco
#326 William St
Port Chester N.Y.

July 23, 1933

My dearest children,

I am well and so I would wish you the same. Be good because I will send you a beautiful costume, also to Silvio. Today I have sent Silvio an Indian costume and I hope he will receive it.

Kisses from your Papa

I love this postcard. *Kisses from your Papa.* I could just hear my grandmother reading it to my father and uncle and seeing their little faces light up for a moment. What mixed feelings Luigi must have had. What else could my grandfather do? He had to try to bridge that 1,800-mile gap between him and his boys. So, he bought them both Indian costumes to show his long-distance love.

That same year, Nicoletta sent Luigi a photo of the three boys and a tender note from Silvio.

Dear Daddy,

We are in good health, only we miss you a whole lot. We hope you will hurry and come home, so we could be happy with you. I go to school now and listen to my teacher and try hard to learn good.

Lots of love and kisses,

Silvio

So we could be happy with you. To me, this is such a beautifully simple and direct sentiment coming from the heart of a child; a son needing his papa. This must have brought tears to my grandfather's eyes. How could my grandmother possibly explain their father's absence to her little boys?

"Mama, where is Papa?"

"He is 1,800 miles away on a mountain carving George Washington's eyes."

It would be surreal enough for an adult to absorb, but a 7-year-old? This would be the first of many letters filled with bittersweet longing between a man and his loved ones.

The year of 1934 shows no record of my grandfather being at Mount Rushmore. It's possible he was there; the records at the mountain have been known to be spotty at best. There is, however, one interesting note in 1934 from Borglum to John Boland that bears mentioning. On May 18, Borglum wrote to Boland about preparations for the season.

Metropolitan Club
Washington, D.C.

May 18. 1934

My dear Mr. Boland,

I have your letter regarding funds: on which I am depending - and have written our Supt to assemble his leaders - Foreman - Johnson, also - tool man and Blacksmith [illegible] Friday 25th prepare frame cables winches - [illegible] scaffold swings. and pipe lines engines - compressors and be ready to put full force at work Monday morning - May 28th beginning the first day of week =

I shall be there to see the work is begun and always followed =

I am bringing Bianco, and Lincoln: and will add an understudy for Lincoln - maybe two - young sculptors and when I can find him a man like Bianco:

Yours truly
Gutzon Borglum

Confidential.
Roosevelt will probably visit us in July -

May 13, 1934

Metropolitan Club

My Dear Mr. Boland,

I have your letter regarding funds which I am depending and have written our Supt. to assemble his leaders from Johnson, also tool man and Blacksmith (?). Friday May 25 prepare and examine cables and winches, scaffolds and swings and (?) (?) engines, compressors and be ready to put full force work Monday morning. May 28th beginning the first day of week.

I shall be there to see that the work is begun and orders followed.

I am bringing Bianco and Lincoln and will add an understudy for Lincoln, maybe two young sculptors and when I can find him a man like Bianco.

Yours truly,

Gutzon Borglum

Confidential

Roosevelt will probably visit us in July.

Apparently, Borglum had every intention of "bringing" Bianco back to Rushmore in 1934. He also was hoping he could find another man like my grandfather, a sentiment he shared in another memorandum in 1933. Did Luigi come?

One thing is for sure: Borglum wanted Bianco there and wanted more men like him.

One document that always gave me pause is the daily record that is on display in the workers' museum at Rushmore.

DAILY RECORD---Men-on-the-Granite Drilling and Carving

Mount Rushmore National Memorial

Daily---Reported to Gutzon Borglum, Sculptor Engineer

Luigi del Bianco, CARVER	Location	Progress		
O. E. Anderson, DRILLER 8	Location Jefferson	Approximate Feet Drilled 40'	Completed and Shot 40'	
James Payne, DRILLER 8	" "	30'	30'	
Alton Leach, DRILLER 8	R Collar	20'		
Elton Gordon, DRILLER 8	" "	8'		
Ray Grover DRILLER 8	Jefferson	27'	27'	
Merle Peterson, DRILLER 8	L Collar	30		
George Hesnard, DRILLER 8	Collar front	20'		
J. Payne 8	Chest	65'	65'	
C. Vranich 8	L Shoulder	65'		
			230'	8 1933 finished + shot
Alfred Berg, POWDER MAN B Eilbeck 8		Drilled Areas Shot 6 lines	Wired and Not Shot	
M. I. Cindel, BLACKSMITH	No. Drills Sharpened 86	12 8 Bits		

Reported and Signed J. A. Johnson Foreman on Granite

Date June 15 1934

Superintendent of Works

I always found it puzzling that Mount Rushmore never listed my grandfather as working on the mountain in 1934. Yet, there is Luigi, listed at the top and the year 1934 at the bottom of the page—displayed in the Rushmore Museum, to boot. If he wasn't there in 1934, wouldn't Mr. Johnson, the foreman, have crossed his name out or made a note stating his absence for the record?

After seven months of separation in 1933, Luigi must have seen the effect it had on his family. The vast majority of the men who worked on Rushmore were local guys who could be with their wives and children at the end of the day. Their quality of life in that regard was never sacrificed. Evidenced by the family's correspondence, Luigi had to have deeply felt that familial void. I think that's why, when the 1935 season rolled around, he convinced my grandmother and his sons to pack their bags and come to live with him in South Dakota.

Luigi and Silvio, Caesar and Vincent, circa 1935.

CHAPTER NINETEEN:

HERE COME THE DEL BIANCOS

THE OLD TIMERS IN Port Chester used to tell me that, as children, they stood on the sidewalk watching the Del Bianco family pack up their green Chevy for the long trek to the Black Hills. It must have taken a great deal of charming negotiation on my grandfather's part to convince my grandmother to uproot herself and her children. A New York Italian-American family going to live out West during The Depression? But they did it. Like any traditional Italian, my grandfather must have really wanted to keep the family together.

Traveling halfway across the country in a car during The Depression with three boys under the age of 12 must have been challenging, to say the least. Without modern plumbing, just the bathroom breaks alone had to have been memorable. I only wish my grandmother had lived long enough for me to hear her stories.

When the Del Biancos finally arrived in Keystone, they settled into their little cabin. My family was by no means wealthy, but they were all used to modern plumbing back in Port Chester. In Keystone, there was none of that. I can just hear my grandmother shout, *What? No toilet? Oh, God help me!* Worse yet, the one store in Keystone, Halley's General Store, had none of the vegetables and ingredients my grandmother needed to make the Italian meals the family was used to. (There were not many Italians living in Keystone.)

Bob Hayes, whose father was Edward Hayes, the tram operator for Rushmore, knew the Del Bianco family well and cemented a friendship with my dad that lasted until the day my father died. On Bob's website, he fondly remembered my grandmother and how frustrated she was with the "culture shock" she experienced in Keystone, particularly the issue of not having the right macaroni or basil for her cooking. According to Bob,

Nicoletta had her Italian items shipped from New York on a weekly basis, so every meal would feel like home. In short, my grandmother did not like living in South Dakota.

On the other hand, my father and uncles loved it. For my father especially, it was as if every western he loved seeing at a Saturday matinee was brought to life before his eyes. The tree-covered terrain, the western architecture and even the local Native Americans added to the mystique of the "Wild West" that my father was so enamored with. I remember as a boy sitting on the floor, enthralled by my father's recollections of the year he spent living in the Black Hills.

> *"I loved it. My brother Silvio and I would spend every day in the woods. We'd make our own fires, cook potatoes or heat up our sandwiches. We went to the school there with the kids of the workers on the mountain. It was one building and one teacher. She would work with all the grades, from kindergarten to high school, all by herself.*
>
> *There were only 20 kids, tops. That's all. School was easy out there. It would get so hot in the summer that we would swim in the big ponds there before school, after school, even during lunch. The boys would take off their clothes and swim in the pond bare assed. The girls would keep their underwear on. So what? We were kids. We didn't care. When it was time to go back to New York, I felt lousy."*

Silvio, Caesar and Vincent in Keystone, South Dakota, circa 1935.

My father also remembers the time he visited Gutzon Borglum's ranch in Hermosa, which was not far from the mountain.

> *"Borglum had a beautiful horse. He was a show horse, so nobody was supposed to go near him. One day, I got on top and tried to ride him. Borglum came up from behind me, yelling like a bastard. He grabbed me and threw me off the horse, and then started kicking me in the ass. Oh, he really let me have it. Then my mother came out of the house because she saw what happened. My mother was only 4'11", but she walked up to Borglum and said, 'If you touch my son again, I won't let my husband come back to finish your faces!'*
>
> *"Borglum looked down at my mother and he laughed, 'Ok, Mrs. Del Bianco, whatever you say.' After a while Borglum let me ride the horse, but only when he was there."*

Vincent on his favorite horse.

My father's fascination with Native Americans went far beyond what he watched on television. He really admired their spirit and the fact that they wanted to live their lives free and independent from any central authority. When Vincent found out that my grandfather had befriended the chief from the local reservation, it was like he had died and gone to heaven. Vincent recalled all too well his father Luigi's special bond with the Lakota Sioux.

> *"The Indians out there, they were shunned. They were nuthin'. My old man, he fell right in with them. He put them at ease."*

My father used to love showing me the scar on his thumb, representing a unique rite of passage for an Italian American boy from New York.

> *"One night we went to the reservation, and they did a blood brother ceremony. The chief cut his thumb, then my old man's. He put them together and they became blood brothers. Then my brother Silvio and I became blood brothers with the chief's sons."*

I truly believe if my father had to pick the top 10 moments in his life that moment would have been one of them.

Luigi on the mountain with his unlikely friends, the Lakota Sioux.

I also believe my grandfather felt the same way. The connection he had with the Sioux was something exceedingly unique: the joining of Italian and Native American cultures. The best indication of this was the Sunday Italian meals my family used to have at the reservation. My father told me about it like it had happened yesterday.

> *"We'd go to the reservation and my mother would make the gravy and four or five pounds of macaroni for the whole tribe. Forty to fifty people. They always asked for my mother's gravy. Then they learned to cook it themselves."*

As an artist, my grandfather was also inspired by his new friends. My father told me:

> *"He liked the way they looked. He was always doing little drawings of them. He also made little carvings and would give them away. Oh, the Indians loved my old man."*

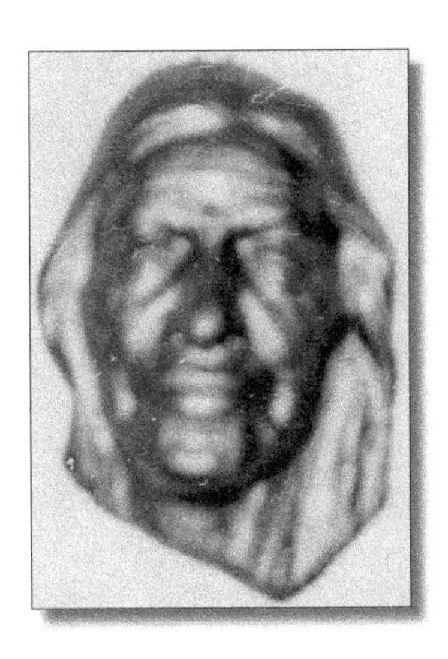

A small head my grandfather made for the Chief of Pine Ridge Reservation.

When I went back to Mount Rushmore in 1988, I was tempted to visit Pine Ridge Reservation. I wanted to go from house to house, hoping to find one of my grandfather's carved heads sitting on a mantel. I might also discover a Native American family eating a time-honored recipe of macaroni and gravy, taught to their ancestors by a kindly Italian mother who wanted to share her culture and love of cooking with them. I never did. I should have.

What about Vincent's recollections of Mount Rushmore? My father had clear memories of Luigi and Borglum constantly arguing about the best way to transfer the five-foot models in the studio to the 60-foot faces on the mountain. As my father explained:

> *"Borglum and my old man would have fights. Borglum would say, 'Christ, Bianco, you're stubborn!' My father would say, 'I have to be with you!' Borglum respected my old man because he knew stone. My father would say to me, 'Don't worry. I'll get him to change his mind.' And he usually did."*

When asked if Luigi respected Borglum, my father said, *"Are you kidding me? He loved Borglum. Borglum taught my old man a lot. Don't say anything bad about Borglum. He was The Master. The Master."*

Luigi studying the models in Borglum's studio.
Photo: Del Bianco Family Collection.

Luigi posing with an unidentified female figure.
Photo: Del Bianco Family Collection.

My father's face became the most animated when he talked about the mountain itself.

> *"One time Papa took my brother Silvio and me up to the top. We had to walk up all those wooden stairs. Christ, it took forever! When we got to the top, I was scared. I'll never forget it."*

He also recalled what it was like to see Mount Rushmore from the ground.

> *"When we would come home from school, me and my brothers and the other workers' kids would go to the bottom of the mountain and wave up to our daddies while they worked. I could see them real well 'cause my old man gave me a pair of binoculars."*

The 706 steps that led up to the faces on Mount Rushmore.
One trip up was like walking almost halfway up the Empire State Building.
***Photo from Rex Alan Smith's,* The Carving of Mount Rushmore.**

My father didn't share much, but man, he sure could talk about his life in Keystone. I loved watching my father's face light up as he talked about those days in 1935. Until the day he died, my Dad still used Western phrases like *I reckon* and *Thank you kindly*, all because of the one-year stay in South Dakota. Seven-year-old Vincent really fell in love with the life out there. He absolutely did not want to go back to New York. When he did, Vincent continued to emulate the Native Americans and Western natives of the Black Hills.

Vincent in sixth grade, seated as the Indian Chief at Washington Elementary School in Port Chester, NY.

If you believe in past lives, you can imagine Vincent having once-upon-a-time been a Lakota Sioux warrior. In the present, he remained a 7-year-old kid having the greatest adventure of his life.

CHAPTER TWENTY:

HOW DID THEY CARVE THOSE GIANT FACES?

WHILE VINCENT'S MOTHER NICOLETTA was home cooking and he and his brothers were exploring the woods or swimming in Battle Creek, his father Luigi was propped 500 feet in the air, putting the soul into iconic faces.

Under the direction of Gutzon Borglum, Luigi was a major part of the process of transforming a blank mountainous canvas into four fully finished 60-foot granite faces.

Many people at the time thought Borglum was crazy. After all, this had never been tried before, so there were bound to be challenges. Fortunately, Borglum was not only a great artist but also an ingenious engineer, a skill that played a big role in achieving a seemingly impossible task. Borglum used his engineering prowess to devise a five-part process to bring those faces to life. Luigi was one of the most important people entrusted by Borglum to see this unique process through.

1. POINTING

Pointing is probably the most important element of stone carving. It is the transference of measurements, or "points," from the sculpted model to the finished product. As a classically trained stone carver, Luigi came to Rushmore already an expert in this field.

Here is a photo of Mount Rushmore before any of the faces were there.

Mount Rushmore before the big transformation.

To transfer these points, Borglum constructed two different pointing machines. Let's use the head of Washington as an example. (Refer to the illustration below).

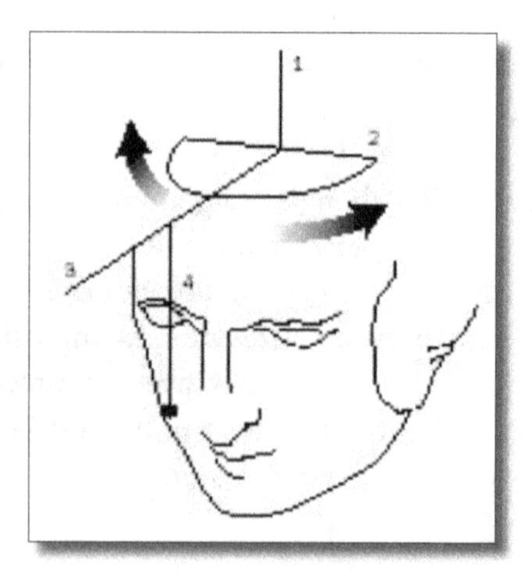

One machine sat on the head of the model, and the other, much bigger machine sat on the head at the mountain. Because the model was 5 feet and the granite head was 60 feet, measurements had to be done in a ratio of 1:12.

At the center of Washington's head (#1) is the master point. The right to left angles (#2) work like a protractor. The horizontal measurement is on the boom, which is the beam that juts straight out from Washington's face (#3). The vertical measurement is on the plumb bob, which is the weight hanging at the bottom of the rope (#4). Measurements 2, 3 and 4 combine to make one measured "point." Let's say Luigi wanted to find a measured point at the tip of Washington's nose. He'd simply move the plumb bob (#4) right to the tip of the nose on the model and leave it there. Then he would measure the angle the bob was at (#2), then measure how far in the plum bob was (#3) and finally measure how far down the plumb bob hung (#4). Then Luigi would go to the 60-foot granite head and take those same three measurements multiplied by 12. That would give him the similar measurement or point on the granite head. Now Luigi would know how much stone would have to be removed to get to that duplicated point. After thousands and thousands of points measured and transferred, the granite head would eventually resemble the model.

One point was calculated by taking three measurements: The angle (#2 in the above illustration), the height (#4) and the depth (#3). All three measurements combined made one measured point. Luigi would take that measurement from the 5-foot model, multiply by 12, and transfer that point to the 60-foot face.

The large pointing machine on top of Washington's head.
***Photo from Rex Alan Smith's,* The Carving of Mount Rushmore.**

Obviously, this was a very crucial part of the process. Borglum entrusted my grandfather to supervise the men when pointing was being done. There was absolutely no room for error. Once you measured the points and then removed the stone, you couldn't put it back like clay or plaster. The memo from Borglum below shows how Lincoln Borglum, who was trained by his father to be a very capable chief pointer, was told to "assist" the much older and more experienced "Bianco" when pointing. (Continue to keep in mind that the vast majority of men who worked on Rushmore were untrained. Lincoln, who was in fact trained, was one of many who Luigi took under his wing during the project.)

Lincoln Borglum Pointer in charge.

You will hold yourself in readiness to assist Bianco in all pointing (the taking of measurements necessary on the sculpture work on Mount Rushmore) until further written orders.

I want the work on the face of Washington finished (by Bianco) beginning ten inches from the hair line procede downward. I want all this work accurately pointed over the surface, every inch on the model, every twelve inches on the Mountain.

Tallman will aid you and Bianco with scaffold and men in every way, promptly as necessary. Be careful in setting the winches to the back of Washington's head. Billy has a floor of loose stone where the new work-shed will be and he will find it difficult to fasten his winches to this floor. No work must be done now without points!!! Suggest to him laying down two heavy timbers and drill deep and hold these timbers down, then bolt winches to these timbers, get book for record of points, and keep a separate page for each set of points with date.

2. BLASTING

Believe it or not, a vast majority of the stone removed from Mount Rushmore was not done using chisels or even drills. It was done using dynamite. To remove the stone any other way would have taken many years; so Borglum hired two experienced powder men to surgically blast off the stone using a precise measured amount of explosive. The technique of rough carving using dynamite had never been attempted before. Mistakes were unacceptable. Any stone dynamited off the mountain could not be put back. After a certain amount of trial and error, the powder men became extremely adept at the exact stone removal down to the inch. Below is a photo of Lincoln slowly starting to appear after the area had been blasted over and over.

***Photo from Rex Alan Smith's,* The Carving of Mount Rushmore.**

3. DRILLING

Once the stone had been sufficiently blasted, it was time for the drillers to get to work. The following photo shows workers drilling on the face of George Washington. The drill bits had to be sharpened several times a day because the granite was so hard. If you look closely, you can see the exposed lines made from drilling straight in to the stone after the excess stone had been broken off. Depending on what part of the face they were working on, every drill went down to about six inches from the final measured point. With so many points to measure, you can imagine how many holes had to be drilled to slowly shape the faces.

***Photo from Rex Alan Smith's,* The Carving of Mount Rushmore.**

4. HONEYCOMBING

The fourth part of the process, honeycombing, is one that my grandfather utilized quite a bit. On the next page is a photo of Luigi drilling a series of holes close together and then another of him breaking off the stone. Each hole is drilled down very close to the final measured point. The drilled holes could be of varying depths, depending on the topography on that part of the face. Honeycombing was a very useful technique because carvers like Luigi could have optimal control when they broke off each bit of honeycombed stone. It's the same idea as perforated paper. It is much easier to rip the paper cleanly with a tight line of holes to aid you. Without those holes, you have very little control over how you want the paper to tear.

***Photo from Rex Alan Smith's,* The Carving of Mount Rushmore.**

Luigi honeycombing.
Photo: Del Bianco Family Collection.

5. FINISHING

Gutzon Borglum was a true pioneer. He created innovative techniques for carving images in stone on a grand scale. One such technique was in finishing the faces to give them that fleshy, life like appearance. In *The Carving of Mount Rushmore*, Rex Alan Smith does a fine job explaining this final phase of the process:

> *"This was done by carvers using 'bumpers'—light, handheld pneumatic hammers driving short steel shafts tipped with four stubby fingers that chattered against the granite and removed it by a fraction of an inch and by the ounce.*
>
> *As part of the finishing, carvers bumped away the polka dotting of round freckles left by the holes drilled in honeycombing, and they smoothed away the roughness created by breaking the stone between those holes."*

In the end, it was Borglum and mostly Bianco who shaped those subtle nuances on the stone faces, particularly where the eyes, nose and mouth needed classically trained hands. In fact, in the final phase of carving, five-foot plaster models of the faces were hoisted up to the mountain. The models were placed right next to the 60-foot faces so my grandfather could have the perfect reference point as he gave the presidents their "refinement of expression." In the photo below, you can see Luigi with the five-foot model; to his right is the cheek and jaw line of the 60-foot Abraham Lincoln.

Luigi finishing the Lincoln face. Photo: Del Bianco Family Collection.

When Luigi was done finishing, he ended up with something like the face below. Not bad, eh?

Lincoln's mostly finished face.
***Photo from Rex Alan Smith's,* The Carving of Mount Rushmore.**

This five-part process was revolutionary, and it served as a model for future sculptors who wanted to carve stone on a grand scale. As evidenced in previous documents about Lincoln Borglum, Luigi was not only finishing the faces, but also had to supervise the men and instruct them in the finesse of pointing, drilling and carving. The excerpt below is yet another example of how Borglum put even his trained men alongside Bianco, so they could learn from him. William Tallman, a talented sculptor who knew my grandfather back in Borglum's Stamford, CT days, was one of those men. (I'm providing the text only because the original handwriting is very hard to read.)

SCULPTURE NATIONAL MEMORIAL

MOUNT RUSHMORE

Instructions for Pointing and Drilling

Date: September 22nd, 1933

To: Mr. Tallman,

"I will give you as much time personally with Bianco. He is the only man here on the mountain who understands granite and this work as sculpture—you will learn much and you will be of great help to him and the work itself. I need this kind of assistance you alone can give him."

Gutzon Borglum

Time and again, Borglum made it very clear that Luigi was much more than a "worker." "Bianco" was of singular importance to the work not only as a carver but also as a teacher and mentor even to the few trained men the mountain had.

You also have to understand that Borglum spent a good deal of time away from Rushmore. He was constantly shuttling back and forth to Washington, DC to lobby for the funding that the project so desperately needed. During The Depression, this must have been a monumental task for Borglum. As a result, he greatly depended on my grandfather to supervise the carving and anything else of consequence while he was away. Borglum didn't trust many people. He knew he could trust "Bianco."

Luigi del Bianco

I shall be away for possibly two weeks and wish you select two helpers from the men and take up the pointing.

1st. of Washington's head - the top and bak, also the sides, especially the side towards Lincoln.

2nd. Begin 10" below the hair and point and carve the forehead of Washington down to the brow. If this is done before I return, you will finish the side of the temples like the model - Washington.

3rd. I would like you to point the rest of Washington's face as closely as possible, Lincoln helping you. I have instructed him to check all pointing and be with you in fixing any important points. They can rough off the hair and forehead of Lincoln, but go down only as far as you approve. I intend to stop carving from a swing. The work is too important. Bill will get lumber right away for scaffold.

GUTZON BORGLUM

Borglum put Bianco in charge of every aspect of the carving. For a perfectionist and control freak like Borglum, it was high praise that he entrusted Luigi with his masterpiece.

It is also interesting to note that during this time Borglum would stop "carving from a swing" because "the work is too important." Many people don't realize that when Borglum started carving Mount Rushmore, he was already 60 years old and not exactly in the right time of his life to be scaling a mountain and carving giant faces. By the mid-1930's, Borglum was pushing 70. I think it is safe to assume that the designer of Mount Rushmore realized that he could give his body a rest and leave the finishing to my grandfather.

And finish Luigi did. In particular, the most vital parts of the faces, meaning the eyes, nose and mouth. Throughout most of the project, Borglum left those parts untouched until Bianco was there to do them.

When Luigi wasn't at the mountain, Borglum would say the same thing: *"The eyes, the nose, the mouth and chin, where the hair touches the face, will not be touched until men capable of handling such work are welcomed to the work."*

Luigi putting the soul into one of the presidents' eyes.

Borglum had an especially brilliant approach when it came to carving the eyes. When he and his son, Lincoln, were traveling on horseback to find the right mountain to carve, Mount Rushmore became the perfect choice. For one thing, the mountain had a strong eastern exposure to the sun, so when it traveled across the sky throughout the day, the sun would create a myriad of effects on the granite surface. Borglum saw this as a great opportunity to use chiaroscuro on a surface. He devised a way to carve the pupil of the eyes as a shaft of granite that jutted out from the eye like the piece on a sundial. Anyone who has been to Rushmore will attest that if you look at the eyes of the presidents at 10 AM and then again at 2 PM, the expression seems different; the shafts of granite in the eyes in conjunction with the changing sunlight creates an interplay of shadow and light that gives the faces a unique and almost touching quality. This was Borglum's ingenious idea. He trusted no one but Bianco to perfect it for him. It's of Luigi bringing one of the presidents' eyes (possibly Washington's) to life. As a child, I always used to imagine my grandfather singing and talking to the presidents while he worked.

CHAPTER TWENTY-ONE:

MONEY PROBLEMS AGAIN

THE INGENIOUS DESIGNER AND his Chief Carver worked side-by-side. By 1935, much progress had been made. At the end of July, the issue of getting paid once again reared its ugly head. On July 29, Luigi sent this letter to "The Master" in Italian. Mary Borglum, Gutzon's wife, was fluent in Italian and probably translated it.

Keystone South Dakota
29-7-1935

Egregio Signor Gutzon Borglum.

Sono già sette settimane che
lavoro nel National Memorial per solo
8.00 al giorno
Voi mi avete promesso $12.00 al giorno
così se voi volete che io continui
lavorare per voi dovete pagare $12.00
il giorno altrimenti col I Agosto sarò
obbligato a sospendere il mio lavoro
che tanto mi dispiace dopo tanti anni
che ho lavorato per voi.

rispettosi saluti
vostro Luigi Del Bianco

Translation of Bianco's letter

Keystone, South Dakota.
29-7-1935.

Hon. Gutzon Borglum;-

It has already been seven weeks that I have been working on the National Memorial for $6.00 a day.

You promised me $12.00 a day, so if you want me to con-time to work for you, you will have to pay me $12,00 a day, otherwise on the first of August I shall be obliged to stop my work, which will cause me great regret, after all the years that I have worked for you.

Respectfully yours,

Luigi del Bianco

This was obviously a painful letter for Luigi to write. He clearly wants to stay and continue the work he was destined to do. But he had a wife and three children to feed, and the same problem that occurred in 1933 was happening again.

This must have been especially difficult for my grandfather because he had already uprooted his wife and sons to live out in the Black Hills with him, and now he was considering leaving again. Keep in mind it had only been seven weeks. A family having to acclimate to a strange, new life would have to pack up and leave again.

I always imagine what my grandparents had to talk about when these issues arose. I'm sure my grandmother had mixed feelings. On one hand, she would have loved to get in that Chevy and drive right back to New York. On the other hand, she now knew that her husband was part of something big; something very important for our country.

Borglum never had mixed feelings about my grandfather. He needed him. By the evidence of these many primary source documents, he needed him badly. The very next day, on July 30, Borglum sent a memorandum to William Tallman reiterating Luigi's role and importance as Chief Carver.

July 30,1935

Re-organization No.2.

William Tallman

Please post this in the dining room for the men.

All drilling of all kinds, roughing, finishing and carving of features must be directed by the chief stone carver on the work and his directions followed.

The chief carver will be held responsible for the ways and the means for removing and finishing the sculpture.

No work must be put in hand for drilling or finishing not concurred in by the pointer chief and the sculptor.

The carver chief will select from the drillers the most experienced men for finishing.

I have appointed Luigi Bianco for this most important task. He will call upon the pointers to supply at call any points necessary to carry on the work and Arthur Johnson, foreman of the job on the mountain will give him immediate assistance in the supply of men, tools, scaffolding in advance of needs.

July 30, 1935

Re-organization No. 2.

William Tallman

Please post this in the dining room for the men.

All drilling of all kinds, roughing, finishing of features must be directed by the chief stone carver on the work and his directions followed.

The chief carver will be held responsible for the ways and means for removing and finishing the sculpture.

No work must be put in hand for drilling or finishing not concurred in by the pointer chief and sculptor.

The carver chief will select from the drillers the most experienced men in finishing.

I have appointed Luigi Bianco for this most important task. He will call upon the pointers to supply at call any points necessary to carry on the work and Arthur Johnson, foreman of the job on the mountain will give him immediate assistance in the supply of men, tools, scaffolding in advance of needs.

Luigi working on what is possibly Jefferson's forehead.

All drilling of all kinds, roughing, finishing and carving of features must be directed by the chief stone carver on the work and his directions followed. That's it in a nutshell, isn't it? This document covers everything my grandfather did on Mount Rushmore to help make it the incredible sculpture it is today. Borglum wanted this posted "in the dining room" so everyone would know that they must answer to Bianco before they made a move on just about every phase of the project. I'm sure, because of Borglum's advanced age that he depended on Luigi to be his Chief Stone Carver, and this memorandum clearly shows that.

This document also suggests that Borglum might have ironed out the salary issue with Bianco, but that was not the case. Below is a very dramatic letter from July 31, the day after the memorandum was posted. In it, Borglum makes some very powerful statements about my grandfather actually resigning and the terrible lack of trained carvers on the work. (I've highlighted the most important statements.)

MOUNT RUSHMORE
NATIONAL MEMORIAL COMMISSION

COMMISSION
Fred W. Sargent, *Chairman*
Charles M. Day, *Vice-Chairman*
John A. Boland, *Secretary*

A. Boland
Budd
les M. Day
ella Greenway
Gurney
Hanna

Royal C. Johnson
Peter Norbeck
Fred W. Sargent
Lorine J. Spoonts
Margaret S. Strawn
William Williamson

A. K. Thomas, *Treasurer*
Doane Robinson, *Historian*
M. A. Wasser, *Clerk of the Works*
W. S. Tallman, *Superintendent*

EXECUTIVE OFFICES

Rapid City, South Dakota
July 31st, 1935.

EXECUTIVE COMMITTEE
John A. Boland, *Chairman*
William Williamson, *Secretary*
D. B. Gurney
L. B. Hanna
Fred W. Sargent

COMMITTEE ON DESIGN AND PUBLICITY
Gutzon Borglum, *Sculptor and Engineer*
Lorine J. Spoonts, *Secretary*
Charles M. Day
Peter Norbeck
Margaret S. Strawn

Dear Mr. Boland:-

I have read the report of Mr. Terrill twice and once aloud to Billy and Lincoln. Its observations are amazingly accurate, as checking with our own and it is interesting to have his corroberation of our figures, regarding amount of air needed, produced, delivered at the compressor tanks and at the outlets and that we are producing every pound of air our power will permit and delivering that air where we need it - it reminds me of what the boy said:" he telling us?"

His solutions, however, and recommendations are amateurish. I doubt if he's an engineer of practical service experience. His cursory observations regarding the Rushmore power plant are curiously familiar and according to his own statement of no value, yet he proposes conditions for hocking up not at all [illegible] ind and should and would never be tried by anyone of practical experience or acquainted with the conditions he comments upon. His comments on the possible cost of parts are problematical and cannot be known until the engine is taken down and properly examined. As it stands, however, two engineers and Mr. Uppercu locked it over last summer and Uppercu offered me $4500 cash for it. As it had been abandoned by the commission and given to me with the compressors and other material, I wrote you for a definite release of the engine, if it was not to be used. I received no answer that I could act upon, so that was lost.

I have had that power property examined by three different experts and I still maintain that no proper examination has been made by anyone whatsoever, therefore no reliable opinion exists as to the value of the engine to the Memorial or the expense necessary to put it in repair . The power plant did serve us in the beginning and also delivered power to Mr. Byron's mine for three months and 21 days. Of course it has suffered from delibertea injury, robbed of valuable parts and our own neglect; with that all against us and the fact that it was an obsolete engine, I still maintain that there is a chance of putting it in working order buying a new compressor and running it as a separate unit in connection with Byron's power, and will give us all the power we need, cheaper than any other plan proposed.

Youhave always opposed repairing our engine and preferred to buy power. I have no objection to that, although I disapprove of that kind of economy. My concern is to get power and I am opposed to any makeshift of any kind. I am returning the Rand-Ingersoll report. I want to compliment you on having it made. It should be kept on file and contains figures and data in a form that we have not [illegible]ulated and it corroborates our own knowledge of our own power pla nt.

I have just received a note from Bianco, resigning tonight. I called Billy, Bianco and Lincoln together and discussed the situation. This quitting revives the old policy of "penny wisdom and pound foolishness" that has threatened the wreck of the Black Hills mountain sculpture from its beginning. No work that I have ever been in charge of has been subject to such petty economies or, in the aggregate, been so wasteful and expensive. And I must tell you this wasteful amateurish practice of trying to create a great national memorial to America in sculptured granite in a pile of largely decayed, ancient, cracked up rock is not a child's undertaking and if I am not permitted to employ even a few trained stone men and carvers for the finishing of the features of these great men, their features will not be finished.

In the absence of a highly trained competent executive who knows sculpture, I yesterday posted an order, dividing the responsibility of the work under the two or three trained minds that I have on the mountain, placing the removal of all granite, methods of removal, form and use of tools, under Bianco; all measurements of every kind whatsoever and the full responsibility of any faults in measurements not provided for drillers on Lincoln. Handling the work preparing the scaffolds, providing tools, under Johnson. Billy to remain as general aid to all and special assistant to Lincoln, he asked for that. I am sure that you cannot realize the seriousness, the exactness necessary in every phase of this work, the constant vigilance required in the removing of stone, the protection of the stone that is not to be removed from any form of injury, the nature and character of the use of powder and how every blast is a form of carving and must be considered as a separate and individual operation. I say, you can't possibly know these things, no man can, unless he has had long experience and great intelligence. Billy doesn't know it; Johnson doesn't know it; Red, the powder man doesn't know it. Lincoln has stopped two blasts that would have wrecked a serious portion of our work, approved of by two men in authority there, who should years ago have known better. I have given orders that no powder shall be used or shots fired that are not approved by both Bianco and Lincoln.

I don't know what we are going to do about ever finishing the work without trained carvers. We have got three first class assistants there now that can work right along with carvers and four more who make very fine seconds to the first three, but this work cannot go on in this manner. I have worked under a contract that was conceived in bad faith, dishonest in its draft, and dishonest in its administration. I knew that, of course, but frankly I never looked at it for three years, had to ask you for a copy of the contract. When Tucker was obliged to leave I accepted the trap I had been caught in and I have worked out of it alone at only my own personal expense and labour as best I could, with the worst tools ever given a man, without aid and without funds.

I have no intention of abandoning Rushmore nor failing in the trust the nation and Washington has in me. That is one thing that will not happen. On the other hand I am not going to carry this work on to an injurious and amateurish finish for the lack of intelligent assistants.

As far as I am concerned I shall let Bianco go. I am not going to make up his wages, nor the wages of anybody else. I have spent the last money that I shall spend, running into many, many thousands, for the sole purpose of lifting a standard here, a burden I should never have had to carry and cannot continue.

His leaving will stop all work on thw features of Washington and Jefferson.

Yours truly,

Gutzon Borglum

After reading the highlighted sections, you can only come to one conclusion: Luigi Del Bianco was the *only* carver capable of finishing the faces. Without him, all finishing work had to stop. Who better to make that determination than Gutzon Borglum? No one. It would appear from this document that Bianco took his wife and sons back to Port Chester, never to carve on Mount Rushmore ever again. Thankfully, that is not the end of the story.

On August 7, John Boland, secretary of the Mount Rushmore Commission, sent out this request to the director of the National Park Service to increase Bianco's wages from .75 cents to $1.50 an hour.

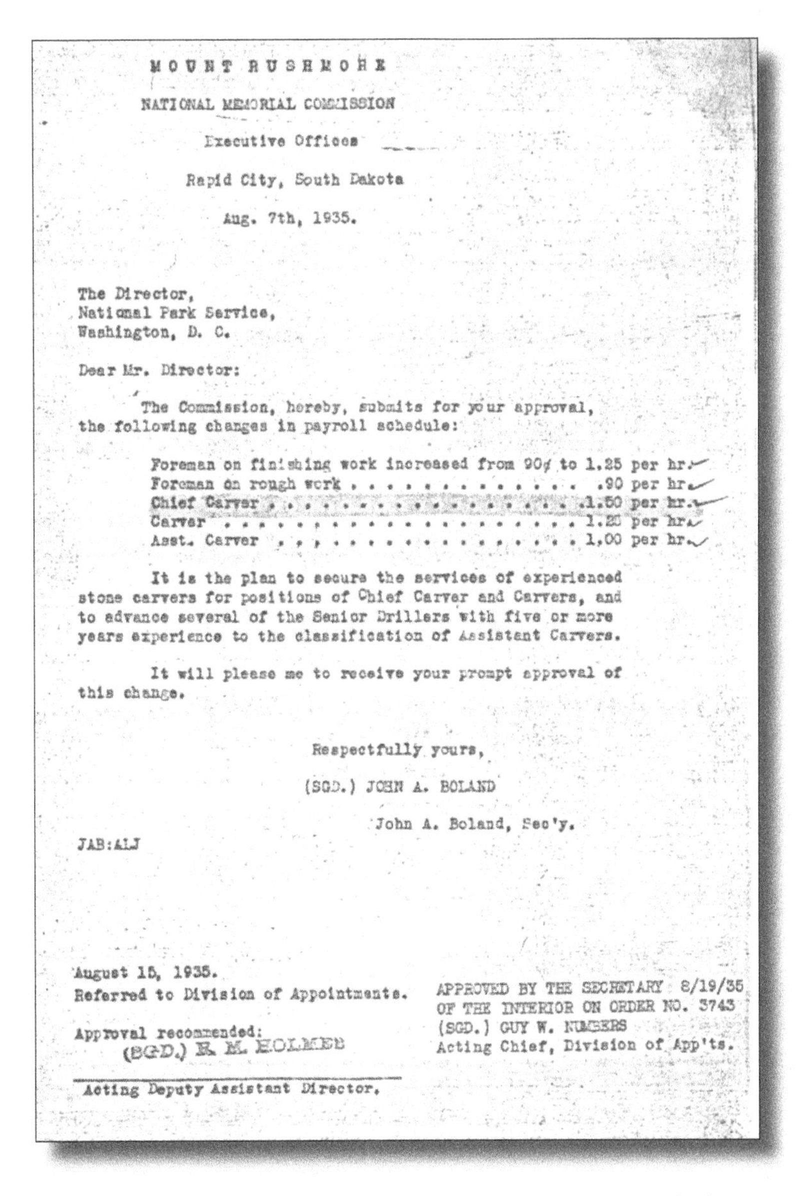

MOUNT RUSHMORE

NATIONAL MEMORIAL COMMISSION

Executive Offices

Rapid City, South Dakota

Aug. 7th, 1935.

The Director,
National Park Service,
Washington, D. C.

Dear Mr. Director:

The Commission, hereby, submits for your approval, the following changes in payroll schedule:

Foreman on finishing work increased from 90¢ to 1.25 per hr.
Foreman on rough work . . . . .90 per hr.
Chief Carver . . . . 1.50 per hr.
Carver . . . . 1.25 per hr.
Asst. Carver . . . . 1.00 per hr.

It is the plan to secure the services of experienced stone carvers for positions of Chief Carver and Carvers, and to advance several of the Senior Drillers with five or more years experience to the classification of Assistant Carvers.

It will please me to receive your prompt approval of this change.

Respectfully yours,

(SGD.) JOHN A. BOLAND

John A. Boland, Sec'y.

JAB:ALJ

August 15, 1935.
Referred to Division of Appointments.

Approval recommended:
(SGD.) R. M. HOLMES
Acting Deputy Assistant Director.

APPROVED BY THE SECRETARY 8/19/35
OF THE INTERIOR ON ORDER NO. 3743
(SGD.) GUY W. NUMBERS
Acting Chief, Division of App'ts.

Something obviously happened between July 31 and August 7. Borglum and Bianco must have had a real heart to heart or, in my father's words, a real *fight*. As much as my grandfather worshipped Borglum, "The

Master," he was his own man and wasn't about to be taken advantage of. After all, Borglum needed Luigi, who, in Borglum's own words, was "worth any three men in America for this particular type of work." The mutual love and respect these two artists had for each other always seemed to erupt in chaos, and then resolve into mutual understanding. Because of his love for Borglum and this great privilege granted him, Bianco decided once again to stay.

Soon after, Borglum sent these two memos to John Boland:

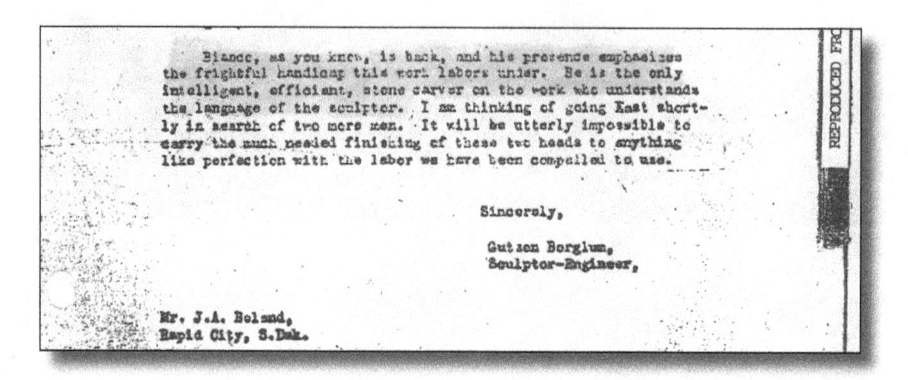

Bianco, as you know, is back, and his presence emphasizes the frightful handicap this work labors under. He is the only intelligent, efficient, stone carver on the work who understands the language of the sculptor. I am thinking of going East shortly in search of two more men. It will be utterly impossible to carry the much needed finishing of these two heads to anything like perfection with the labor we have been compelled to use.

Sincerely,

Gutzon Borglum,
Sculptor-Engineer,

Mr. J.A. Boland,
Rapid City, S.Dak.

I returned Bianco to his work this morning as Chief Carver, and granite expert, at a dollar and fifty cents per hpur.

He will have complete charge of the practical ways and means of dealing with the finesse of carving and instructing the other carvers, in the ways and means of handling this particular stone. I am arranging for two other carvers I have located one on New York and one in Denver, who worked for me at Stone Mountain. These men will be paid a dollas and 25 cents an hour - standard carvers wages, for general work.

In conference with Tallman, Bianco and Lincoln, we have agreed to create two other classes of carvers: a dollar an hour class and a ninety cent class.

There are five men on the mountain that have earned this distinction. Tallman will give you their names in the next month's pay roll.

CHAPTER TWENTY-TWO:

PORT CHESTER REUNION

LUIGI STAYED THE REST of the 1935 season and performed his many duties as Chief Carver. His wife and children stayed with him until the end of the season. Eventually, they all got into that green Chevy for the 1,800-mile ride back to Port Chester. For my grandmother, it was a relief. She could resume the life she was accustomed to: family, friends and church. My father and brothers were nothing but disappointed. For them, this was the end of a great adventure out West. Good friend Chet Risio once recalled, as a child, seeing that Green Chevy pull in the Del Bianco driveway completely covered with thick dust from the long journey back. Chet remembers very well all the tales my father told him and the other local kids of his adventures with Indians, horses and walking up to the top of Mount Rushmore. My Dad must have felt like a celebrity. My Uncle Silvio, three years older than my Dad, was much more soft spoken about his experiences and didn't share much. I became very close to Silvio, but he never told me about his childhood in Keystone. He passed away when I was 12. When the family lived in Keystone, my Uncle Caesar was only 4 years old. His memories were vague images of the mountain and the long car ride to South Dakota. It was my father who became the keeper of all the Rushmore lore, and those stories will always represent my fondest connection to my Dad. When he talked about those days, a side of him was revealed that I rarely saw.

Back in Port Chester, life for Luigi and the family returned to relative normalcy. There were tearful reunions up and down South Regent Street with the extended family: the Cardarellis, Scafas and good "compare" like the Terenzis, Risios, D'Ottavios, Meccas, Marianaccis and Acerbos. My grandmother got back to cooking her macaroni and gravy, escarole and beans and pasta fagioli. My father and uncles tuned into "Jack Armstrong,

All American Boy" and played Ringalevio in the streets of Washington Park. Luigi resumed his memorial carving business, although with The Depression in full swing, business had to be slow. Thank God, he had Borglum and Rushmore.

In December of 1935, *The Daily Item* ran a wonderful article about Luigi. I discovered it on microfilm and as such, it's not an easy read, so I've added the actual text of the article. You get a real sense of the time period and the way my grandfather felt about this historic sculpture taking shape before his very eyes. Whenever I read the part below where my grandfather regards Rushmore as "something close to sacred," I get a lump in my throat.

> *"Like all good artists, Mr. Del Bianco put his heart and soul in his work. The Mount Rushmore memorial is regarded by him as something almost sacred and it is no wonder he is impatient to get back to the job."*

THE DAILY ITEM

PORT CHESTER, N. Y., SATURDAY, DECEMBER 14, 1935

DEMANDS HARRISON PROB

Sets Of Twins Attend Schools In Port Chester

Peace Plan Stirs Rift In League

Local Resident Helps Hew Memorial To 3 Presidents On Dakota Mountain Side

Luigi Del Bianco At Work Two Years Directing Carving Of Faces Of Washington, Lincoln And Jefferson; Project 6,600 Feet Above Sea Level

Has Novel Job

LUIGI DEL BIANCO

Club Ca For Inqui Into Char

Committee U To Investigat Accusation

Boils Over, Cob Youth ly Burned

R. H. Tingley, Noted Engineer, Dies Suddenly

Woman Facing Trial To Test Liquor Taxes

THE DAILY ITEM PORT CHESTER, N.Y. SATURDAY, DECEMBER 14, 1935

Local Resident Helps Hew Memorial To 3 Presidents On Dakota Mountainside

Luigi Del Bianco At Work Two Years Directing Carving Of Faces Of Washington, Lincoln And Jefferson; Project 6,600 Feet Above Sea Level

If Luigi Del Bianco, of 108 South Regent Street, could wish time away, it would be April now instead of December and he would be more than 1,000 miles away from here.

He would be out in the Black Hills of South Dakota, directing the carving of the heads of George Washington, Thomas Jefferson and Abraham Lincoln out of the rugged side of Mount Rushmore, one of the highest peaks in the Hills.

For the last two years the Port Chester man has been directing the carving on the huge Mount Rushmore memorial, designed by Gutzon Borglum, of Stamford, known as one of the greatest sculptors in the country.

Like all true artists, Mr. Del Bianco puts his heart and soul in his work. The big Mount Rushmore memorial is regarded by him as something almost sacred and it's no wonder he is impatient to get back on the job.

A Test For Nerves

Carving the big heads out of the mountainside is a job that tests a man's nerve as well as his skill. The stonecutters work on narrow scaffolds and one slip means certain death on the rocks hundreds of feet below.

So far the rough carving on the heads of Washington and Jefferson have been completed. One can get some idea of the huge task the job is by the measurements of the faces. They average 60 feet from the chin to the forehead and the noses average 16 feet each. The eyes are from 10 to12 feet across.

The memorial is 6,600 feet above sea level. When completed it will be clearly visible at a distance of 25 miles. Blasting work was started in 1929 and the stonecutters have been working on the job for the last two years. It is estimated that it will be completed by March 1937 at a cost of about $750,000. So far $200,000 has been spent on it.

The most the men can work on the project is five or six months a year. Sixty were employed last year, but it expected that 40 more will be added when work is resumed in March. All carving is done with machine drills.

Most of the men on the job last year were married and had their families with them. Mr. Del Bianco's wife and their three sons are as anxious as he is to get back to the Black Hills.

Village Nearby

Keystone, a thriving village, is close to where the memorial is being carved. The nearest city is Rapid City. There has not been a serious accident in connection with the work, as far as Mr. Del Bianco can recall.

Mr. Del Bianco was born in Italy 43 years ago and began stone carving at an early age. He studied the art in Venice for two years and two years in Vienna.

He first came to this country in 1908. He returned to his native country in 1913 and fought for Italy in the World War. He came back to the United States in 1920.

He went to Barre, Vt., where he obtained a position as a marble carver. Later he met Mr. Borglum. Among his works is The Governor Hancock in South Carolina and the World War Memorial at Newark, New Jersey.

Mr. Del Bianco established his own stone-carving business at 20 Clinton Street, Port Chester in 1927. Like many others, he was forced out of business by The Depression. But has hopes of re-establishing it as soon as the Mount Rushmore memorial is completed.

CHAPTER TWENTY-THREE:

LUIGI MEETS A PRESIDENT

WHEN THE **1936 SEASON** rolled around, Luigi was ready to go. He and Nicoletta decided that she should stay home with their sons in Port Chester. The time out in South Dakota really disrupted the boys' schooling in New York. As a result, Silvio and Vincent had to repeat their grades another year. Much to my father's disappointment, it was best for them to stay home and get their lives back in order.

On May 1st of that year, Luigi sent a telegram to John Boland in the business office that the season had started and that Borglum wanted him out there as soon as possible. Depending on how rough the winters were in South Dakota, a season of carving could start as early as March or as late as June. Below is the telegram my grandfather sent. You'll notice that my grandfather makes sure he will be getting the wages he was promised. I can't say I blame him.

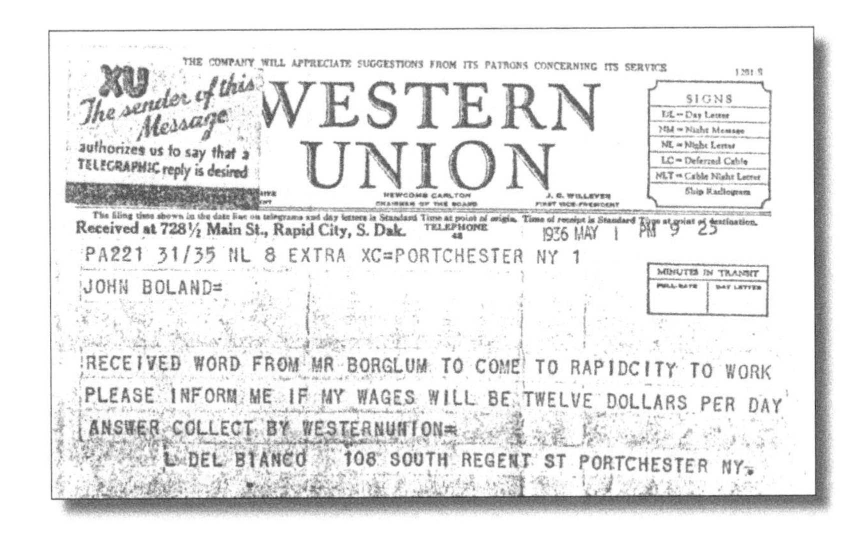

THE COMPANY WILL APPRECIATE SUGGESTIONS FROM ITS PATRONS CONCERNING ITS SERVICE

The sender of this Message authorizes us to say that a TELEGRAPHIC reply is desired

WESTERN UNION

SIGNS
DL = Day Letter
NM = Night Message
NL = Night Letter
LC = Deferred Cable
NLT = Cable Night Letter
Ship Radiogram

Received at 728½ Main St., Rapid City, S. Dak. TELEPHONE 48 1936 MAY 1 PM 9 25

PA221 31/35 NL 8 EXTRA XC=PORTCHESTER NY 1

JOHN BOLAND=

RECEIVED WORD FROM MR BORGLUM TO COME TO RAPIDCITY TO WORK
PLEASE INFORM ME IF MY WAGES WILL BE TWELVE DOLLARS PER DAY
ANSWER COLLECT BY WESTERNUNION=
L DEL BIANCO 108 SOUTH REGENT ST PORTCHESTER NY.

Here is another daily record from July 15, 1936 that shows Luigi again as Chief Carver finishing the head of Washington.

DAILY RECORD—Men-on-the-Granite Drilling and Carving 15

Mount Rushmore National Memorial

U. S. Department of Interior

Daily—Reported to Gutzon Borglum. Sculptor Engineer

	Location	Progress		
	Location	Approximate Feet Drilled	Completed and Shot	
Leach	R Cheek Lin		12-4	
Gordon	" L Temple	40	15-4	
Jim Payne	" Nose	Channel 43	35-4	
Vanrick	" Forehead	43	30-4	
Jack Payne	Wash L Shoulder	30	25-4	
Brandt	Lin Front	64	16-6	
Champion	Wash L Shoulder	42	49-4	
Gust	Between L & J	80	25-6	
Carl Baird	" "	72	35-6	
Anderson	Wash L Shoulder	75	21-6 6-1	
Watson	Wash Forehead	finishing		
Maxwell	Lin Front	60	15-4	
Gardner	Jeff Front	32	33-4	
Madill	L Shoulder	70	32-4	
Bianco	Wash Forehead	finishing		
POWDER MAN Henry Berg Denton Wilkerson		Drilled Areas Shot all	Wired and No. Shot	46 sticks Powder
BLACKSMITH Nicholas Canfield	No. Drills Sharpened 310			

Date 7/15 1936

Reported and Signed Fred Borglum Foreman on Granite

George Rumple Foreman of Works

I wonder what my grandfather was thinking on that 30-minute walk down the mountain at the end of an eight to 10-hour day of carving. Was he thinking about his next paycheck? Or was it the mysterious people in the Rapid City office who were always giving him trouble? I'm sure it was the latter, but mostly he must have been missing his family, knowing that when he got back to his little cabin exhausted and covered with dust, no one would be there to greet him. He must have missed my grandmother's strength and quiet resolve. He must have missed Silvio's sweet nature, Vincent's spunk, and Caesar's charm. As important as this work was, the Del Bianco family had to sacrifice a lot in those days.

Luigi had to distract himself, but how? For one thing, I know my grandfather was a real man's man. He was also ahead of his time. Thirty years before Clint Eastwood and the Spaghetti Western came roaring onto the silver screen, Luigi loved to dress up like an authentic cowboy. My grandfather was living proof that the Italians love the West.

Luigi in cowboy garb playing the part. He wears it well!

My grandfather also became adept at riding a bucking bronco. The photo below is an absolute classic. The Italian cowboy!

Luigi: what a man!

When Luigi wasn't riding horses, he loved to box. I believe my grandfather boxed in Italy in his youth. According to my father, he was also given a lot of pointers from his paesan, Primo Carnera. Here he is with an unidentified man who might be Jack Payne of the Payne brothers. Jack was a driller and carver on Rushmore and also state boxing champ of South Dakota. My father told me Luigi used to spar with Jack.

Luigi boxing with worker Jack Payne.

Aside from the mention of Jack Payne, it didn't seem like my grandfather socialized much with the other workers. I know they must have respected him. After all, Luigi was an artist in stone and an invaluable teacher for the men. Still, the culture clash might have made the local Keystone boys and "Bianco" a little uncomfortable. Maybe that's why my grandfather gravitated more toward the Native Americans; after all, they were outsiders, too, right? If you're looking for Luigi in this photo, you won't find him; he's not there.

A group of workers on Mount Rushmore.

The year 1936 found my grandfather bouncing back and forth among all the faces, training the men and finishing the granite features. It was a very productive season for Luigi as far as the refining of the faces was concerned. This is according to the annual report for the Mount Rushmore National Commission:

> *"Much of the work was confined to the roughing out and removing of excess stone on the bosom of Washington; beneath the chin of Jefferson; between the shoulder of Washington and the face of Lincoln; and over the entire face of Roosevelt. Other work was confined to the details on the heads of Washington and Jefferson and the brow, nose and eyes of Lincoln. Most of the work of the season of a nature as to probably indicate little progress to laymen."*

Because Luigi was the only carver charged with the "refinement of expression," it is safe to say the most important details in the faces were done by him.

On August 26, a telegram was sent to Washington reporting, among other things, that Bianco is "getting highest wage on schedule." Money problems again? Did Luigi and Borglum have another row about his wages? It's certainly possible, given the history of my grandfather and the "office at Rapid City." If anything, this telegram only reinforces the obvious: that an artist with Luigi's ability, performing the singular role as Chief Carver, should get paid what he deserves.

STANDARD FORM No. 14A
APPROVED BY THE PRESIDENT
MARCH 10, 1926

TELEGRAM

OFFICIAL BUSINESS—GOVERNMENT RATES

FROM INTERIOR DEPARTMENT

BUREAU

CHG. APPROPRIATION

AUGUST 26 1936

JOHN L NAGLE
ROOM 1036 NAVY BUILDING
WASHINGTON D C

RECOMMENDATIONS CHIEF POINTER ONE DOLLAR FIFTY PER HOUR ASSISTANT POINTER ONE DOLLAR PER HOUR FORWARDED WASHINGTON STOP REPLY [illegible] BORGLUM FOR ADDITIONAL INFORMATION STOP RUMPLE PAID [illegible] WAGES [illegible] ON START STOP CONSIDERING DAVIS STOP RECOMMENDATIONS ON PETERSON FORWARDED WASHINGTON STOP EILBECK DID NOT REPORT FOR WORK STOP BIANCO CHIEF CARVER GETTING HIGHEST WAGES ON SCHEDULE STOP BORGLUM WAS AWARE OF INTENDED PURCHASE OF DIESEL ENGINE OR PORTABLE COMPRESSOR THOROUGHLY DISCUSSED WITH HIS SON STOP ANALYSIS OF POWER BY LETTER TO ST LOUIS S LAST MONDAY

SPOTTS MT RUSHMORE NATIONAL MEMORIAL COMMISSION

NIGHT LETTER
PAID
GOVERNMENT

The dedication of the Jefferson head on August 30th was a big day at the mountain. While not completely finished, it was far enough along to show to an adoring public. The most exciting news was the fact that the president himself, Franklin Delano Roosevelt, would make a public appearance and say a few words. Luigi Del Bianco would be there that day, too.

My grandfather loved photos and often carried a camera. Although the quality is not great, here is an original photo taken of the President by Luigi from the viewing stands.

F.D.R. in the passenger seat of his car at the Jefferson dedication. Photo: Del Bianco Family Collection.

A crowd gathered at the base of the mountain. At noon, shots were fired and a flag large enough to drape over Jefferson's face dropped to reveal his visage to the cheering people. President Roosevelt gave a wonderful speech that is worth repeating here:

> *"I had no conception, until 10 minutes ago, not only of the mountain's magnitude, but also of its permanent beauty and importance. I think that we can perhaps meditate on those Americans of 10,000 years from now…meditate and wonder what our descendants…and I think they will still be here…will think about us. Let us hope that they will believe we have honestly striven every day to preserve a decent land to live in and a decent form of government to operate under."*

After the ceremony, Borglum wanted the President to meet his Chief Carver. According to family lore, F.D.R. asked Luigi, "Del Bianco, is that Italian?" Apparently, my grandfather puffed out his chest with pride and replied, "One hundred percent."

CHAPTER TWENTY-FOUR:

POLITICS AS USUAL

AT THE END OF the season in 1936, an exasperated Borglum wrote to Superintendent of the National Park Service John Nagle. Borglum expressed his frustration with local political cliques who had controlled the bloated services that Borglum needed to run his project. Money that should have gone to pay trained carvers like my grandfather was instead going to pay inflated overhead costs. I've highlighted the sections that address this issue, along with the repeated statement made by Borglum that Bianco and the blacksmith were the only "master workmen on the entire job." It is also heartening to read where Borglum praised his small group of loyal, untrained miners.

UNITED STATES
DEPARTMENT OF THE INTERIOR
NATIONAL PARK SERVICE

Mount Rushmore National Memorial Commission
Rapid City, South Dakota
November 19th, 1936.

My dear Mr. Nagle:

Enclosed you will find the pictures sent to the Department while you were here - plus, such as I have been able to secure by local photographers. You'll see, not of the class of our own regular photographer. However, they show the progress with the amount of stone removed. - Approximately an average of 140 tons per day. This is by 40 percent the largest average of measured stone ever removed per 8 hour day for sculpture purposes from a mountain cliff.

You'll find in No. 395 a sketch made by Lincoln with figures on the back, showing cubic feet removed between the dates of July 7th and November 6th, 1936.

In making any just estimate of our work here consideration must be given first, to the awkward and hazardous position of 80 percent of our actual drillers; only the finishers are in cribs. I've tried every form of detaining and holding men in the position of their work, and the swinging cage, following the leather swing, has proven the most efficient. The scaffold is useful but closes in the work too much to permit study as you proceed, and I have found no model can be made that will fit the lighting, the position finally determined upon in the rock in place, that can be followed mechanically. Constant change from the original is imperative unless you want to produce a dead, artificial, meaningless mask, regardless of light, location, etc. And the condition of the stone is constantly interfering with design and location. This I explained to you while you were here.

I have as fine, as efficient as loyal and honest a group of workmen as can be developed out of the untrained, forgotten men found in our small mining camps and out of some two or three hundred I've developed a small group who make their time, earn their wage and will carry on. Our success here, admitted by all who are at all familiar with the work, is due to trusting my men, looking after their personal comfort and safety, and promoting and paying them as they deserve, of course instructing them.

There are only two men on the entire job who came to us as master workmen; those are Bianco, carver, trained by me for the past twelve years in the east and our blacksmith, a master of his job. All the rest have been

Page - 2

apprenticed on this work and trained to their present efficiency. Efforts are constantly being made to break down the morale by the Rapid City political racket. This year they presented 60 new applicants for work; they have delivered such worthless and corruptible men from the beginning of this work, that I look with suspicion on all their suggestions.

I don't know what else I can add. I contracted to do this work in four years, was under penelty for any delay, chargeable to me. The Commission became as a commission, as Norbeck humorously described it, a "defunct commission," which explains why I urged the National Government to give me a resident aid. I undertook this work with plans for 40 or more drillers, our own power, all of which I provided. Sabotage wrecked our engine as soon as a local company was in a position to sell us. We made or can make power for 1½ cents per K. W.; we are now paying 4 cents or from seven to nine hundred a month and tied to an interminable time, because of inability to increase our working force. We cannot, no one can, do more with what we have, but we have a ridiculous over-head, which is not efficient, with the gang half size - and I have railed against this from the year we began. That is, we could handle twice our force.

Locally there is no understanding as to what it is all about. The only reaction we have here is by the measure of their business balances through tourist influx, growing in leaps and bounds; gas companies report a hundred percent increase in three years traffic is cutting their roads to ribbons. Happily we got rid of a governor who has been fighting us and all west Missouri growth.

There is one condition I want you to note; that local state park, a beautiful development, the life work of Senator Norbeck. The board has been planning and scheming for years to grab Rushmore, farm it out in concessions and make it a part of their local machine. I've resisted that and some day some one will look into the unrecorded acts and find why and how we are in the National Park system. I want the monument to stay there. I have two reasons for that: local politics are fitful, changing, split to pieces by graft, jealousies and worse and Custer Park is the hide out for as indifferent a group of useless human beings as I ever met entrusted with money and property. And so it would be disastrous to have a Federal work of this kind become the prerequisite of their petty local rackets. One of my big disagreements here has been and still is, I will not permit my studio to be farmed out to a local clique - a shop for geegaws of every description. I've answered, "wait just a little longer, and if Washington lets you, you can make a night club, a brothel if you please - but not while I'm here. Norbeck, Boland, Chamber of Commerce all enlisted to put a Jewish group in charge.

Now you are in and in to stay for the National Park system, thank God. I've no disagreements with Spotts except when his departmental red tape trips

Page - 3

up our efficiency, and that's not serious. I want Rushmore to be a part of our National Park work and Iwant you to be proud of it. You and I can't have any differences - sensible men do not have.

The local pictures are not what they should be, so Lincoln and I took more yesterday. Can't promise any better, but whatever the result I'll send. Thanksgiving is near. I'm giving the men an elk, wish I could give you a chunk, including Spotts - I'll try.

Sincerely yours,

/s/ Gutson Borglum

Mr. John L. Nagle,
Sup't National Park Service,
St. Louis, Mo.

Photo's sent separately - and Elk ordered - send you shortly.

It is interesting to read that the "local machine" that appeared to have ties to the Mount Rushmore Commission Board was trying get local people jobs on the mountain no matter what their ability. It's no surprise that a well-paid "outsider" like Luigi would rankle their plans to keep local control. Borglum also showed great concern that the board might try to use political muscle to privatize Mount Rushmore for their own financial gain. He wanted Rushmore to remain under government protection with the National Park Service. You have to commend Borglum for sticking to his guns. This was obviously a very big obstacle for him to constantly contend with.

CHAPTER TWENTY-FIVE:

"MY DEAR MASTER"

EVEN THOUGH IT TOOK 14 years to complete Mount Rushmore, Borglum also made it clear that he "contracted to do this work in four years." Wow, four years? The money problems, working around bad granite, the lack of trained men and supposed political corruption all must have contributed to the dragging out of the project. Luigi was always working on the mountain during the most productive times or when the money was available. It's safe to say my grandfather's contribution to a project originally projected to last four years was based on quality, not quantity. When he wasn't there (as Borglum has stated) the features on the faces were left "unfinished" until he returned.

At the beginning of the 1937 season, Luigi wrote to John Boland in the business office inquiring about the upcoming budget for the new season. Since Luigi was educated only in Italian, this letter was written in English by my grandmother.

L. DEL BIANCO
GRANITE AND MARBLE
MEMORIALS
108 SO. REGENT ST., PORT CHESTER, N. Y.
TELEPHONE 643-J

Port Chester N. Y. April 13- 1937

My dear Mr. Boland:

Just a few lines to take the liberty of asking you a question regarding the work out in the black hills this year. If it is not asking to much I would like you to let me know just about how much money they have in the bank this year towards the work out there. Hoping to hear from you in the near future

I remain your friend

Luis Del Bianco.

Port Chester, N.Y. *April 13, 1937*

My dear Mr. Boland:

Just a few lines to take the liberty of asking you a question regarding the work in the black hills this year. If it is not asking to much I would like you to let me know just about how much money they have in the bank this year. Hoping to hear from you in the near future.

I remain your friend,

Luigi Del Bianco

Luigi was of course concerned about the issue of money, and I'm sure he wanted to avoid more problems once he got out there. Here is John Boland's response:

UNITED STATES
DEPARTMENT OF THE INTERIOR
NATIONAL PARK SERVICE
MOUNT RUSHMORE NATIONAL MEMORIAL COMMISSION
RAPID CITY, SOUTH DAKOTA
April 19, 1937

L. Del Bianco,
108 So. Regent St.,
Port Chester, N. Y.

Dear Mr. Bianco:

To answer yours of the 13th instant, will say that there is now $30,000.00 to carry on the work at Rushmore and it is hoped and expected that an Appropriation of $100,000.00 will be made available July 1, 1937.

Sincerely yours,

John A. Boland,
Secretary.

For reasons we can only suspect, Boland's information was not satisfactory to my grandfather. He must have thought about the $100,000 dollars being released in July— "I'll believe it when I see it." A month later, Luigi received a letter from Borglum wanting him to return. I don't have that letter, but here is Luigi's response:

L. DEL BIANCO
GRANITE AND MARBLE
MEMORIALS
108 SO. REGENT ST., PORT CHESTER, N. Y.
TELEPHONE 643-J

Port Chester N.Y. May 16th 1937

Dear Mr. Borglum:

Received your letter and appreciate the fact very much your wanting me to work with you again this summer, but am sorry to say that I cannot take this trip again this year for that salary, if I could receive at least fourteen Dollars then I could consider starting for out there again. Mr. Borglum you already understand that I have always been on your side working for you and being obedient to your

L. DEL BIANCO
GRANITE AND MARBLE
MEMORIALS
108 SO. REGENT ST., PORT CHESTER, N. Y.
TELEPHONE 643-J

desires at all times, therefore
I think that if you speak
again to Mr. Tiegle and make
him understand that I am
really needed importantly by
you for that work but then
then maybe he will consider
giving me that raise in
salary that I need very
much to carry on and take
care of my self and family.
Mr. Borglum if everything
is satisfactory and you send
for me I will come
immediately
Thanking you in
advance I remain
respectfully Del Bianco

Port Chester, N.Y. May 16, 1937

Dear Mr. Borglum,

Received your letter and appreciate the fact very much your wanting me to work with you again this summer, but am sorry to say that I cannot take this trip again this year. For that salary, if I receive at least fourteen dollars then I could consider starting out there again.

Mr. Borglum you already understand that I have always been on your side working for you and being obedient to your desires at all times, therefore I think that if you speak again to Mr. Nagle and make him understand that I am really needed importantly by you for that work out there then maybe he will consider giving me that raise in salary that I need very much to carry on and take care of myself and family.

Mr. Borglum if everything is satisfactory and you send for me I will come immediately.

Thanking you in advance I remain,

Respectfully Del Bianco

To me, this letter really shows the respect and admiration my grandfather had for Borglum. In many ways Luigi treated Borglum like the apprentice treats the master artist: with obedience. Luigi was not an apprentice, far from it, and he made a very strong case for his worth as an artist and just as important, his responsibility to his family. I have no idea how Borglum responded to that letter. What I do know is that less than two weeks later, the powers that be at Mount Rushmore wasted no time recommending that Luigi be released from his position as Chief Carver when he "failed to report for work this season." The memorandum was approved by the Secretary of the Interior on June 28.

UNITED STATES
DEPARTMENT OF THE INTERIOR

MEMORANDUM FOR THE SECRETARY

In re proposed [illegible, crossed out], separation (Cross out those not applicable.)

of L. Del Bianco (No. 10*) of Keystone, South Dakota
(First name, initial, surname) (Legal residence)

as Chief Carver
(Designation)

at 1.50 per hour w. a. e. for
(Probable length of service)

to (if promotion) at per hour w. a. e. / diem w. a. e. / month / annum

to be employed in Mt. Rushmore National Memorial Commission of the National Park Service

and effective close of May 31, 1937 vice

*Justification:

Failed to report for work this season.

APPROVED BY THE SECRETARY OF THE INTERIOR ON ORDER NO. 4309 June 28/37
Guy W. Numbers
Acting Chief, Division of App'ts

Previous Government service:
Recommended: John S. Boland

Hillory A. Tolson
Acting (Signature and title) Associate Director

*Give full information, including necessity for employment, qualifications of appointee, and duties to be performed. (If additional space is necessary, use the reverse side "head to foot", i.e., make the bottom of the obverse the top on the reverse.)

U. S. GOVERNMENT PRINTING OFFICE 8—6726

Why would they release him from that vital position when there was no one to replace him? Seems really hasty to me. There is no letter or any document that my uncle found with Borglum's reaction to this. Maybe Borglum, knowing the frustration both he and Luigi had with the "office at Rapid City," decided to wash his hands of the whole affair. What was Borglum going to do without his Chief Carver? Was Luigi really finished with Rushmore, once and for all?

On July 22 of that same summer, Luigi responded to a telegram from his "Dear Master."

L. DEL BIANCO
GRANITE AND MARBLE
MEMORIALS
108 SO. REGENT ST., PORT CHESTER, N. Y.
TELEPHONE 643-J

Port Chester
July 22, 1937

My dear Master:

Just a few lines in reference to your telegram of last night. It is impossible for me to leave home at the present time, Because my wife is just recuper-ating from a severe case of Quincy sore throat, As soon as she is all well and able to take

L. DEL BIANCO
GRANITE AND MARBLE
MEMORIALS
108 SO. REGENT ST., PORT CHESTER, N. Y.
TELEPHONE 643-J

care of the house and children I will be able to come out there. If possible you might inform me if it will be alright to come out there later on.

Thanking you kindly and with many regards I remain your friend

Luigi Del Bianco

Port Chester

July 22, 1937

My dear Master,

Just a few lines in reference to your telegram last night. It is impossible to for me to leave home at the present time, because my wife is just recuperating from a severe case of quincy sore throat. As soon as she is all well and able to take care of the house and the children I will be able to come out there. If possible you might inform me if it will be alright to come out later on.

Thanking you kindly and with many regards.

I remain your friend

Luigi Del Bianco

From the language in this letter you can tell, in spite of my grandfather being "released from his position," Borglum still pursued Bianco. Once again, my grandfather was put in the untenable position of loyalty to Rushmore over his own family. Even though he says it is impossible to come, Luigi promises to return once his wife is well. Did my grandfather return? We know Borglum wanted him to. There is some very strong proof that he did return for part of the 1937 season. Although this letter was referenced earlier, I must go back to Superintendent James C. Riggs' correspondence with my Uncle Caesar in 1986. He lists 1937 as one of the years Luigi was working on the mountain as Chief Carver. (Refer back to page 14 for the full letter.)

7. Gilbert Fite refers to your father being employed first in 1933 as Chief Carver. Our records show the following information:

1933 - Chief Carver; worked on Washington and Jefferson figures.

1934 - No record of Mr. Del Bianco working at Mount Rushmore.

1935 - Chief Carver; salary raised to $1.50 per hour. (See enclosed letter approving payroll changes)

1936 - Chief Carver; finishing work on Washington figure. (No details)

1937 - Chief Carver; finishing work on Washington and Jefferson figures. (No details)

There is also a personal organization list from the end of 1937 that lists Bianco as the Chief Carver. According to this document, Luigi was put back on the payroll.

1937

DEPARTMENT OF THE INTERIOR

Personnell Organization List

Bureau: National Park Service | Unit: Mount Rushmore National Memorial Commission | Fiscal year: 1937 | (page 1)

Position Number	Position	Grade	Salary	Name		Appropriation Item
	EMERGENCY					
1 p. m.	Superintendent		$250.	Vacant: Vice W. S. Tallman		Mt. Rushmore National Memorial Commission
63	Treasurer & Spec. Disb. Agt.		---	A. K. Thomas		do
64 p.m. wae	Timekeeper		125.	~~John C. Merrick~~	9/3 Rep 5-15-37	
2 p. m.	Secretary		100.	John A. Boland		do
3 "	Clerk		75.	M. A. Wasser		do
55 p.m. wae	Watchman		~~75.~~	~~H. B. Baird~~	Rep 7-[illegible] 7/7	do
4 p.m.	Custodian		60.	Gale Wilcox		do
10 p.h. wae	Chief Carver		1.50	L. Del. Bianco		do
6 "	Foreman, Finishing Work		1.25	~~Vacant: Vice J. A. Johnson~~ George Rumple	7/7	do

According to the above document, Luigi did in fact keep his promise to Borglum and returned to work in 1937. Borglum must have been relieved. At least for now, he had his Chief Carver back. The question was, could he keep him once and for all?

CHAPTER TWENTY-SIX:

RUSHMORE 1938. WHERE IS LUIGI?

IN FEBRUARY OF 1938, Borglum wrote a letter to Fred W. Sergeant, Chairman of the Mount Rushmore National Memorial Commission. One paragraph in particular talks of Borglum's frustration with the way my grandfather was treated, and why he will never return. Once again, you can see what Borglum felt he had to deal with.

For the purpose of Washington's "red tape," a portion of our better men are designated as carvers; there are no carvers on the mountain - there never has been but one, and he refused to return because of the chronic sabotage directed at him by influences in Rapid City, and the Park Department. We have no men on the mountain except my son who can read or understand contours, curvatures, and sculptural modeling necessary to direct the carver. Work on all the heads has been automatically stopped where the carving of the features required an intelligence not available in Rapid City or by local workmen.

"For the purpose of Washington's 'red tape,' a portion of our better men are designated as carvers. There are no carvers on the mountain — there has never been but one, and he refused to return because of the chronic sabotage directed at him by influences in Rapid City and the Park Department. We have no men on the mountain except my son who can read and understand contours, curvatures, and sculptural modeling necessary to direct the carver. Work on all the heads have been automatically stopped where the carving of the features required an intelligence not available in Rapid City or by local workmen."

This paragraph sums up everything my grandfather experienced on Mount Rushmore:

1. He had the distinction and burden of being the only classically trained stone carver.
2. "Sabotage was directed at him" from the powers that be.
3. After 1937, it appears he refused to return to Rushmore.
4. As in prior instances, finishing work on the features automatically stopped when Luigi was absent from Rushmore.

Sabotage is a very strong word. What exactly was done to my grandfather besides withholding the wages he deserved? Borglum is never more specific than "insolence, petty dickering over wages." We can only speculate, according to Gutzon Borglum, the "influences in Rapid City" made Luigi Del Bianco's life so miserable that this great privilege granted to him was not worth what he was being put through. I know my grandfather was a very strong individual, and it would have taken a lot for him to throw in the towel. Was it because he was an immigrant, the other? Did the political racket simply want his salary to go to one or more of their own? Perhaps it was a combination of both. There certainly is well-documented bigotry toward Italian Americans in the 1930's. Still, we may never know. What we do know is that by 1938, Gutzon Borglum could only go so far without Luigi Del Bianco.

For the next two seasons, it appears "Bianco" was not working at Mount Rushmore. James C. Riggs, in his letter to my Uncle Caesar in 1986, admitted the National Park Services records were limited after 1937, and nothing was found in the Borglum papers that said he was on the payroll in 1938 and 1939. Was my grandfather back in Port Chester, carving memorial headstones? Was he at Rushmore?

CHAPTER TWENTY-SEVEN:

LUIGI RETURNS!

N MARCH 4, 1940, Borglum received this interesting response letter from Bianco:

L. DEL BIANCO
GRANITE AND MARBLE
MEMORIALS
108 SO. REGENT ST., PORT CHESTER, N. Y.

Telephone 4054-W

March 4,1940

Dear Mr. Borglum:

I received your interesting letter sometime in October and sent you a telegram immediately that I understood your requests.

Now I am waiting for the details of the marble alter or the call to come there and serve you.

I hope you send me the pictures so that I may study them carefully about the work that has to be done on the upper lip of Jefferson.

This is all I have to say except to wish you lots of luck on the job.

Yours truly,

Luigi Del Bianco

L. Del Bianco

LB:AA

The mention of "the marble alter [sic]" reveals that Luigi must have been doing other work for Borglum outside of Rushmore. The most striking line pertains to "work that has to be done on the upper lip of Jefferson." Did this mean Luigi was coming back to Rushmore? Did Borglum and Bianco have another heart to heart? This question is easily answered by the next letter, dated April 18, 1940.

Rapid City
~~XXXXXXX~~

April 18, 1940.

Mr. L. Del Bianco,
108 South Regent Street,
Port Chester, New York.

My dear Bianco:-

You better be here by May 1st, and I am glad you will come. You will have to work for me and for Lincoln, and nobody else will trouble you.

Very truly yours,

Gutzon Borglum
Sculptor-Directer
Mount Rushmore National
Memorial Commission.

You will have to work for me and Lincoln, and nobody else will trouble you.

This certainly harkens back to the "sabotage" that Borglum wrote about in a previous document. We know there were efforts to undermine my grandfather's salary, but the details of this sabotage remain to be seen. It is clear that Borglum was doing everything he could to make Bianco feel comfortable and protected.

On May 7, Borglum sends another letter to Luigi, this time with a real sense of urgency.

Rapid City
XXXXXX

May 7, 1940.

Mr. L. Del Bianco,
108 South Regent Street,
Port Chester, New York.

Dear Bianco:

I wish you would come as soon as you can if you want to be of help to me. I must finish the faces by the 1st of July- and all of them. I need you.

Your pay will be exactly what it was before, and there will be no reductions from it. You are the only man who is on that pay.

Sincerely yours,

Gutzon Borglum
Sculptor-Director
Mount Rushmore National
Memorial Commission.

To me, this letter is pivotal in that it supports the fact that the faces, while mostly carved, were not finished with that "refinement of expression" so necessary in transforming them from giant copies to breathing works of art. *I need you* sums up Borglum's feelings at the time. He was a proud man. Admitting that he needed help from someone must have a taken a lot. According to this letter, Borglum needed Bianco to trust his promises, finish the faces and possibly make up for the time he hadn't been there in 1938 and 1939. All along, this is what my grandfather was hired to do. Time after time, Gutzon Borglum made it crystal clear that Bianco was the only one who could perform this crucial last step in the carving of Mount Rushmore.

In July of 1940, Borglum reached out to his old friend and sometime adversary Hugo Villa. Borglum had been cutting a large room in the back of the mountain called the Hall of Records. This room was to contain important American documents and some artwork of Borglum's choosing. It looks like he wanted Villa to construct a model of the Hall of Records for him. Even though Mount Rushmore has no record of my grandfather on the payroll in 1940, Borglum proves that he was there by mentioning, "I have Bianco with me…"

Rapid City, July 6,1940

My dear Villa:-

We have been too busy to adjust our plans as I promised in my last letter, but we now are ready with our big studio, the second studio, and I want to make a model of the large room or Hall of Records, that is to go into the mountain. We have cut the entrance way 74 feet and we shall soon be taking it up again now.

I would be very glad if you will come to Rapid City and help me in this work for several months in the summer. I can promise you work at a dollar and a half an hour, an eight hour day. You have a car so I advise you to come up in your car. You will like the work and the room we have to work in and there will be no interference with the work at all. I have Bianco with me and plenty of good helpers.

There is no need to tell you that I have no relations at all with Boland. He has been treacherous and dishonest in all our work and he has been dishonest with me. He keeps up his friendship with two or three men that have been dismissed for dishonesty. He never comes near the work, of course nor does he have anything to do with my loyal friends. The government took the money away from his bank when he was dismissed and it is now in Washington. We deal directly with Washington. I am telling you this only that you may know the situation here.

I hope you are very well.

Sincerely yours,

Mr. Hugo Villa,
San Antonio, Texas

Salutâ anche dalla grande mere. Mary-Ellis a un bambinò three months old.

You get the feeling Borglum mentions my grandfather hoping it will help convince Villa to come. Villa and Luigi were fellow Italians and both worked for Borglum for years. It was to be the first time he would have more than one artist of a high caliber assisting him on the mountain.

What about the mountain? The faces? Who else was actually carving them in 1940? If you are assuming it was only my grandfather, you are right. Richard Cerazani wrote an absolutely stunning book titled, *Love Letters From Rushmore*. The book lovingly chronicles the correspondence between Richard's dad, Arthur Cerazani, and his mother. Arthur was a talented sculptor who worked in the studio at Rushmore with Villa and my grandfather in 1940. His beautiful letters to his wife detail the trials, tribulations and joys of working at Rushmore. In one of his letters, Cerazani tells of his admiration for Villa and that the only man working on the faces is "Bianco."

AUGUST 3

The place is as silent as a tomb. There is only one man working on the faces and that is Bianco. I am still working with Villa. Its hard work but I like it. I am trying to study when the boys are not trying to make me drunk. I am drinking every night, and can I take it.

AUGUST 5

Well, darling, here it is Monday and I am still busy working with Villa. I like my work very much. I pray I may work for a long time with Villa, he is the tops as an artist and a friend.

***From Richard Cerazani's book,* Love Letters from Mount Rushmore.**

There is only one man working on the faces and that is Bianco.

It is one thing to see 30 to 40 men climbing those giant faces, but to look up at the great expanse of Rushmore to discover just one tiny person alone carving an eye, finishing a lip…what a sight. My Grandpa Luigi.

It makes sense. If finishing the faces is what was required by 1940, then you only needed Luigi Del Bianco to do the job.

Luigi Del Bianco with Arthur Cerazani at the base of the models in the studio. Photo from the Richard Cerazani Collection.

In addition to finishing the faces, there was one important task that Borglum charged my grandfather to perform: fixing a terrible crack in the lip of Thomas Jefferson. In earlier correspondence, Luigi responds to a letter from Borglum about the crack in the lip, and he asks for a photo to be sent so he could study the crack. Here is that photo.

Photo: Del Bianco Family Collection.

Luigi climbed the 706 steps to a scaffold set up in front of Jefferson's lip and with an assistant, removed that giant crack. Using steel pins, he shaped a fresh piece of stone and surgically inserted it into the hole he made. Here is a great photo of Luigi actually repairing the lip with something you didn't see much of on Rushmore: a hammer and a chisel. Only a trained artist used those tools.

Photo: Del Bianco Family Collection.

In the end, Luigi used his talents as an artist to make that lip look like the crack had never happened. See for yourself.

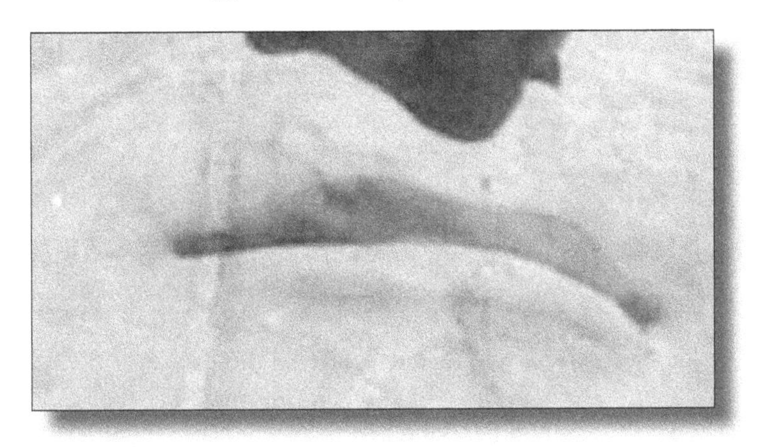

Jefferson's lip looking just like new.

As the Park Ranger told the crowd during my visit to Rushmore in 1988, the work my grandfather did on that lip was the only successful repair job ever done on the whole of the four faces. However, the park ranger had no idea who did it or who my grandfather was. That's a thread that has run throughout Luigi Del Bianco's time on Rushmore: **the unknown immigrant artist not credited with doing the most important carving on America's most iconic sculpture.** The photo below typifies my grandfather's role on the mountain. There is Borglum and his son posing in the forefront, and there is Luigi way in the background quietly saving Jefferson's lip. My Uncle Caesar used to look at that photo and say, *Look at my old man. It's like he's in the shadow of the mountain.*

Lincoln and his father, Gutzon Borglum, in the "bucket." Bianco is in "the shadow." Photo: Del Bianco Family Collection.

The countless decades of Luigi Del Bianco's anonymity in no way disparages Gutzon Borglum. Actually, it's quite the opposite. There would be no Rushmore without him. What's more, without him my grandfather never would have had this incredible opportunity. In fact, my family will be forever grateful to Borglum for putting pen to paper and dictating so many memos about his dear "Bianco." What valuable evidence he has given us, evidence that should give our grandpa his rightful place in American history.

In 1940, the evidence once again proved Luigi's worth. He returned to Rushmore to, in Borglum's own words, "finish the faces." This time he had the whole mountain to himself. With no one to train, no one to distract him or, worse, harass him, Luigi could spend the entire 1940 season doing what he did best: carve the "refinements of expression" on Washington, Jefferson, Roosevelt and Lincoln.

By 1941, it looked like the future of Rushmore was uncertain. The funds that the United States Government had been allocating diminished with each passing year. What's more, the pegmatite stone spread throughout the entire lower half of the mountain made it next to impossible to carve what Borglum had originally envisioned, as seen in this photo of the full model.

Borglum's original model of the way he wanted Rushmore to look, with full torsos. Photo: Del Bianco Family Collection.

Isn't that amazing? If finished down to his waist, Washington would have stood 465 feet tall. Because of the difficulty of carving faulty pegmatite stone below the faces, it was not meant to be. Besides, Borglum in 1940-41 was not well; in February of 1941, Borglum had to have prostate surgery. He eventually put his son Lincoln in charge of the faces. This 14-year project seemed to be nearing its end.

CHAPTER TWENTY-EIGHT:

BORGLUM AND RUSHMORE LEAVE TOGETHER

FROM NOVEMBER 1940 TO February 1941, Luigi corresponded with Borglum about an altar Luigi was to carve and erect in the chapel at Saint Luke's Hospital in Kansas City, Missouri. In one of the letters, Borglum complains about being sick: "I have got influenza or malaria or something else; it doesn't matter. It gives me an excuse for loafing and I'd rather loaf than anything." Luigi wrote back that he was so sorry his Master was "not in good health."

For a powerhouse like Borglum, who could never sit idle, something must have been seriously wrong. Very soon after that correspondence between the sculptor and his favorite stone carver, Borglum passed away on March 6, 1941. If any of his projects, (namely Rushmore) were to continue, they would now be in the hands of his son, Lincoln.

On March 13, the *Daily Item* talked to my grandfather about his beloved Master.

THE DAILY ITEM, PORT CHESTER,

Borglum's Death Grieves Del Bianco, Sculptor's Right-Hand Man For 20 Years

When Gutzon Borglum, nationally-known sculptor, died a week ago, the most profoundly shocked man in Port Chester was Luigi DelBianco, Mr. Borglum's right-hand man on the huge Mount Rushmore Memorial to Washington, Jefferson, Theodore Roosevelt and Lincoln, which is being carved out of solid rock on the South Dakota mountain side.

Mr. Borglum's passing meant more than the loss of his boss to Mr. Del Bianco; it meant also the loss of a true friend of 20 years and a fellow artist.

Now Mr. DelBianco is awaiting a telegram from Mr. Borglum's son, Lincoln, who will carry on the work recalling the Port Chester man to South Dakota to continue his job as soon as the weather becomes warmer. The huge monument, started in 1927, will take another estimated five years

as a carver for Mr. Borglum, but also served as his model on many occasions. He is a big man with a fine, well-proportioned body and classic Roman features and when Mr. Borglum was creating the huge World War Memorial for Newark, N. J., Mr. DelBianco was his model for about 20 of the 48 figures.

In 1928, Mr. DelBianco left Mr. Borglum and was engaged by the late John D. Rockefeller to do extensive marble work at the oil magnate's Pocantico Hills home. Five years later he went back to Mr. Borglum and stayed on. As chief stone carver on the Rushmore project he received $16 a day and was able to earn a considerable amount "on the side" by selling small figures he made in his spare time.

Mr. DelBianco was born in Italy

studied in Venice and Vienna. When home from the Mount Rushmore job, he conducts his own stone carving business on Clinton Street.

5 From Harrison In March 18 Quota

Five men from Harrison are included in the 21 to be sent for induction March 18 by Draft Board 747, comprising Harrison and parts of White Plains and North Castle, it was announced today.

Two of the five are volunteers. They are Anthony Barrego, of 165 Lakeview Avenue, Silver Lake, and John J. Sarni, of Anderson Road, Purchase.

Selectees from Harrison will include Guiseppi U. Fiore, of 141 Adelphi Street; Arthur J. Lamn, 34 Oak Street, and George R. Gasparrini, of Colonial Place.

MINE BLAST KILLS FOUR

REVLOC, Pa., (AP). — Four men were killed early today by an

THE DAILY ITEM, PORT CHESTER, N.Y.
THURSDAY, MARCH 13, 1941

Borglum's Death Grieves Del Bianco,
Sculptor's Right-Hand Man For 20 Years

When Gutzon Borglum, nationally known sculptor, died a week ago, the most profoundly shocked man in Port Chester was Luigi Del Bianco, Mr. Borglum's right-hand man on the huge Mount Rushmore memorial to Washington, Jefferson, Theodore Roosevelt and Lincoln, which is being carved out of solid rock on the South Dakota mountainside.

Mr. Borglum's passing meant more than the loss of his boss. To Mr. Del Bianco it meant also the loss of a true friend of 20 years and a fellow artist.

Now Mr. Del Bianco is awaiting a telegram from Mr. Borglum's son, Lincoln, who will carry on the work, recalling the Port Chester man to South Dakota to continue his job as soon as the weather becomes warmer. The huge monument, started in 1927, will take another estimated five years for completion, and Mr. Del Bianco hopes to be there when the job is completed, and especially he wants to get back as soon as possible to do the hand of Lincoln, one of the most difficult parts of the entire job.

Back in 1920, Mr. Del Bianco was working as a stone carver at Barre, VT, when a friend introduced him to Mr. Borglum and the famous sculptor gave him a job. Since then, with the exception of a few years, Mr. Del Bianco has been with Mr. Borglum on all his important projects.

Mr. Del Bianco is Chief Carver at the Mount Rushmore job, having 32 men under him and being responsible for the faithful transfer of the figures of the four national heroes from the models to the side of the vast mountain.

The local artist talks of walking on the lip of Washington and carving the eye of Lincoln, yet he has profound respect for his subjects. Operations can go on only about five months a year because of the weather, but during that time, Mr. Del Bianco says, he loses at least

15 pounds climbing over the huge figures with the aid of ropes and supervising the large scale though delicate carving operations. The figures are scaled one foot to one inch from the models and one bad error with high powered drills and dynamite would be likely to ruin years of work, so Mr. Del Bianco carries a lot of responsibility with him as he clamors around the features of the figures.

Mr. Del Bianco not only worked as a carver for Mr. Borglum, but also served as his model on many occasions. He is a big man with a fine, well-proportioned body and classic Roman features and when Mr. Borglum was creating the huge World War Memorial for Newark, NJ, Mr. Del Bianco was his model for about 20 of the 46 figures.

In 1928, Mr. Del Bianco left Mr. Borglum and was engaged by the late John D. Rockefeller to do extensive marble work at the oil magnate's Pocantico Hills home. Five years later he went back to Mr. Borglum and stayed on. As chief stone carver on the Rushmore he received $14 dollars a day and was able to earn a considerable amount 'on the side' by selling small figures he made in his spare time.

Mr. Del Bianco was born in Italy 48 years ago and started stone carving at an early age, and then studied in Venice and Vienna. When home from the Mount Rushmore job, he conducts his own stone-carving business on Clinton Street.

Like so many other articles and letters, we continue to hear phrases about Luigi being Borglum's "right hand man" and that his role as Chief Carver carries "a lot of responsibility." The most touching part to me, though, is how "shocked" Luigi was to hear about the passing of this force of nature he called "Master."

Borglum must have seemed invincible to "Bianco": a great teacher, mentor and I'm sure a father figure to a young immigrant newly arrived in this country seeking direction for his talents. Borglum not only provided that direction but also respected Luigi for his own expertise as a granite carver. A 20-year relationship in the art of sculpture had come to an end.

On April 2, Luigi wrote a note to Gutzon's wife, Mary Borglum. Here is the original in Italian and the translation is below:

Port Chester 2· Aprile 1941

Mia Carissima Mrs Borglum.

Mi farebbe molto piacere se questa
mia lettera vi trovasse calma e in
buona salute.
io vi scrissi già una lettera poco dopo
la morte del mio Caro Maestro.
ieri sera ho ascoltato alla Radio
il vostro Caro figlio. Capisco che lui
sarà quello che porterà il lavoro
avanti.
Mia Cara Signora ora vi domando
se dovrò andare avanti coll'avoro
che il mio Maestro mi avveva
ordinato, cioè ALTAR CHAPEL. ST. LUKES
OSPITAL KANSAS. CITY. MISSOURI
vi prego di scrivermi; un vostra lettera mi
sarà molto cara.
vi saluto con tutto il Cuore
sempre devotissimo Luigi Del Bianco

Port Chester April 2, 1941

My Dear Mrs. Borglum,

I would be very pleased if my letter finds you calm and with good health. I already wrote to you a letter shortly after the death of my Master.

Yesterday evening I listened to the radio and heard your beloved son. I understand that he will be the one that will bring the work forward. My dear lady, I now wonder if I should go forward with work that my Master had ordered i.e. the altar in the chapel of St. Luke's Hospital in Kansas City, MO. There you can write me a letter but it will be very expensive. I wish you well with all my heart.

Your eternally devoted,

Luigi Del Bianco

I have no idea what became of the St. Luke's Chapel altar, or whether my grandfather finished it. What appeared to be finished was Mount Rushmore. Without Borglum, how could it go on? I guess it was up to Lincoln to decide whether it was worth it. As I said before, difficulties with pegmatite stone, World War II and certainly the passing of Gutzon Borglum contributed to a major slowdown of the work. On October 31, 1941, the last scaffold was removed and the last drill put away. Mount Rushmore was considered officially finished.

CHAPTER TWENTY-NINE:

LIFE BACK IN PORT CHESTER

FOR MY GRANDFATHER, IT was time to go back to his memorial stone carving business in Port Chester. This talented artist never sought great commissions like Borglum did. Certainly, his status as an immigrant put him at a disadvantage in the art world. At the time, there were so many gifted artisans in that very same position. To be honest, I'm not even sure Luigi was interested in that kind of career. He was an artist with a workingman's mentality: give me the work, and I am happy. And Luigi worked. When he wasn't carving and setting headstones, he was crafting and installing finely made marble fireplaces for the wealthiest families like the Rockefellers of Westchester. You would also find Luigi in his little studio garage carving pieces for a varied clientele. I love this photo of his shop at the end of his driveway on 26 Clinton Street.

Luigi's studio. Don't you love the little busts strewn all over?

Here are some pieces my grandfather created before and after Rushmore. Some were lost. Some we still have. The ones we've managed to keep, we will never sell.

From top left, George Washington; Teddy Roosevelt; and one of 500 headstones carved at St Mary's Cemetery in Rye Brook, NY. The lettering is supposed to resemble tree limbs. The top half isn't finished.

Abraham Lincoln mosaic

Charles Lindbergh

*From top left, bust of Silvio Del Bianco, age 16;
the only painting we have by Luigi;
and one of the many plaster copies
Luigi made of Mount Rushmore.
I love this piece because it looks like a
freestyle version of the actual model.*

Luigi's gorgeous self-portrait in white marble.

People used to ask me, *Why didn't your grandfather ever carve a statue that is on permanent display in Port Chester*? I was never sure what to tell them. While Luigi was a stone carver and not a sculptor, I'm sure there are many statues of his at St. Mary's Cemetery. That was Luigi's calling in Port Chester. I can't tell you how many times the old timers used to come up to me and say, *Your grandfather, God bless him. He carved my mother's headstone.* People couldn't wait to tell everyone in the room that the man who was the Chief Carver on Rushmore also carved a headstone for their family member with a little angel statue on top. That's what I find so special about my grandfather. He had his feet in both worlds: the world of Gutzon Borglum and a much smaller place called Port Chester, NY. How graciously and humbly he walked between those two worlds.

CHAPTER THIRTY:

THE FAMILY WELCOMES A NEW BABY

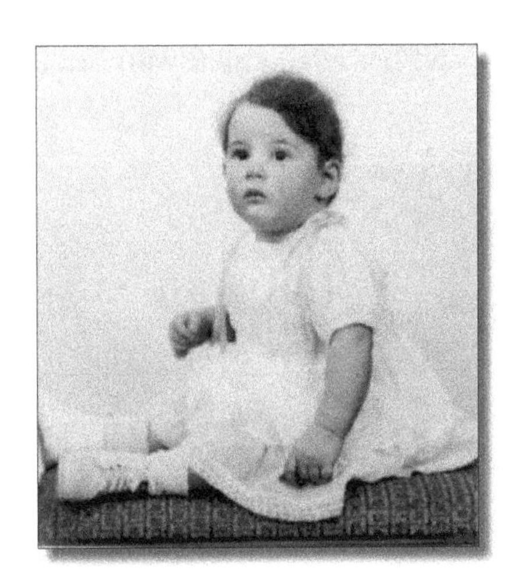

Baby Gloria Del Bianco, circa 1946.

IN **1946,** A LITTLE miracle occurred in the Del Bianco Family—My Aunt Gloria was born. Was it planned? Absolutely. Even though my grandmother was now in her early to mid-forties, she pined for a little girl. After 20 years, Nicoletta still missed her dear Teresa.

My grandfather was concerned for all the obvious reasons. At 44, Nicoletta was in a very risky part of her life to have a child. A previous pregnancy 10 years earlier resulted in a miscarriage. Luigi was 10 years older at 54. He didn't feel right becoming a father at a grandfather's age. My grandmother won out in the end.

On March 8, 1946, Gloria Teresa Del Bianco came into the world. Nicoletta named her Gloria for "Gloria in Excelsis Deo"— Glory to God in the Highest! This change of life baby would keep everybody on their toes, including the three brothers who were 15, 18 and 21 years older than their little sister. "Gloriooch" would get everything she wanted from her much older brothers.

Nicoletta doted on her baby girl. And just as with Teresa, the daughter they lost years ago, Gloria became the apple of Luigi's eye.

My parents spoiled me rotten, my aunt used to tell me. *I did whatever I wanted.*

Gloria remembers the tantrums she would throw because she wanted to go with her father to watch him work. Wouldn't you? When Luigi did take his daughter, those outings became some of the best childhood memories of Gloria's life. But I'm getting ahead of myself. You're going to hear lot from "Gloriooch" and her relationship with her Daddy at the end of this book.

Gloria "on the job" with Luigi. She is sitting right where a statue would be set at Corpus Christi Church.

CHAPTER THIRTY-ONE:

POST WAR YEARS

GLORIA IS BORN IN 1946, the war is over and Port Chester, like so many other communities, is welcoming back its returning veterans. My Uncle Silvio is one of them. He spent 1944 to 1945 on a submarine chaser in the Mediterranean. Unfortunately, Silvio saw a lot of action.

I also found out recently he was one of many "darker skinned soldiers" used as guinea pigs and experimented on with mustard gas. Apparently, the U.S. Military assumed that Black, Hispanic and Italian soldiers had "heartier skin" and could withstand the mustard gas better than the "white soldiers." God only knows the effects this testing had on my poor uncle; it probably contributed greatly to his early death.

When my uncle returned home from the war, he decided he wanted to follow in his father's footsteps in some way. Luigi took Silvio under his wing, hoping to help him get over the war by learning some sort of craft. Here is an article from the *Daily Item* in 1948 that shows father and son together. The article also mentions something interesting about Rushmore.

A MINIATURE MOUNT RUSHMORE MEMORIAL took shape in Port Chester two months ago in exact proportion to the original stone monuments carved out of the Black Hills in South Dakota under the expert hands of Luigi Del Bianco (left) of 26 Clinton Street, who has a monumental and statuary business in the village. Reading from left to right are the fifty-six year old sculptor, his son Luigi, who is studying stone carving under his father, and the Presidents Washington, Jefferson, Teddy Roosevelt and Lincoln. The elder Del Bianco, who was once in charge of all close drilling and carving of the Jefferson head at the national memorial, is awaiting a call for further assignments on it. Other reproductions of Mount Rushmore carved by the Port Chester sculptor have been shown in the Capitol Theater, the YMCA of Port Chester, and the County Center.

—Staff Photo

It appears "Luigi" (the reporter meant Silvio) was actually studying stone carving under his father. It's nice to see that Port Chester honored Luigi back then by displaying his work. The most interesting part of this news article is the reporter mentioning that Luigi is "awaiting a call for further assignments" on Rushmore. Was Lincoln Borglum trying to get the project started again? It never happened. The way the mountain looked back then is exactly the way it looks now and will probably always look. Maybe this was just wishful thinking on my grandpa's part?

The post war years were very good to my grandpa. He had lots of work and was able to build his own house on Clinton Street. Around this time, the late 40's and early 50's, Luigi started to feel the pull of the Old Country. He hadn't been back in years and sorely missed his family, friends and the culture that shaped him. For the next decade and a half, Luigi would make many pilgrimages to Italy and his little village of Meduno. As Gloria grew older and more independent, Luigi would stay for months at a time. Earlier on, I'm sure the trips were much shorter. Here is a lovely postcard he wrote to Nicoletta from Italy in 1953.

December 24, 1953 Trieste

My dear Nellie,

I am well. My dear ones here love me very much. Soon after the holidays I will go to Meduno. You can write me there. Kisses to all but especially to Gloria and Andreina.

Your Gigi

I guess my grandpa was very secure with who loved him. "Andreina" is actually my oldest sister, Andrea. She was born in 1953 and was Luigi's first grandchild. Here are some photos of Luigi in Italy.

Postcard of Meduno, the little village of Luigi's childhood.

Luigi and his cousin, Luigia. He is standing proudly in front of the home he was raised in.

One of my all-time favorite photos of my grandfather. Here he is with his sister Maria in Piazza San Marco in Venice. Look at the way he is clutching his big sister's hand.

I've always been especially fond of my grandfather's photos of his visits back to Italy. I wish I could have gone with him. Better yet, I wish I had been older or that he lived longer so I could have known him better. I wish he could see the man I've become. I would tell him, *Grandpa, I'm an actor and storyteller. I became an artist, just like you.* What conversations we could have had about his life and our mutual love for the arts. I still have dreams at night about what we could have shared.

What I do have, though, is a valuable connection to him that I try not to take for granted. I think we all want to know where we come from; we all have a desire to explore the lives and the stories that led to our existence. I'm sure Luigi's many trips back to Italy took him beyond his present-day family and friends. I'm sure he connected to the people and the stories that came before him.

Also during this time, my grandfather received a great honor. In 1956, the National Sculpture Society recognized Luigi's contribution to the art of stone carving. He was awarded a plaque that must have made him so proud. Imagine receiving such an honor as an American.

Even though "The Master" had been gone for years, Luigi never lost his strong connection to the Borglum family. Here is a photo of Lincoln Borglum and my grandfather. Luigi probably visited Lincoln at the "Borgland" estate in Stamford.

Lincoln Borglum and Luigi Del Bianco.

CHAPTER THIRTY-TWO:

THE CRUELTY OF GRANITE

THROUGHOUT THE 1950'S AND early 60's, as Luigi traveled more, he tried to maintain a steady work schedule. But breathing became harder for our talented stone carver. I'm not sure when Luigi was diagnosed with silicosis. It's no surprise that he got this terrible disease, since it was a leading killer of anyone who worked with stone. After years of carving with granite and the accompanying silica dust that it creates, my grandfather's lungs became filled with the dust, and it is next to impossible to expel it from the body. The silica dust literally becomes embedded in the lungs. Over time, breathing becomes more difficult, persistent cough sets in and fatigue takes over. This is what started happening to Luigi as he got older.

Why didn't my grandfather wear some sort of protection? A dust mask, perhaps? Unfortunately, back in the day most of the stone carvers and stonecutters didn't. I don't think any of the workers on Rushmore did. Before the 1950's government protections were not in place. Some of those guys got so sick with silicosis they never made it to 50.

Dust masks existed, but they were pretty cumbersome. Here is a rare photo of my grandfather wearing one at Rushmore.

Luigi Wearing a gas mask. Photo: Del Bianco Family Collection.

Why didn't my grandfather, or any of the other men, for that matter, wear masks all the time? I was told they were very difficult to work in and even harder to see through. Imagine my grandfather trying to refine the faces on Rushmore wearing that contraption. I'm sure it really hindered his ability to carve proficiently. Until better masks were designed, Luigi toughed it out and took his chances. Now, he would pay the price.

My father told me years ago that one of the reasons my grandfather went to Italy so often was because of a popular sanitarium there, where he would go and try to get the dust literally blown out of his lungs. It helped temporarily. My aunt also said her dad preferred the air quality of the Italian Alps, and it was easier for him to breathe there. Still, there was no cure for silicosis. It would only be a matter of time. In spite of that fact, my grandfather never showed the pain he went through. Luigi came from tough Northern Italian stock. He never lost his energy or charm or desire to flirt with the ladies. The strongest image of my grandfather I have is from the old timers in our town. They remember a tall, well-dressed gentleman walking the streets of Washington Park, tipping his fedora to everyone and captivating them with his wit and charm.

Luigi ready for another walk through Port Chester.

During the 1950's through the 1960's, my parents, Vincent and Angie, became quite prolific in the baby-making department. By 1963, Vincent had already given Luigi four grandchildren. They were all girls. I know my grandfather loved my sisters, but Italian men tend to prefer grandsons. When my mother became pregnant again, guys in Port Chester started placing bets as to whether this time it would be a girl or a boy. On May 31, 1963, I was born. The streak of girls was finally broken. When my grandfather got the news, he was in Italy. According to my father, he wired a telegram that said, "You must name him Luigi." My mother wanted to name me Mark. The next day, another telegram came. My grandfather decided to sweeten the pot. "If you name him Luigi, I will give you $1,000 dollars." My mother offered a compromise to name me Louis. Luigi agreed and gave my parents $500 dollars. Sounds fair to me.

The next year, my mother got pregnant again and gave birth to my sister, Amy, in 1964. The family rounded the number of children to lucky seven when Valerie came along in 1967. Luigi now had seven grandchildren, six girls and one boy.

In 1966, the *Herald Statesman* came to do what would become my grandfather's last newspaper interview. The article is so big that I thought it best to provide you with the text below in two photos.

Luigi DelBianco Recalls Danger And Glory Of Mt. Rushmore

He Carved The Face Of History

LUIGI DELBIANCO, who celebrated his [illegible] birthday just a week ago, stands beside a bust of himself which he carved in [illegible], when he was [illegible].—Staff Photo by [illegible]

Luigi posing with his self-portrait for the Herald Statesman. The light in his eyes is unmistakable.

THE HERALD STATESMAN. YONKERS, NEW YORK, SATURDAY MAY 14, 1966

Luigi Del Bianco Recalls Danger and Glory Of Mount Rushmore

He Carved the Face of History

by Marguerite Gibble

The face of Abraham Lincoln is more familiar than the image of his friends to Luigi Del Bianco of 68 Grant Street.

"I know every line and ridge, each small bump and all the details of that head so well."

His sensitive, long fingers gently were tracing the outlines of Lincoln depicted on the yellowing pages of a 36-year-old magazine spread open on the table before him.

Mr. Del Bianco could have said the same thing about George Washington, Thomas Jefferson or Theodore Roosevelt, whose names recall the years of hard, frustrating and dangerous work as head stone carver at the Mount Rushmore memorial in South Dakota.

He'd Do It Again

But to Mr. Del Bianco it is superbly satisfying to have had an important part in creating a national memorial which may endure a million or so years.

"I'd do it again even knowing all the hardships involved. I would work at Mount Rushmore even without pay if necessary," he said emphatically and added: "It was a great privilege granted me."

Every April for nearly 14 years, work was taken up at the memorial site, S.D., and carving continued until winter winds and snow made the sheer cliff too dangerous for the men suspended from the mountain top by cables and straps to continue chipping and smoothing the surface of the rock.

Mr. Del Bianco, named "head carver" at the memorial in 1933, has been described as, "one of the most competent men ever employed at the mountain."

The Great Borglum

He was called simply "Bianco" by the renowned designer of the "Four Presidents," Gutzon Borglum, with whom he was associated not only at Mount Rushmore, but also, earlier, at the sculptor's studio in North Stamford, CT and at the controversial Stone Mountain project in Georgia.

For Mr. Del Bianco, the presidents immortalized at Mount Rushmore were so long an important part of his life that he still feels he knows them intimately and understands what they stood for.

He studied from every angle the models of the heads created in the studio under the direction of Mr. Borglum and then saw them day by day, translated in proportion on the mountain peak.

It was Bianco who brought life-like light to an unseeing, dozen foot wide stone eye in the 60-foot-tall head of Lincoln (the president's figure would be 465 feet high if carved full length in the same proportions.)

First the Dynamite

When the first head was started at Mount Rushmore, Borglum was able to have his men get within a foot of the planned carving surface with dynamite. Later, blasting techniques were worked out by which dynamite removed rock within a few inches of the proposed surfaces of the faces before the carvers went to work bringing the features out of the mountain stone.

The dust from blasting had barely cleared away when the winches housed at the mountaintop began groaning and cables were reeled out to lower the narrow platforms or strap seats for the carvers to reach the work area on the cliff.

Describing how it was, he raised one hand as if to touch the rock cliff before him and brought the other arm up in back of his head in mock preparation for striking a blow on a chisel, then leaned back as far as possible in his chair.

"I could only see from this far what I was doing, but the eye of Lincoln had to look just right for many miles distant."

Any View Is Perfect

In The Black Hills, Robert Casey wrote, "from the studio near at hand or...from a peak five miles away you will see the four presidents gazing at you with the same majestic calm...free from even a hint of distortion."

Mr. Del Bianco is an artist, sculptor and worker in stone in a variety of forms. Several years ago the Port Chester library had an exhibition of some of his smaller works. Busts of presidents have been favorite subjects, but he carved "A Blind Beggar" in South Dakota, made "Desperate Man" bookends and did a figure of a cousin of Crazy Horse, among other sculptures. His works range from realistic to modern to symbolical in style.

He had his own stone-cutting shop for years at Clinton Street in Port Chester. About 500 of the gravestones at St. Mary's cemetery were made by him from rough Vermont marble.

Learned From Father

Luigi Del Bianco was born aboard a ship near Le Havre, France, while his parents were returning from the United States to Italy. When he was a small boy hanging around the woodcarving shop of his father at Meduno, Udine province, men of the village used to say, "Look how curious the little one is!"

In time, Vincent Del Bianco became convinced that his son was interested in carving and had more than ordinary ability. He took the 11-year-old boy to Austria to study under a skilled stone carver. Luigi later studied in Venice and Vienna. Although he came to the United States at 17, he returned during World War I to serve with the Italian Army. Back here after the war, he worked for a time as a stone cutter at Barre, VT.

His brother-in-law, the late Alfonso Scafa, a Port Chester stonecutter who was doing some work for Gutzon Borglum, introduced Luigi Del Bianco to the noted sculptor. Bianco then began working at the Stamford studio and the association of the two men continued until the death of Borglum in 1941.

> *In 1922, after Mr. Del Bianco married Nicoletta Cardarelli of Port Chester, the newlyweds lived for some time in a cottage on the grounds of the Borglum estate in North Stamford.*
>
> *The three sons of the Del Biancos, Vincent, Silvio and Caesar, remember happy and exciting days of summer at the site near Keystone. The flurry caused by important visitors arriving to see progress on the national memorial, the clouds of smoke rising after blasts of dynamite, and watching the men who looked so small from a safe distance below as they carved, all were fascinating. They liked, too, the family excursions by car into the country when their father was free from work.*
>
> *They feel a little sorry for their sister, Gloria, a student at the American Academy of Dramatic Art, because she is too young to have known those happy days.*
>
> *Although Borglum was a controversial figure, Bianco has only praise for him.*
>
> *"It was a sad, sad day when my master died," he said with eyes misted and voice filled with emotion. "The world lost a great genius."*

How cathartic it must been for my grandfather, at the end of his life, to share his fondest memories of Mount Rushmore. He relays such a strong feeling of devotion for the mountain; when he talks about the Presidents' heads, he might as well be talking about members of his own family. Clearly, Rushmore was an extremely transformative part of my grandfather's life, and Gutzon Borlgum had a profound effect on Luigi as an artist and a man. I'd like to think the feeling was mutual.

In 1967, my grandfather turned 75. The family gathered at 68 Grant Street to celebrate. Below are six of Luigi's grandchildren with him. (Valerie, the seventh grandchild and the youngest, wasn't born until November of that year.)

Luigi and his grandkids, circa 1967.
From left, Linda, Nancy, yours truly, Amy, Andrea, Luigi and Maria.

Valerie, circa 1970.

Not many people of that generation who worked in granite lived to be 75 years old. As I said before, many Vermont stone carvers, as well as Rushmore workers, died in their 40s. For that reason alone, this milestone birthday must have been very special to my grandpa. As strong as his will was to live, the dreaded silicosis was beginning to win the fight. In 1968,

Luigi had to be put in a nursing home so he could have access to machines that would aid him in his breathing. During this time, my grandmother was suffering gravely from the complications of diabetes and heart trouble. Luigi and Nicoletta had to be separated. In a way, Rushmore was once again the culprit.

My grandmother passed away first. My Aunt Gloria, who traveled back from California for the funeral, had the burden of going to the nursing home to tell her father that his dear Nicoletta was gone. It had been 48 years since they were first introduced by Alfonso Scafa. Now Luigi, who was slowly dying, had to say good-bye.

Just six months later, in 1969, my grandpa breathed his last breath. He finally surrendered to the disease that had been slowly stealing his breath for many years. Luigi Del Bianco lived for his art. He also died for it.

PART III:

DEFENDING LUIGI

CHAPTER THIRTY-THREE:

WAIT UNTIL THEY SEE WHAT I FOUND!

I'M NOT EXACTLY SURE when we sent those incredible documents that Caesar found to Rushmore. It had to be soon after the second or third trip to Washington in 1991. It was during those trips and a subsequent one with his dear friends Jim and Judy Sapione that Caesar found what he considered gold. At the time, Dan Wenk was still the Mount Rushmore superintendent and Jim Popovitch the Chief of Interpretation. I met them both during my visit in 1988. My uncle and I were filled with anticipation waiting to hear how impressed they would be to read Borglum's own words about Luigi.

"Worth any 3 men in America…"

"The only one besides myself who understands the language of the sculptor."

What I do remember was an angry phone call from Caesar.

"I just got off the phone with Wenk. It was bad, Louis, very bad. He didn't care about the papers we sent! He doesn't understand. I have to get off the phone now. This is making me very nervous."

Apparently, Mr. Wenk was not impressed with any of the documents, even the ones that praised my grandfather above all of the other workers on the mountain. He said something that my family would hear for the next 25 years.

"Your grandfather was classified as a worker. The workers on Mount Rushmore were a team. They are credited as a team. The only two who receive special recognition are Gutzon Borglum and his son, Lincoln."

Well, my uncle would not accept that, and I can't say I blame him. Still, I got the feeling that the discussion had gotten a little acrimonious. I knew my uncle. He was a very passionate man. I worried that Caesar might have overstepped his bounds and insulted the superintendent.

I decided to call Dan myself in an attempt to undo any damage my uncle might have done. I wish I'd had the foresight back then to document my phone call conversations; I can only rely on my memory, which, I must say, is pretty solid. I recall the conversation with Dan starting amicably. I asked him about the documents and what he thought of them. He gave no clear answer. I asked again about Rushmore's willingness to change their policy and take my grandfather out of "worker" status and finally acknowledge him as Chief Carver. He responded with the party line: *"Your grandfather was classified as a worker. The workers on Mount Rushmore were a team. They are credited as a team. The only two who receive special recognition are Gutzon Borglum and his son, Lincoln."*

I felt my body start to tense. I don't remember what was said after that. I do know we both went back and forth until the conversation started to escalate to a more unpleasant tone. With all due respect to Mr. Wenk, he got under my skin. He made me feel like a gadfly who was pressuring him to do something that would be unfair to the other workers. All I wanted was for my grandpa to get the recognition he deserved, nothing more, nothing less. I had to get off the line and fast. The only thing I do remember saying at the end of the call was, "Well, I don't give up easily. You'll be hearing from us again and again until the right thing is done." I remember Dan saying in a supercilious tone, "You do what have you have to do." Click.

After I hung up, I thought to myself, now I understand why my uncle got so angry! The superintendent saw primary source documents that said Luigi Del Bianco was the Chief Carver, and instead of thanking me for bringing this to his attention and promising to correct this error of omission, he did the opposite.

Why couldn't Mount Rushmore officials do the right thing? What were they afraid of? Were they worried that giving my grandfather his rightful title, a title he deserved, would cause resentment among the other living workers? This idea of offending the other workers and their families was a theme that would play out over and over again. The fact is, Luigi *was* in another category from the other men. Even Lincoln Borglum admitted that in a taped interview.

Focusing on the brick wall we both hit with Dan Wenk wasn't getting Caesar and me anywhere. I decided to talk to Jim Popovitch. After all, he was the Chief of Interpretation. Surely, he would be able to interpret the documents that read, "Chief Carver," right? Actually, there was nothing to interpret. I was giving Jim a gift on a silver platter. When he answered the phone, there didn't seem to be any hint that Jim knew about the confrontations with Dan Wenk, although I'm sure he was aware. I reviewed the documents and restated that the Del Bianco family was only asking that Luigi be given what Borglum gave him: the title of Chief Carver. Despite the irrefutable evidence that Bianco was the most important carver on the work and a trained artist, Jim responded that Rushmore was a team effort and it wouldn't be fair to give my grandfather more attention than the other workers.

Was this going to be the Dan Wenk conversation all over again? Just before I started to defend the documents, Jim threw me a curve ball I couldn't ignore. "You know, we are in the planning stages of erecting a workers' museum. Do you have any photos of your grandfather you can send me? I will do my best to make sure the photo is properly displayed when the museum is complete."

Okay, I wasn't ready for that. I told Jim I would be happy to send him photos on the condition that my grandfather is identified with the title of Chief Carver under the photo.

"I'm sorry, I can't promise that. Let's take one step at time and make sure a photo of your grandfather gets in the museum."

Even though this seemed like another brush off, the fact that Jim was reaching out at all felt like a little ray of hope. It was something we could build on. I agreed thinking we could negotiate the name and title later on.

CHAPTER THIRTY-FOUR:

ANNIVERSARY TIME

DURING OUR CHALLENGING TALKS with Dan and Jim back in 1991, Rushmore was gearing up for the 50th Anniversary of the project's completion. The buzz about the anniversary was pretty exciting. A host of dignitaries and celebrities would be there, including President George H. W. Bush.

Caesar was planning on going but backed out at the last minute. The thought of flying was just too much for him. I wanted to go, but I was in the middle of recording my first song and story cassette for children and just couldn't reconcile my schedule. I was launching my career as a kids' recording artist, and I had to prioritize.

Fortunately, my father booked a flight, as did my Aunt Gloria. I knew my father had been yearning to go back to the Black Hills for many years. He would be interested mostly in riding horses and reliving the magic of his childhood haunts. My Aunt Gloria, on the other hand, wanted very much to help in our mission to discover more about her father's Rushmore experiences. Maybe she could talk to some living workers? If anyone could work a room, it was Gloria.

Not too long ago, I discovered some photos from that trip. Here is my favorite one. Below is a traditional Lakota pow wow held in a nearby high school. It doesn't surprise me that my father wanted to be around Native American people again. They profoundly touched his spirit all those years ago. Just look how happy he is.

Vincent dancing with the Lakota Sioux. He is truly in his element.

I even found a photo of my Dad doing something he had wanted to do for many years: ride a horse again in Keystone.

Vincent reliving his old Rushmore days.

I love the way my father looks in this photo. This trip to Rushmore gave him the chance to come full circle and reconnect with his version of paradise. He never wanted to leave.

What did Gloria get out of this experience? I'm sure she loved the anniversary; the opportunities to brag about her talented father and hear the President speak. None of it would compare, however, with the man she met before the plane ride back home. His name was George Rumple, and he was one of the carvers that Luigi trained at Rushmore. I'll let Gloria tell you about him:

> *"While I was at the dedication ceremony for The Mount Rushmore National Monument in 1991, I had the pleasure of meeting Sandy Borglum Fawcett (grand-niece of Gutzon Borglum) and her husband, Darryl Watson. After our initial meeting, we decided to visit the sites the following day.*
>
> *We were at the Mount Rushmore Museum when I noticed an elderly man surrounded by and talking with people about Mount Rushmore. He had a t-shirt on emblazoned with the Mount Rushmore image. I waited until he was free, and Sandy and I approached him. I introduced us and asked if he knew my father, Luigi Del Bianco. He said, 'Your father?' I replied yes and he paused, looked at me awhile and blurted out, "L. Del [his nickname for Luigi], you can't really be his daughter." He choked up and with that both Sandy and I also began to cry. It was a very emotional moment for all of us and one that I will never forget!*
>
> *He proceeded to tell us how happy he was to meet Sandy and me. We talked a little longer, and I asked him if he could come again tomorrow so I could video tape him and have a conversation about Mount Rushmore and my father. He said, 'Of course I'll be here.' I arrived early the next morning, and he was already waiting for me. I proceeded with this taped video. I was so happy and touched to run into George Rumple, such a special man. What a great and unusual opportunity this was. He was alive, knew my father, called him 'friend.' As it turned out the event was more timely than I realized as George Rumple passed away not too long after that chance encounter."*

Below are excerpts from George Rumple's wonderful video:

"My name is George Rumple; I'm an old man now. I'm 86 years old. When I first got to Mount Rushmore, I heard they were hiring men up there and I went up and saw Mr. Borglum, the sculptor. He said, 'We're hiring. We pay .30 cents an hour and if you furnish your own tools, we'll give you a nickel more.' I said I wanted to go to work.

So, I went to work on the main road that goes all the way to where the studio was to get our equipment in. I worked there a little while, and he came along one day and said, 'George, I see you're a stone man.' I said, 'Yes sir, I am, Mr. Borglum.' He said, "Come into my office 10 o'clock tomorrow, I want to see you.' I said, 'I'll be there, Mr. Borglum.' So, I went in at 10 o'clock and he said, 'George, I'm gonna put you up on the mountain. I'm going to have you start carving because you know stonework. I'll put you up there on one of the faces.'

Well, I worked there a while and there was a lot of men. Mr. Borglum was a very fine man; he was temperamental, but he was a good man to work for. Washington was the only one there when I went to work. They were hiring men and I told them some of the men that I knew. They hired miners, and there were no real carvers there. He said, 'George, I'm gonna have a couple of carvers in from the east. When you get up there, I'm gonna put one of them right beside ya.' I said, 'How would I know him?' He said, "We call him L. Del Bianco." Well, he was a big, husky guy. I was working on the eye and L. Del, he came up to me and told me who he was. I said, 'I'm gonna watch ya and see if I can learn a few pointers.' He said, 'I'll be glad to help ya, George. Ya know, I was even a guard for the Pope. I'm a stone carver now.' That L. Del, he was not only a stone carver, he was a genius. By me working beside him, we become real close friends. I watched him.

On the lip of Jefferson, there was a flaw and Mr. Borglum come up one day and he said, 'L. Del, we're gonna take that out, I'm gonna have you get another piece of stone, a wedge-shaped piece and put it in that lip.' Where I was working on a part of the eye, I could look right down and see L. Del working on that lip. I tell ya, he was a genius. He just went to work there. He knew what he was doing 'cause he was a carver, a sculptor. I think he was one of the top men and he became a real good friend of mine.

He made a little model of Washington. He said, 'I'm gonna give you this little model that you can work with up here.' It was the death mask of Washington, and I still have it to this day. I worked there from 1932 to 1941. So, L. Del, he left in the meantime and I lost track of him. I didn't know where he went but he made me this mask of Washington and I still got it. On the bottom, it says, "L. Del Bianco, 1939." I cherish that thing. I wouldn't take a thousand dollars for it. I felt real bad, cause I lost track of him. He taught me lots of things. He was not only a carver, he was a genius. I think he could have took Mr. Borglum's place and finished that himself.

Anyway, after I come back, I come back every year. I met his daughter, and we had quite a conversation. I'm trying to tell her a little bit about her dad. She'd never have to be ashamed of her dad. He was all man. He walked tall. He had lots of friends out here and everybody loved him. He was a lovely man. He was a big fella, ya know, he looked more like a prizefighter. Boy, he knew what he was doing when he was working on the faces; he worked on different faces on the mountain. Anyway, first thing I know, he was gone and I lost track of him. But I'm talking to his daughter; this is the year 1991. I was really glad that I met her. I just feel like she's my relation, too, cause L. Del, he was such a close friend to me. Oh, I can't give him praise enough. A lot of the men liked him but he didn't mix too much in conversation with the men. But he was a close friend of mine.

I know Mr. Borglum was paying L. Del a little extra. The most they ever paid up there; I got to be foreman and the most I ever got was a dollar and a quarter. That was a top wage. I think Mr. Borglum should have doubled L. Del's money. He should have been getting $3 dollars an hour for the work he was doing because he was an artist. He was not only a stone carver but he was an artist, a friend; well, you just name it, that's what L. Del was."

I don't know how my aunt was able to hold that video without shaking. She must have been so overwhelmed with such elation. Here was an actual worker who assisted her father on Rushmore. George could not have been clearer about my grandfather's importance.

"I think he could have took Mr. Borglum's place and finished that himself."

Along with Borglum's writing, this was without a doubt an incredibly powerful and touching testimony to Luigi Del Bianco. As pleasant as George was, you not could help but notice his little hints about my grandfather not "mixing in conversation with the men." George was not an unemployed miner. He was not in that clique. I was starting to see a pattern develop here:

- Rex Alan Smith wrote a book with a strong narrative about untrained miners from Keystone doing the impossible—carving Mount Rushmore. Luigi Del Bianco, Chief Carver, is not mentioned.
- Both Wenk and Popovitch are both very resistant to that narrative being disturbed by recognizing a "ringer" with special ability to finish the faces.
- George Rumple makes it very clear that while Luigi got along with the miners, he did not mix with them. He did, however, mix well with Rumple, who was not part of that miners' clique; the same clique that Alan Smith, Wenk and Popovitch appear to be so protective of.

It was starting to make sense. If Rex Alan Smith's "hook" was about untrained miners carving a masterpiece, surely my grandfather would have disrupted the theme of his book. So, what does he do? He decides not to mention the Chief Carver. A Chief Carver would only imply that there were in fact trained hands involved in the finishing of the faces. Also, Alan Smith was from that specific area of South Dakota. The Borglum Papers from Washington are not mentioned once in his research. If you were going to write the definitive book on Mount Rushmore, wouldn't you do your homework and read the writings of its designer, Gutzon Borglum? Rex Alan Smith had to know those papers existed. Instead, he chose to write a book that was solely "Dakota-centric" in its chronicling of the Rushmore experience, leaving out crucial details that would have told the whole story.

You now have an incomplete story with an agenda that Wenk and Popovitch not only embrace but also fiercely protect; **not only does Luigi not fit into Rushmore's incomplete story, he is a threat to it.**

CHAPTER THIRTY-FIVE:

"YOU CAN SEE WHAT YOU'VE GOT UP THERE"

THE 50TH ANNIVERSARY OF Mount Rushmore came with a mixed bag of emotions for my Aunt Gloria. She had to fight her way into a reception she and her brother should have been invited to. Did our arguments with Dan Wenk somehow contribute to that perceived snub? It's possible. All I know is that in 1933, the "office in Rapid City" did not want my grandfather at the mountain. In 1991, they didn't invite his children to Rushmore's 50th Anniversary reception. I want to be fair here, but that incident never felt right. Still, serendipity and my aunt's determination to capture George Rumple on video made the trip an unforgettable experience for sure. Thank you, George.

While fate was in full swing at Rushmore, Caesar and I were experiencing our own form of kismet at home. My good friend, Mary Edwards, called me one day excited to tell me she had made a Rushmore connection. It turned out that her co-worker was the nephew of Matt Reilly, who was a pointer and foreman at Mount Rushmore. Mary had just learned about my grandfather and couldn't wait to tell Jim Reilly the connection. After a quick phone call, it was confirmed that not only did Matt remember Luigi, but they were close friends and always drove out to the mountain together. Luigi and Matt lived only 15 minutes apart.

Unbelievable. Another living flesh and blood worker, and only 15 minutes away!

I will always be grateful to Mary Edwards for making this crucial connection for my uncle and me. After I thanked her profusely, I called Caesar to tell him the great news. Immediately, I had to hold the phone away from my ear.

"Are you kidding me?!" Caesar began screaming. "I've been going crazy trying to find this guy! He lives in Stamford? Oh, Madonna mia... This is the best thing that has ever happened to me. Louis, pick me up *now*. Let's go see him!"

After I managed to talk my uncle down from his elation, I told him Matt would love to meet us and that we could see him the next day.

Matt Reilly was a total gentleman with a real twinkle in his eye. At 80 years old, he was not as vital as we hoped he'd be. I could see that his neighbor and friend, Mary, was there to make sure we did not take advantage of Matt in any way. Good for her. We were, after all, total strangers.

The ice was immediately broken when, early on in the interview, Caesar asked Matt if he knew my grandfather well.

"Well, I knew him well enough to sleep with him."

Matt managed a sly smirk of a smile when Caesar's mouth dropped, and then he burst into laughter. Matt was referring to the many times he and Luigi had to bunk together in the same bed or sleeping bag on the way to South Dakota every season. From then on, we all got along beautifully. Here are some excerpts from that afternoon:

Caesar: The men on Mt. Rushmore, when you were there in '33, '34, '35, '36—those years, did he get along with the men?

Matt: Oh yes—because...he could get along with the men because he had the ability...to fall in with the crowd.

Caesar: Did he hang around with the men, did he drink with the men, talk with them?

Matt: No, he wasn't around like that.

Caesar: He was a loner, wasn't he?

Matt: Loner, pertaining to, uh, the work. The men were all whiskey drinkers.

Caesar: He what?

Matt: I said the men were all whiskey drinkers, mostly.

Caesar: He was a wine drinker.

Matt: Yeah, well, he had his own wine, there. He didn't mix it. [Caesar laughs.]

Caesar: Did you know him very well?

Matt: Well, I knew him well enough to sleep with him.

Caesar: [Chuckles] You slept with him—That's pretty good! Did you get along? Did you like my father? Not because I'm here...Did you, uh, get along very well with my father?

Matt: Oh, yes, because he took me under his wing to make a pointer out of me.

Caesar: He taught you how to point, my father?

Matt: Yeah.

Caesar: My father was a very outgoing personality, wasn't he? Bianco, he spoke a lot, didn't he?

Matt: No, I wouldn't say too much.

Caesar: Not too much, eh?

Matt: No, he was, he was...he knew what...it was just like being a sculptor. He knew what to say and when to say it. He could get along very well with people. He had a mind of his own, too. You could tell when you were talking to him, when you give him an order whether it'd ring or not. If the bell didn't ring right, he let you know it.

Caesar: [Laughs] True. [Laughs again] You got along very well with him, eh?

Matt: Oh, yes.

Caesar: Now, did these guys like Merle Peterson, Red Anderson, the so-called carvers, but they're not skilled, did they work on the eyes?

Matt: The eyes were finished by Borglum, and usually, with Bianco.

Caesar: That's right...that's right.

Matt: Cause Bianco he would, uh, take the orders from Borglum of how much to take off, how much to—

Caesar: And did Bianco, was Bianco, would you say that Bianco was the main carver, taking orders from Borglum, rather than Anderson and Peterson, who weren't as skilled?

Matt: Oh, yes. Bianco was—

Caesar: Probably the main carver.

Matt: He was the main carver.

Caesar: [Pause] You don't know how good this makes me feel...

Lou: So just like you, Borglum had respect for Bianco.

Matt: Oh, yes, he respected Bianco.

Caesar: So, would you say Bianco probably, was the uh—

Matt: He was the main carver.

Caesar: You would say he was the best carver?

Matt: Oh, yes. You can see what you got up there.

You can see what you got up there.

If I had to bank on one statement above all the rest, it would be that one. Here is an actual worker who my grandfather took under his wing, telling my uncle that when you looked up at the faces on Rushmore, you of course saw the collective work of those 400 men for sure; nobody would argue with that. But I think it's clear what Matt really meant. Those faces look so real, and they emanate a humanity that could *only* be brought out by the skilled hands of the *only* classically trained stone carver on Rushmore. Borglum said it over and over again in his papers. Now Matt Reilly was saying it: *You can see what you got up there.*

What you got up there was the work of "Bianco." To say my uncle was beside himself would be an understatement. Because of his tendency to be neurotic, he always worried that maybe his father wasn't as important as he thought. *You know, my old man liked to exaggerate.* The fact was, Luigi never talked to his children about his Rushmore experience, so there was nothing *to* exaggerate.

That didn't matter anymore, because we were now finding people to speak for Luigi, and it was pretty exciting. First Gutzon Borglum, then George Rumple and now Matt Reilly; all people who had first-hand contact with my grandfather and his work on those four faces.

As happy as we were about this, there was a double-edge sword in operation here. It wasn't like Rushmore was ignoring Luigi's importance because he wasn't important. They were ignoring him because he *was* important. Obviously, he was a little too important. The more evidence we gave them, the more likely they were to resist. My biggest suspicion was solidifying: Luigi Del Bianco's great contribution does not fit into the narrative of those unemployed miners at Rushmore.

I remember sending video and audio cassettes to Rushmore so they could see and hear from actual workers with positions of authority on the mountain praising Bianco. My uncle insisted on following up himself. I let him. For one thing, we were at two very different times of our lives. I was 28 trying to grow my career, and as torn as I was, I had to prioritize. Caesar was 60 and semi-retired. He had lots of time to devote to correspondence with Rushmore. I have no specific recollection of any feedback from Rushmore about what they thought of George and Matt's testimonies. I do remember my uncle's frustration at hitting wall after wall. In spite of these major setbacks, a Luigi fan club was slowly growing. Founding members included my wife Camille, Jim and Judy Sapione, Peter Sgroi and now Mary Edwards. Of course, "fan club" is tongue in cheek, but these wonderful people all wanted to help my uncle and I find Luigi. The list would continue to grow.

CHAPTER THIRTY-SIX:

THE UNITED STATES POST OFFICE TO THE RESCUE

OUR NEWEST FAN CLUB member in 1991 was the President of the Port Chester Historical Society. Her name is Goldie Solomon. She fell in love with Luigi a few years before when she found out he built the base for our Spanish American War memorial. Goldie wanted to memorialize Luigi in honor of Mount Rushmore's 50th Anniversary.

"If Mount Rushmore won't recognize your grandfather, we'll do it right here in Port Chester!" she declared.

Goldie is a passionate woman who cares deeply about preserving local history. She worked with Caesar and I, along with the local Port Chester Post Office, to create a special hand-cancellation stamp; stamps that are usually created to honor a specific person or a moment in American history. I remember clearly our first meeting to map out what the stamp would look like. Caesar and Goldie were very funny together, like two peas in a pod. I was boxed in between two strong-headed extroverts. I had to step in a couple times to bring focus to our meeting.

In the end, Goldie made the stamp happen. On the day it was released, villagers lined up to get their mail officially stamped with the image of Luigi carving on the mountain. This was a once-in-a-lifetime opportunity to have a government agency like the Post Office create a special endorsement for such a momentous occasion.

My family will be forever grateful to Goldie, not only for believing in my grandfather's unique story, but for her generous efforts in helping get him due recognition.

When you care passionately about something, as Caesar and I did, people start to gravitate to you; not just family and good friends but those watching from the sidelines. Your dedication becomes contagious. Add to that our struggle with the National Park Service, and you have a recipe for what began to happen: More and more people wanted the United States Government to recognize Luigi. Maybe we can't change the tax laws, but can we change the historical record?

CHAPTER THIRTY-SEVEN:

"YOU ARE FURLAN—BE PROUD!"

THE YEAR 1992 WAS filled with ups and downs. The people at Mount Rushmore made their stand very clear. There appeared to be no way around it. I decided to take Caesar out to lunch to discuss what our next strategy might be. He told me he would eventually write a book about Luigi and Rushmore. I shared some ideas about turning our struggle into a human-interest story for television news magazines like "60 Minutes."

He said, "I don't want to share the documents with anyone right now. I don't want anybody to steal my ideas!"

"If we go to the national media, and they cover the story," I countered, "it will help develop a banner following. Then when we pitch your book to a publisher, we will already have an audience. It's a win-win."

Caesar strongly disagreed.

I knew our talk was getting a little too spirited when people in the restaurant started looking toward our table. When you had any kind of discussion with Caesar, good or bad, it was going to draw attention. In the end, I decided it was best to give in to Caesar. I backed off from pursuing any national media attention at this point. I knew my uncle was very serious about this work. He was very protective of the research papers and I had to respect his point of view, even though I didn't agree. I would continue to help him in any way I could.

I got home feeling a little frustrated. The officials at Mount Rushmore would not budge. I guess we would have to wait for Caesar's book to come out. But what do we do in the meantime? As I pondered the next step, my phone rang.

"Hello, I am Pietro Vissat. Is this Luigi Del Bianco?"

My true name. Every time I'm called that I feel my grandfather's presence in some mythically transcendent way. I told him my name was Lou, but Luigi was fine.

"I am the President of the Famee Furlane. Did you know your grandfather was Furlan? Did you know you are Furlan? You should be proud!"

Famee Furlane? What's that? It doesn't sound Italian, I thought to myself. Then I remembered. Yes, the part of Italy my grandfather was from. Friuli. The people there speak Italian, but they also speak a language fused with Italian, Latin and ancient German. Many of the vowel endings are dropped. Furlan people don't say, "vino," they say, "vin." And don't ever say to someone from Friuli that they speak a dialect. No! Furlan is a written language, and don't you forget it. I was impressed with the gentleman on the other end of the line. He continued to explain the reason for his call.

"I hear about your grandfather, Luigi Del Bianco, and his great work on Mount Rushmore. The Famee Furlane is so proud of him! We want to honor him at our club in Queens. We would like your family to come. Please, will you do this? We would be so honored."

Of course, I said yes! We'd hit an impasse with Mount Rushmore; at the same time, an organization representing my grandpa's birthplace comes hat-in-hand and treats us like royalty.

"Pietro," I said, "I would love to come. I will ask my family to attend as well. Thank you so much for recognizing my grandfather. You have no idea what this means."

I hung up the phone and thought, *I don't even know how these people found out about Grandpa.* It didn't really matter. Luigi's fan base was growing. His story was beginning to take on a life of its own.

Most of my family, unfortunately, couldn't make it to Queens for the ceremony. When I asked Caesar, he gave me his classic, *Let me think about it* response that always ended up as a no. To my surprise, my father wanted to go with me. He was really into the idea. This was his old man, after all. My father must have felt a pride about his Papa. He just couldn't express it the way Caesar and I did. The rest of my family, in particular my six sisters, felt a pride as well. Up until now, they had been cheering from the sidelines, but not actively involved. When my youngest sister Valerie insisted on coming, I was really thrilled. I had no idea she had such a strong connection to her grandfather. Then I remembered how excited she was when I showed her and my other sisters those documents after my trip to Rushmore. I realized that I was so into my own thing, I forgot how much my siblings cared.

When the three of us entered the club, a sea of suits and dresses ran to embrace us. It was something I'll never forget. *Ah, Del Bianco! Del Bianco!* was shouted over and over again followed by hugs, kisses and the kind of affection you get when you're home. To these people, we were home.

My sister Valerie loved every minute of it as she made her way through the crowd, charming everyone she came in contact with. My father was overwhelmed. I don't think he really knew what to do. I think, in his own way, he was touched by all of these proud people. I can't put it any other way. One couple in particular, Vinny and Lucy Maraldo, made their way over to our table when things quieted down a little. Vinnie Maraldo couldn't wait to tell me that his grandmother was a Del Bianco. "We must be related," Vinny said as he shook my hand, squeezing it tight. Lucy was a pleasure to spend time with, and I fell in love with her mom, who reminded me of my Great Aunt Vilma. The Maraldos would prove to be the most wonderful champions of Luigi.

After talking to the Maraldo's, something happened to me that I'll never forget. I went to get a drink and out of nowhere an old man grabbed me by the shoulders. With misty eyes, he exclaimed, "Del Bianco, Godammit!" Then this man wrapped his arms around me.

Have you ever smelled something, tasted something or even felt something that thrusts you back to another time in your life? It could be as simple as smelling stale Italian bread in a breadbox. All at once you are a kid again in your grandmother's kitchen smelling the stale bread she is about to make meatballs with. It's a profound emotional experience called sense memory: when sensory stimuli like smell and touch trigger memories. That's exactly what happened to me. There, that night, that old man's voice, his accent, his elderly arms embracing me. I was 5 years old again being hugged by my grandpa.

I was overwhelmed. Little did I know there would be more sense memories to come.

After dinner and dancing, Pietro Vissat asked my father, sister and I to join him in front of the admiring crowd. Pietro talked about how his paesani were unique in that so many of them were artisans in wood, stone, mosaic and terrazzo.

"Luigi Del Bianco is a great representative of the Furlan People. Like all of us here, he came to this country to practice the skills God gave him.

To do what he did on Mount Rushmore had never been done before. We salute one of our own. We salute Luigi Del Bianco!"

The crowd cheered as Pietro presented my father with a beautiful plaque and gold medallion. Pietro insisted my father say a few words. *Oh, no!* I thought. Can he handle this? I'd never heard him speak in public before. I suddenly felt like a parent about to watch his son in a school play, wracked with panic and praying he wouldn't stutter or struggle for the words. My father was fine. Absolutely fine. I can't tell you I remember everything he said, but the one thing I do recall most was him clutching that plaque and saying, "You people make me feel so good," as his newfound paesans applauded.

My sister Valerie beamed. Who knew that Vinny could work a room so well? I learned something that night; I wasn't the only one in my family who wanted to know where I came from. Maybe my father and sister did, too. To what extent, I really didn't know. I'm just really glad they decided to be a part of this.

From left, Ida Miletich, Pietro Vissat, Valerie Del Bianco, Vincent Del Bianco, and myself.

CHAPTER THIRTY-EIGHT:

BORGLUM, MORE ARGUMENTS, LECTURE TIME

CAESAR AND I SPENT the early to mid-90's visiting various works by Borglum all over the tri-state area. Dear friend "Nicky Ply" Tenaglia was always available to help out, earning him membership into the Luigi Del Bianco fan club. It didn't hurt that Nick knew my grandfather well and recalled having many stimulating conversations with him about Italian art and culture.

Caesar hamming it up with Borglum's "Seated Lincoln" in Newark, N.J.

In addition to pilgrimages to Borglum sites, Caesar also started writing essays about his father and Rushmore, hoping to get them published. Sometime during 1996, my Aunt Gloria called to ask why we weren't pursuing Rushmore anymore. I told her that until power changed hands, it seemed like we would only be spinning our wheels. My aunt offered to talk to Rushmore officials. I gave her my blessing. The next day she called me, just as irate as her brother and I were five years earlier.

"I talked to Jim Popovitch. He wouldn't budge. I told him if Wenk and he didn't give my father the credit he deserved, I would sue Rushmore!"

Sue Rushmore? Is that even possible to do? My aunt laughs about that now. "I was very emotional. Naïve, too. I was just so frustrated!" I always gave her credit for trying.

Soon after, Caesar called me.

"I want to put together a lecture about Mount Rushmore. I'm going to call it, 'In the Shadow of the Mountain,' cause my old man worked in the shadow of everyone else, capisci?"

"What about the book you're writing?" I asked.

"I'll get to that later."

While I thought the book was a priority, I couldn't argue with the idea of a lecture, which could also garner a lot of attention. Caesar once again enlisted his friends Jimmy and Judy Sapione to help put the lecture together. Since these were the days before Power Point, Jim had to take all the photos and convert them into slides to be run on a carousel projector. Our newest member to the fan club, Phil Maniscalco, offered to run the projector during the lecture.

I was so happy for Caesar because he could really focus on this latest project: getting up in front of a crowd and talking about his Papa. Caesar was an experienced performer, so this would not be a problem. His first lecture was at Westchester Community College for the Italian Department, under the direction of Professor Carlo Sclafani. Carlo was and is one of the most passionate and charismatic advocates for Italian culture in America. Unfortunately, because of my work schedule, I could not attend the lecture. I heard only great things about Caesar and his professorial approach to the subjects of Rushmore, Borglum, the workers and "Bianco," Chief Carver.

His next lecture was at the Port Chester Public Library, where folks from Port Chester and beyond packed the room and applauded my uncle for his very meticulous and somewhat scholarly talk. It wasn't until the Q&A when Caesar began to charm the crowd with his great sense of humor. The evening came to a warm and touching close as family and friends from Washington Park reminisced about the great stone carver they all knew, loved and admired. Perhaps my favorite part of the evening was when Caesar ended with—"To my nephew, Louis, who helped me so tremendously all these years."

Caesar would give his lectures all over Westchester County for several years. Not only was he spreading the word, but also giving himself the opportunity to be taken seriously for his work, his research and his love for his Papa's achievements. Even though we were frustrated with Rushmore, both my uncle and I, along with the growing number of people helping us, would continue to find other ways to tell Luigi's story. If Grandpa was able to persevere through his Rushmore experience, then so could we.

CHAPTER THIRTY-NINE:

"MEET THE BORGLUMS"

IT WAS BECOMING APPARENT over the years that my uncle didn't have a book in him; he wrote an article instead, and used the same title, "In the Shadow of the Mountain." The late 90's were mostly about Caesar, his lectures and repeated attempts to get the article published. Good friend and writer Peter Sgroi was a huge help in editing my uncle's writing. Rejection letters from various magazines like *Smithsonian* and *American Heritage* came one by one with the same boilerplate response: *Thank you for sending you query on Luigi Del Bianco. Unfortunately, your idea does not meet our editorial needs...*

How these American history publications were not interested in such a unique American story was beyond me.

In 1999, Caesar called. When I picked up the phone, the first thing I heard was, "Ya gotta come over, right now!" Caesar never wasted time with the usual niceties. I got in my car. I had no idea what my uncle wanted to see me about. Whatever it might be, it would be something different and interesting:

- *I got a chain letter in the mail and it's making me very nervous.*
- *There's a hum coming from the telephone pole outside my bedroom window, and it's driving me nuts. You gotta move my bed into the kitchen.*
- *The bulb in my ceiling looks strange to me. I don't want to get electrocuted. Can you change it again?"*

The good thing about my uncle is that he could usually muster up a sense of humor about his neurosis. *"I get nervous before I get nervous!"* he used to love to say. *"I'm King Nutt, double T!"* We always had a good laugh about it. I wondered what he was worried about today.

When I entered his apartment, he was standing with a brochure in his hands, which were shaking. Caesar had recently been diagnosed with early Parkinson's disease.

"Louis, the Stamford Museum is having an exhibit of Borglum's paintings and sculptures. Borglum's daughter, Mary Ellis and his grandchildren are going to be there. You gotta take me!"

Caesar was in love with the Borglums and was dying to meet Borglum's daughter. For him, it would be the equivalent of a Beatles fan meeting Julian or Sean Lennon. Actually, I was excited to go, too; I was curious to meet Borglum's descendants as well.

I took Caesar and my wife Camille to the Stamford Museum. When Borglum's daughter, Mary Ellis, saw my uncle, she actually recognized him. Mary Ellis smiled and her eyes grew misty. "The last time I saw you, you were such a little boy." It was amazing.

She remembered my uncle as a 4-year-old living with his family in Keystone back in 1935. It was a 64-year reunion for the two. My uncle and Mary Ellis embraced. Caesar was thrilled beyond words. It was touching to see. We also met Borglum's grandson, Jim, and granddaughter, Robin.

For Caesar, it was all about Mary Ellis. He spent the rest of the evening following her around like a puppy, asking question after question. Mary Ellis patiently answered what she could. I know this was an unforgettable evening for my uncle. He could see Gutzon Borglum's work up close, as well as meet the descendants of "The Master." Here is a photo from that night.

Caesar with Mort Walker and Mary Ellis Borglum. Mort is the cartoonist of "Beetle Baily." He had his studio on what was originally "Borgland," the Borglum Estate in Stamford.

CHAPTER FORTY:

"CHIP OFF THE OLD BLOCK"

IN 2000, *THE SOUND Shore Review* did a wonderful article on Caesar and his father. Other articles had been written on my uncle in the past, but this one typified him.

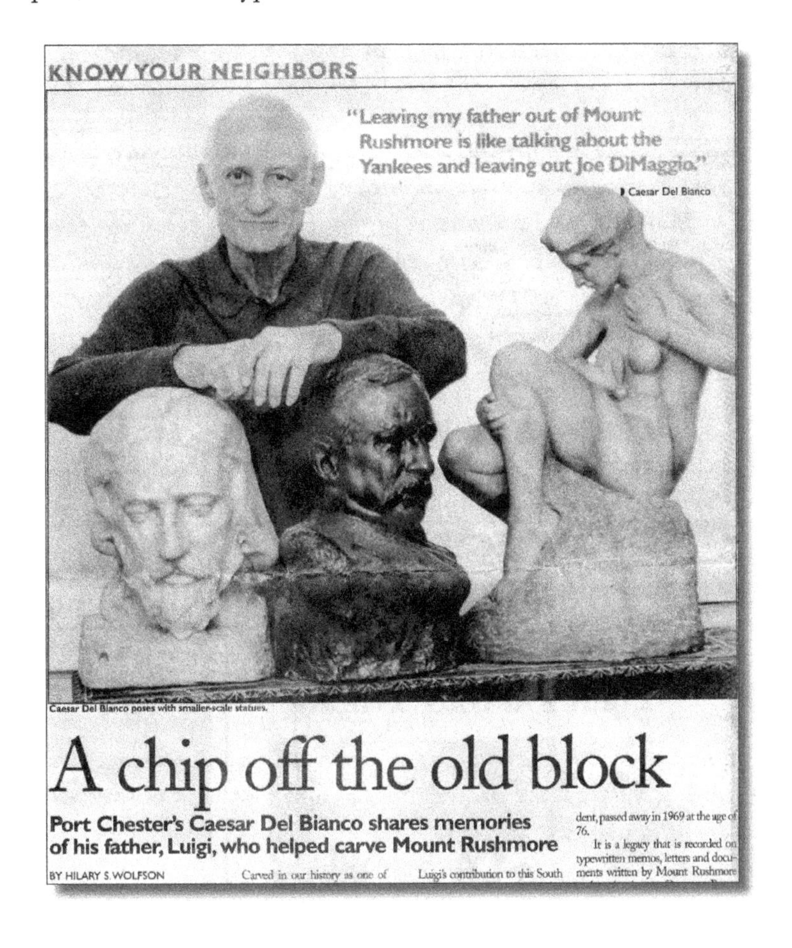

KNOW YOUR NEIGHBORS

"Leaving my father out of Mount Rushmore is like talking about the Yankees and leaving out Joe DiMaggio."

Caesar Del Bianco

Caesar Del Bianco poses with smaller-scale statues.

A chip off the old block

Port Chester's Caesar Del Bianco shares memories of his father, Luigi, who helped carve Mount Rushmore

BY HILARY S. WOLFSON

Carved in our history as one of

Luigi's contribution to this South

dent, passed away in 1969 at the age of 76.

It is a legacy that is recorded on typewritten memos, letters and documents written by Mount Rushmore

THE SOUND SHORE REVIEW

"Know Your Neighbors"

April 2000

No faces on a mountain loom as large as these. Spanning 60-feet from the tops of their heads to the ends of their chins, Mount Rushmore's presidents: Washington, Jefferson, Roosevelt and Lincoln, epitomize "America the Beautiful" and its glorious rich history of democracy and leadership.

Carved in our history as one of the nation's grandest monuments, Mount Rushmore stands at the pinnacle of man-made achievements. Begun in 1927 and completed in 1941, Mount Rushmore is the sum parts of many and the master of a few, including one artisan, Luigi Del Bianco, a stone-cutter and carver born in the Friuli-Venezia-Giulia region of Italy.

Luigi's contribution to this South Dakota monument is deeply etched in the heart and soul of his son, lifelong Port Chester resident, Caesar Del Bianco. Caesar (who's turning 69 on Friday the 13th) worked for years as a drill press operator for an airplane parts manufacturer, but has virtually dedicated his life to keeping his father's legacy alive. The senior Del Bianco, a former Port Chester resident, passed away in 1969 at the age of 76.

It is a legacy that is recorded on type-written memos, letters and documents written by Mount Rushmore sculptor/engineer Gutzon Borglum—papers that are now safely housed at the Library of Congress and National Archives in Washington, DC.

"I needed to find out as much as I could about my father," said Caesar. "Especially after Rex Allen Smith's book came out in 1985. Here was this author writing a book, The Carving of Mount Rushmore, *and nowhere in this book did he mention my father. I just couldn't believe it. It was like all of his contributions on this monument were erased from history. I needed to make sure that my dad received the recognition he was entitled to."*

People in the community can hear for themselves what this devoted son and researcher discovered over the past 10 years. Caesar will be giving a lecture at the Port Chester Council for the Arts CASTLE on October 13th at 7:30 PM titled "The Making of Mount Rushmore." Admission to the lecture is $5.

"Leaving my father out of Mount Rushmore is like talking about the Yankees and leaving out Joe DiMaggio," said Caesar, whose propensity for baseball metaphors comes from a love for the sport and his need to emphasize the importance of "every team member."

What this proud son will also tell you—in no uncertain terms—is that the sculptor Gutzon Borglum was "the true master and genius of Mount Rushmore. He had the last word on the mountain. No one did anything without Gutzon Borglum knowing about it."

The tapestry of people, place and things that were Luigi's life with Mount Rushmore is as rich and colorful as the man himself. Luigi, who reminded his son of Maurice Chevalier, was this tall, dashing charismatic figure that made his presence known simply by walking into a room.

Born in a little town in Italy called Meduno in 1892, the young Luigi went to Austria to apprentice under an Austrian stone carver, working with sculptor Borglum beginning in 1920. Moving to Borglum's Stamford estate in 1922 with his new bride, Nicoletta Cardarelli, this man "who could do magic with his hands," drove his car to South Dakota in 1933 to begin his first seven-month season to begin carving on the "new Jefferson head."

"When my father came out there was only one head," said Caesar. "It was Washington. To the right was the original Thomas Jefferson, which was only half done. They found a lot of bad rock on this head. So, when my father came, he started the new Jefferson on the left. He stayed there for seven months and came back again in 1935, 1936, and again in 1940 to repair Jefferson's lip."

Luigi was employed by Borglum to carve the "refinement of expression," or detail, in the faces, said Caesar. This meant, in part, sculpting the eyes which were designed to be visible from long distances.

"To highlight the pupils," said Caesar, "my father would carve wedge shaped stones and imbedded them into the eye cavities. The eyes would then reflect the light, making them sparkle and more lifelike. This idea was probably Borglum's, but my father was responsible for executing it."

The idea to do Mount Rushmore in the first place, said Caesar, didn't come from Borglum, but rather from Doane Robinson, the state historian for South Dakota. Back in 1923, Robinson wanted to attract tourists, said Caesar, and originally wanted to have a sculpture with the likenesses of western heroes, like Bill Cody, Lewis and Clark, and Indian Red Cloud.

They wanted to do something "with a more serious theme," said Caesar, "so the idea evolved into the U.S. presidents."

Borglum's son, Lincoln, who was the chief pointer on the project, was the one who completed Mount Rushmore after his father's passing in 1941.

"As the chief pointer and one-time superintendent," said Caesar, "Lincoln was the one who calculated the measurements of the faces, which second to Borglum's job, was the most important. The thing that most people don't realize though is that every carver, like my father, is also a pointer. My father didn't have anything to look at when he was carving except these five-foot plaster models of the faces. He'd be up on the scaffold, hanging in his harness, staring at the space, and then carve it. He'd know how to do it simply by gazing at this large face. How he got any perspective is beyond me. He just knew and he did it."

Caesar said that during his father's lifetime, two other great national monuments had the Del Bianco hand carved stamp on them. His father also worked with Borglum on "The Wars of America Memorial" in Newark, NJ, which is one of the largest bronze castings in America, and the "Stone Mountain Project" in Stone Mountain, GA.

Luigi eventually settled in Port Chester where he set up a stone carving and stone cutting studio on Clinton Street. There he carved statues and gravestones, said Caesar, setting many works as well in the community, such as the statuary at Corpus Christi Church and the Our Lady of Fatima statue at Holy Rosary school.

Rushing around a few days prior in preparation for his Friday lecture, Caesar sounded tired but pleased. He referred to his papers, which could be heard rustling in the background, quoting Borglum in one of his papers to the Honorable John A. Boland in Rapid City, SD about his Chief Carver.

Caesar read, "We could double our progress if we could have two like Bianco."

"What did I tell you," he added wistfully. "He was quite a man."

My uncle was in his best form in this article: charming, charismatic and funny. His lecture for the Port Chester Council for the Arts, an organization my wife Camille helped found, was a resounding success. This time, Caesar wanted a "real podium." Luckily, we had one. I guess all these lectures under his belt were making him feel more and more professorial. Once again, family, friends and more new members of the Luigi fan club were there to cheer on my uncle. I even convinced Caesar to bring the white marble bust of his father so everyone could see it up close. It was a great night. Unfortunately, this would be my uncle's last big push recognizing his Papa. There were tough years ahead for the both of us.

CHAPTER FORTY-ONE:

FAMILY LOSS AND THE PASSING OF THE BATON

THE LAST TIME MY uncle was at Mount Rushmore he was just 4 years old. He used to say, *I gotta get back there before I die.*

I noticed the Parkinson's tremor strengthening and his walk weakening. He dreamed out loud, *I'll take a train and stay out there the whole summer, you know, walk to the mountain every day, talk to the park rangers, do research. Maybe they'll let me do my lecture a couple times a week.*

It was a great dream for Caesar to have. I can't tell you how many photos my uncle accumulated from friends who all visited Rushmore without him: Nicky Ply, standing and pointing to my grandfather's name on that plaque at Rushmore. It drove my uncle crazy. *I gotta get out there!* He never did. I used to get impatient with my uncle's all-talk, no-action phases. Thinking back, I am amazed that someone like Caesar, who suffered severely from depression and neurosis, got as much done as he did. He would go for months without doing anything, yet when he was well, his passion, drive and dedication bore the sweetest fruit. I didn't always agree with some of his choices, but I always tried to respect him for making them.

Now, in 2001, Caesar's ability to make any choices became more and more a thing of the past. I drove him to Westchester Medical Center to have him admitted for open-heart surgery. His recovery after the surgery was difficult. Rushmore and my grandfather were now the last things on both of our minds.

Tragedy...conflict...struggle...sometimes come in two's or even three's. While I was regularly checking in with Caesar, I was also going to Greenwich Hospital to be with my mother who was dying of ovarian cancer. Angie Del Bianco was the backbone of our family. Our mother was everything to us. Caesar was also crazy about her. I couldn't explain to him what was going on with my Mom, or the fact that I had to leave him because I had an appointment with my lawyer. Yes, my lawyer. Caesar was in the hospital, my mother was dying and I was getting ready to serve my agent with a subpoena for refusing to pay me the $30,000 dollars she owed me. I felt numb, in some sort of dream state; probably a survival instinct. I had no idea what was coming next.

It was my Mom. She passed away on July 12, 2002, with her loving family surrounding her. Ironically, it wasn't my father or uncles who first told me about my grandfather and Mount Rushmore. It was my amazing mother. She is the one who inspired me to look for Luigi.

Over time, my uncle's medications were adjusted. He was able to return home. After some arguing back and forth with a social worker, he agreed to allow a visiting nurse to come to his apartment three mornings a week. Caesar was slipping, slowly but surely. Still, I saw a glimmer of something in those eyes.

In 2004, one of the members of the Famee Furlane, Rudy Magnan, asked me if I wanted to set up an exhibit booth at an Italian Expo he was running at the County Center in White Plains, New York. Thousands of people would frequent the expo throughout the weekend. It would be great exposure for Luigi. Thank you, Rudy. I jumped at the chance. Caesar was hesitant. When I told him I would do it without him, he changed his tune and decided to come. I knew him so well.

The weekend of the exhibit came, and Caesar was a different person.

"Let me do the talking."

"Sure," I said.

For two days, my uncle lectured, laughed and charmed his way through the crowd, which was mostly Italian American. Everyone who came to our booth, where we had Luigi items on display, including that marble bust I remember from boyhood, was blown away. *I had no idea! An Italian was Chief Carver?!* It was the first time in a while we both felt that Luigi pride. At one point, I turned and traced my 41-year-old fingers on that marble profile, just like I did when I was 5. Sense memory enveloped me. The story was alive again.

Caesar and me at the 2004 Italian Expo in White Plains, N.Y. Photo: Del Bianco Family Collection.

Things appeared to be on the upswing. Maybe my uncle could start talking to the people at Mount Rushmore. Surely someone had to have been replaced by now. It never happened. Caesar's second wind was temporary. His Parkinson's was escalating and affecting his state of mind. He became reclusive again.

In 2005, my family was hit with a terrible loss. My youngest sister Valerie died suddenly. My family was shocked, devastated; we didn't really know how to express our grief. It was too much, and on the heels of losing our beloved mother. Val was the baby, "Little Bee," our Dad used to call her. I couldn't begin to imagine how her death affected him. My father had a hard time expressing emotion. *The tears, they don't come.* How do you deal with outliving your own child?

This is what happens when you are passionately pursuing something; the passion frequently gets interrupted by life. Once again, Luigi and Rushmore were the last things on my mind.

As 2005 turned to 2006, the wounds of losing loved ones were slowly beginning to heal.

My father managed one more trip to Rushmore. Because his struggle with diabetes was limiting his mobility, he needed his family with him. Work prevented me from going, unfortunately. My sisters told me my father was in his glory, sitting in a wheel chair and telling stories about his father to all the park rangers. By now the workers' museum was completed, and Jim Popovitch had made good on his promise to display one of the photos of Luigi that I sent to him 14 years ago. It was the one of my grandfather carving the forehead of Washington.

My father got to see that photo, with one glaring omission: There was Luigi's name, but nowhere did it read, "Chief Carver." For all anyone knew my grandfather could have been a driller. There was no way of knowing about his important role. Rushmore managed to keep my grandfather a "worker," just like those 400 unemployed miners. In spite of all that irrefutable proof from the Library of Congress, Rushmore continued to maintain Rex Alan's Smith narrative, keeping Luigi hidden.

A phone call from Famee Furlane member Vinnie Maraldo was a pleasant distraction.

"The club would like to honor your grandfather again. We have dignitaries from Pordenone coming and a gentleman who started a museum in Cavasso Nuovo wants to include an exhibit on your grandfather. Michele Bernardon wants to meet your uncle and you."

It was a relief to hear again from a Luigi fan. This call couldn't have come at a better time.

The event at the club came and went with as much enthusiasm and pride as that evening back in 1992. I met Michele and was immediately taken with his passion and dedication to the history of Friuli. Michele loved Luigi Del Bianco and couldn't talk enough about the exhibit he wanted to do in Italy. I would spend the next few days emailing him photos that he could use. Caesar didn't want to go the Famee Furlane event because his knee had been bothering him. He was willing to have Michele and Vinny come to his apartment.

When Vinny brought Michele to Port Chester, they could tell that my uncle was not well. Michele treated Caesar with so much respect as the son of the Chief Carver of Mount Rushmore. Vinny Maraldo acted as translator.

From left, Michele Bernardon, Caesar, and myself.

Michele thanked Caesar for all he had done for his father. My uncle jokingly replied, "But I didn't do anything!" Caesar laughed. It was nice to hear him laugh. Michele told us that he worked in iron and steel, and now in his retirement he had become a historian for Pordenone and was already a published author. My grandfather would end up in several of Michele's later books. It was a bittersweet afternoon. Michele was so ebullient, so excited. Compare that to Caesar's effort to look enthused. In his own way I'm sure he was, but you could see his aliments were overwhelming him.

The afternoon ended with hugs and kisses. We could now rest with the comfort that in spite of Rushmore's perceived snub, other people, nationally and now internationally, were committed to telling this story and changing the historical record on their own.

Caesar's knee got worse. He had trouble walking and would have to stop every 20 feet, wincing in pain.

"I'm gonna get a partial knee replacement," Caesar told me one day over lunch. "My foot doctor told me not to do it. She said it would exacerbate my Parkinson's, and she would never see me again."

Dr. Carlucci was right. After his operation, Caesar was taken to a rehab/nursing home to rehabilitate his knee. The knee improved, but his Parkinson's and depression grew worse. After a terrible time of adjustment and a new mix of medications, Caesar's state of mind improved greatly. He finally was able to settle into his new home, surrounded by the most loving and caring nurses and aides.

Always the consummate flirt, Caesar found a way to get nurses around him, laughing at his jokes, combing his hair and kissing him on the cheek. One nurse in particular, Nichola Mckensie, became the new love of Caesar's life. When Nicole wasn't around, you could hear my uncle shout, "Where's Nicole? Tell her to get her ass in here!" He was crazy about that woman. The feeling was mutual.

I made sure he was getting the best care possible. The staff all knew me and were always happy to give me updates and trouble shoot any problems. I even bought in a television and DVD player so he could watch old movies. I set up a CD player so he could listen to his idol, Frank Sinatra. Caesar would shout from his bed, *Come in here! I want to you to listen to this.* It was usually some quiet little Filipino nurse or aide standing there politely while Caesar waved his arms waxing poetic about the genius of his favorite singer. *Do you hear that? The tone, the phrasing, nobody interprets a song like F.S.! Do you understand? I want to you to know Sinatra. He's the greatest! Bar none!* The nurse or aide would turn red, giggle and go out of her way to tell me later, *Oh, Mr. Caesar, he love Frank Sinatra. He so funny.*

On other days, my uncle would give impromptu lectures from his wheelchair or bed on Borglum, his father and Mount Rushmore. I'll never forget the day I walked into his room to discover nurses, aides, even custodians, listening to Caesar as he talked about his favorite subject.

One day he said to me, "I wanna do my lecture here at the hospital. You can bring the projector and screen and I could do it for the people here."

He was serious. I was ready to do it. Caesar seemed like he *could* do it. He would say, "Nothing bothers me," which almost convinced me he had one more lecture in him; all the years I'd known him, I'd never heard him say those words.

I knew my uncle would be here for the rest of his life. I decided to slowly start pursuing my grandfather's story on my own. Every time I made a phone call or sent an email I felt guilty. Caesar's friends encouraged me to keep going. I made a connection with the Italian American Museum in Manhattan. Maria Carparelli had joined the fan club. She proposed a full exhibit about my grandfather. It required some oral history. She asked me to videotape the living children of Luigi.

"I've tried to interview my father and uncle in the past but they weren't very cooperative."

"Try again!" she said.

I did. To my surprise, my father agreed, and many of the memories he shared are in this book. My Aunt Gloria also did a wonderful job talking about her Daddy. Before I proposed a video interview to my uncle, I swallowed hard and told him about the exhibit I was planning with the Italian American Museum. I cringed at the thought of his response. This was his baby. "Good, good," my uncle replied. What a relief. Caesar was allowing himself to let go a little. He also agreed to the interview. Though weak in body and voice, my uncle talked about Borglum, Rushmore and his Papa. I asked him how he felt when he found all those incredible papers at the Library of Congress. There was no hesitation. "It was the greatest moment of my life."

The exhibit never happened. It wasn't anyone's fault. This whole journey has certainly had its ups and downs. If I've learned anything from this, it's that nothing is wasted when you are pursuing a goal. If I hadn't met Maria Caparelli, I wouldn't have done those video interviews. I will always be grateful to Maria for that.

In October of 2007, my father passed away, just months after that interview. He had been suffering from Type 2 diabetes for years. I think he also missed my mother terribly. The death of my little sister was a devastating blow. He went peacefully. It was the third major loss in my family in four-and-a-half years. Caesar insisted on going to the funeral. He wanted to see his brother for the last time; the big brother he fought with from the time they were kids. That tall, skinny, stuttering boy who wanted to be an Indian.

Caesar was now confined to a wheel chair or bed. I had to clean out his apartment.

I was left with a mass of photos, articles and artifacts from the family I had never seen. It was amazing. It was then that I decided to create a website dedicated to my grandfather. It would include wonderful photos of Luigi on the mountain, those video interviews of my family, and so much more. Best of all, I would include a link entitled, "Borglum and Bianco," filled with many of the papers from the Library of Congress. Now Rushmore aficionados and anyone for that matter could download these papers. It would be a great tool to generate interest and further build a movement that would force the National Park Service to do the right thing.

When I told Caesar my plans for the website, he was happy. He looked up at me from his bed and said, *You've gotta take this over when I die.* Then he called me something he hadn't in a while—"My Nefoo." I looked down at those twinkling eyes and that twisted nose, and I smiled. Caesar passed away just two months later. *I gotta get to Rushmore!* This time, I bet he does.

CHAPTER FORTY-TWO:

STARRING...LUIGI!

UNCLE CAESAR, THIS FORCE of nature, this truly unique individual, was gone. It would be so strange not having him in my life anymore, inspiring me, fighting me, driving me crazy. Yes, he drove me crazy, and I was crazy about him. Even in the late stages of Parkinson's disease, he would be in his chair, eyes lit up, talking about his "old man." Now he was gone, and even though he couldn't show it, I knew he cared. Even though he cringed when I tried to hug him, I knew he loved me. I knew when he passed he was proud of me and finally ready to let go, ready to let me take the lead.

I was on my own now. For years, it was me helping Caesar. Now I had his much-desired blessing and carte blanche to call the shots. There was so much I wanted to do.

For starters, the website was up and running. My amazingly talented buddy Alex Fidelibus, who designed all of my own promotional materials, did a fantastic job bringing Luigi to life on the Internet. The website was everything I hoped it would be. I titled it "LuigiMountRushmore.com." The site still stands and is updated with every new development. Now that the website was in cyber land, it was great to get emails from people all around the world thanking me for letting them know about the Italian immigrant who anonymously lived the American dream. Anonymous until now, of course. I had to figure out the next step.

I forwarded the website to Mount Rushmore and received no response. I forwarded it again, this time sending the specific link to the "Borglum/Bianco" section that contained all those incredible papers from the Library of Congress. Mind you, all of these documents had already been shared in paper form throughout the early 90's, but now they were consolidated into an easy to follow timeline that told a story. As a storyteller, that's how I love to express myself. I had been doing it for years performing educational one-man shows for children that combine storytelling, theater and music. After the second and third attempt to get Rushmore to hear this story in a different way, I got nothing. The same frustration from years past crept back. It made me want to go in a whole other direction. As an artist, that was how I tried to look at life; if you are stuck on something, get off that track and take another. Find another way. Start fresh. All of a sudden, the answer was staring me in the face.

I'd been telling stories for 25 years. My latest venture was a portrayal of Abraham Lincoln. He was such a perfect fit for me. I resurrected my abilities as an actor and fell in love with living history. That's when it hit me: Why not do the same thing with my grandfather? Like Lincoln, why couldn't I *become* Luigi?

When I was trying to become a children's entertainer on television, I would get the most obnoxious feedback. *You've got to change your name and Americanize it. You sound like a cartage company. You're too big and masculine, you're going to scare little children.*

I found out later, when I was on the phone with my agent, the comments really meant—*A big Italian guy is going to scare little children.*

Well, there you go again, those ridiculous stereotypes that just won't go away. This time around, I was feeling empowered. If I'm going to be accused of being the big Italian guy, I may as well be just that. In Lincoln Borlgum's words, I'll be that "great big Italian." I'll be my grandpa.

I was inspired. It only took a couple months to put together. I did my first show at one of the elementary schools in my hometown of Port Chester. Dressed in a white shirt with the sleeves rolled up, a tie and knickers, I resembled my grandpa the way he looked in the 1935-1936 photo of him standing next to the models. I showed photos on a big screen. I shared my childhood memories of our short but powerful bond: *I am Luigi, you are Luigi.*

I talked about my grandfather's trip to America to live his dream. Then, against that photo of him and the models, I transformed into Luigi for my young audience, complete with mannerisms and full-blown Italian accent. My character was an amalgam of colorful imitations from Caesar mixed with mannerisms my father got from his Papa that were in turn passed down to me. It was a character interpretation straight from my biological and emotional family tree. The kids were spellbound. So was I, actually! To portray my grandpa was totally and unforgettably cathartic for me. Luigi was strong, playful and passionate. The kids loved him. They learned about his time in the Black Hills with his wife and three sons and the important work he did to help Borglum and the 400 workers carve those faces. The show conveyed messages about history, perseverance and honoring your ancestors. After it was over, I had an epiphany. After 25 years of developing my expertise as a storyteller, this was the story I had always been working towards. This was the story I was meant to tell.

I performed my grandpa again and again. Kids of all ages would shout, *Luigi! Luigi!* after the show was over. Teachers would come up to me with tears in their eyes.

Oh my God, this reminds me of my family, and I'm not even Italian! That was the best thing I could hear—my grandfather's story had universal appeal: the immigrant experience.

As the show tightened and became more focused, I added a component at the end about Rex Alan Smith's book omitting Luigi and Mount Rushmore's consistent refusal to honor him in a special way. After falling in love with Luigi and cheering him on, children and adults were shocked to hear of my family's struggles. I told them about our trip to the biggest library in the world and the research we did to prove his importance. The children's immediate empathy for Luigi was palpable. They started asking me how they could help my grandpa. I told them to tell his story to everyone they knew. I told them they could spread the word because sometimes history does not give you the whole story. If someone is being ignored or even bullied, you have the power to find out the truth and advocate for that person. What a great message for today's children to hear: In the cold and desensitized computer age, you can lead with your heart, connect on an emotional level and help change history for the better. Best of all, children were moved to talk to their own living relatives to find out their own unique stories. I felt, in my own small way, I was inspiring children to interact more with their grandparents. Perhaps I would even help some children cultivate more sense memories, long after their loved ones were gone.

I started performing for adults as well. When I was with a more sophisticated audience, I could bring those documents up on my screen and read the history of my grandfather's vital importance. They were spellbound by Borglum's praise, then completely empathetic to my grandfather and his struggles with the "sabotage" directed against him. Every family has had an immigrant experience that made my grandfather's life relatable. Luigi touched a chord.

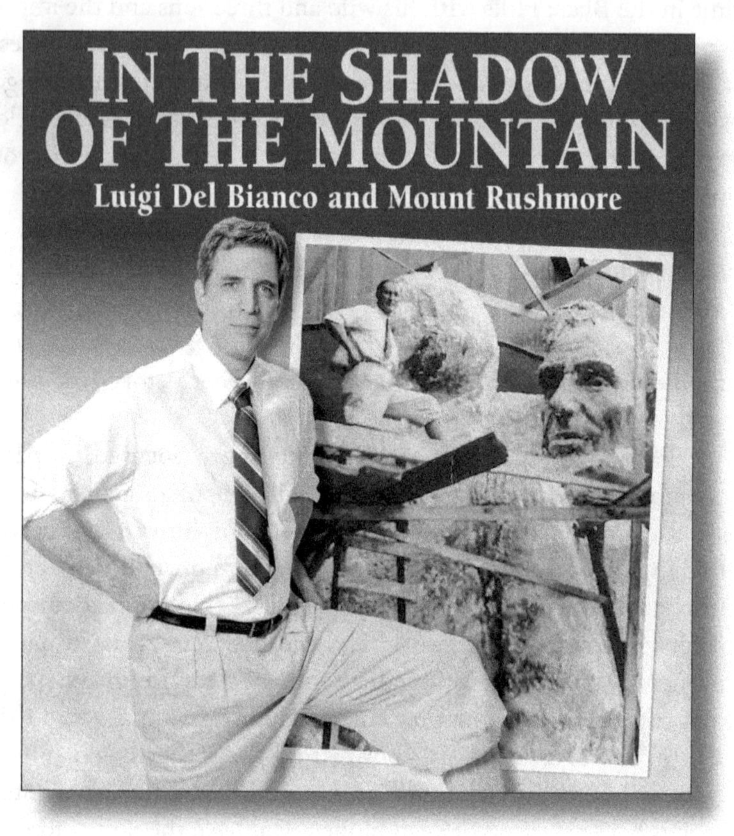

A flyer for my one-man show about Luigi. Flyer designed by Alex Fidelibus. Photo: Mike Pierro of Vita Studios.

One night after a very successful Luigi show, I sat down with my wife Camille, and we talked about the experience of performing my grandpa live. Since we were both lovers of musical theater, we joked about a Luigi musical as the next obvious step after my dramatic portrayal.

"Can't you see your grandfather up in the air, on stage next to a giant face of Lincoln, carving his eye and singing? You can't get more dramatic than that!"

We were joking about it, but we really weren't. It would be a great musical…or a movie.

That was it. I loved movies. I'll write a Luigi movie. Why not? I could write about that one year, 1935, when my grandpa had the whole family out there in the Black Hills. Of course, I knew absolutely nothing about writing a screenplay, but I knew it was possible with little or no experience. I had nothing to lose.

I spent a good month online reading screenplays, one after the other, learning the format, the flow, the arc of each character. I read a couple of books on the subject. Then I just started writing. I brought everything I knew to life: Luigi and Nicoletta, Borglum with Bianco, my father's memories of Keystone, the Lakota Sioux and the "sabotage." The whole story was woven in and around a Sunday visit from 5-year-old me, listening to Luigi share his memories of that year.

Believe it or not, there were agents and producers who were interested to a degree. They loved the story, but were afraid the cost of bringing those faces to life was too high to ensure a profit. Period movies also cost much more to make. Other producers criticized flaws in my writing. I had no problem with that. Still, I was acutely aware of the crappy screenplays that got produced every year. It would be such a wonderful family movie with the best messages for all ages.

I started to feel like I was spinning my wheels with "making it big overnight" in the movies. Not to be discouraged, I decided to explore other more realistic avenues. I was sure I could network my way into the kind of circles that could help me create a movement that would, over time, change Rushmore's stance. I started with all the national Italian American philanthropic groups. Andre DeMino, a past president of UNICO International, loved my grandpa's story and invited me to their national meeting in Hershey, Pennsylvania. I would get 15 minutes in front of 400 representatives from UNICO chapters all over the country. Because of the limited amount of time, I opted not to appear as Luigi, but his grandson, showing photos and proudly proclaiming his accomplishments as an artisan immigrant carving our nation's greatest memorial. When I was done, the crowd leapt to its feet, applauding and shouting, *Bravo, Luigi!* It was electric. They were not expecting this story. Most people aren't.

That's what happened that Saturday in Hershey. UNICO members came up to me and hugged me, thanked me. These were people who were sick and tired of enduring all of the negative stereotypes the media and entertainment perpetuates about Italian Americans on a daily basis. Luigi Del Bianco was an Italian they were thrilled to share with their communities as a positive role model. Once the joy and excitement wore off, the realization always set in for the audience members: *Why won't Mount Rushmore honor him?* When I explained Rushmore's "policy," I'd often heard the same thing. *That is unacceptable! Una disgrazia!* I couldn't agree more.

I went back to New York as if on a cloud. People like Andre DeMino and UNICO were behind me now. Manny Alfano, President of the Italian American One Voice Coalition (IAOVC), pledged to put pressure on the National Park Service to rethink its stance. I also developed a relationship with Dr. Joseph Scelsa and the Italian American Museum in Little Italy in Manhattan. Joe was so moved by Luigi's story that he offered space for a permanent exhibit in the museum.

Luigi Del Bianco exhibit at the
Italian American Museum in Little Italy, Manhattan.
Photo: Del Bianco Family Collection.

People like the gentlemen I just mentioned have devoted their whole lives to honoring their heritage. While Rushmore was choosing to put Luigi "in the shadow," people like Andre, Manny and Joe were bringing him out into the light where he belonged. The movement was growing beyond my local area. Luigi was slowly becoming the star he deserved to be. I wasn't feeling so alone anymore.

One night back in Port Chester, my wife Camille and I were watching one of our favorite reality shows, "Cake Boss." It stars Buddy Valastro and his family who own Carlo's Bakery in Hoboken, New Jersey. They make theme-styled cakes for a variety of customers. One episode involved a cake resembling the Statue of Liberty. As I looked at Buddy's patriotic creation, an image of Rushmore as a cake flashed before my eyes. I said to Camille, "Buddy should make a Rushmore cake and honor Luigi." She loved the idea. Hey, if I can't make Luigi a movie star, I'll make him a television star! A Mount Rushmore cake would be a perfect fit for "Cake Boss." I was convinced that Buddy Valastro, a proud Italian American, would be honored to make such a cake. I got on it right away and contacted High Noon Productions. They told me to download the proposal page and send it in. After months of follow up, I admitted to myself that they just weren't interested. I didn't get it—my grandpa would be so perfect for this show. I had to get over my disappointment and move on. Luigi's stardom would have to take other forms.

CHAPTER FORTY-THREE:

RUSHMORE BREAKTHROUGH! (I THINK)

IT WAS JANUARY OF 2011. Now that a movement was starting to develop, I decided to grit my teeth and try to communicate with the people at Mount Rushmore again. To my great relief, there was finally a turnover in staff, and I could start again on a clean slate. Gerard Baker was the superintendent. The fact that Gerard was Native American gave me hope that maybe Rushmore would be more open to change. After a very cordial conversation with Gerard, it was clear to me he did not have the time to deal with the issue of my grandfather's role on Mount Rushmore. He put me in touch with Nat Singh, the interim chief of interpretation. This was the same position that Jim Popovitch held many years before.

Do you know the expression, "Some things never change?" Mount Rushmore was no exception. Nat was vaguely familiar with my grandfather and vaguely familiar with the incredible documents we routinely sent. I quoted those documents over the phone. Instead of doing his job and interpreting the obvious, Nat once again gave me the Rushmore party line: *Your grandfather was classified as a worker. The workers on Mount Rushmore were a team. They are credited as a team. The only two who receive special recognition is Gutzon Borglum and his son, Lincoln.*

This was starting to feel freaky. Were all new administrators given a sheet of paper with those words and told to read them to people like me?

I'm not going to bore you with the same details. I countered, defending my grandfather's importance as written by Borglum, and Nat continued to remind me that *400 men worked on Rushmore and all contributed to its success.*

It's not that they weren't getting it; they were politely *not allowing it.* They knew exactly what they were doing. Nat Singh was continuing to protect the same narrative as administrators Wenk and Popovitch before him: Mount Rushmore was carved by a group of "workers" that would be credited as a "team." It was Rex Alan Smith's story, and once again Mount Rushmore officials were stubbornly sticking to it.

To say I was discouraged would have been an understatement. But not for long. The very next day I got a phone call from South Dakota.

"Hello. My name is Bruce Weissman, and I am the curator for Mount Rushmore's new workers' museum. I would love to talk to you about your grandfather, Luigi Del Bianco."

Now, this was an interesting call to get after my frustrating call the day before.

"Bruce, I'm all ears."

Bruce proceeded to tell me how moved he was by Luigi's story. He wanted to explore different ways to call attention to Luigi's role at Rushmore. Hearing all this gave me goose bumps. This was the first time a NPS official has ever been so solicitous about my grandfather; and out of nowhere, it seemed.

We talked for a good hour about many things: The Rex Alan Smith book, my uncle's research, our struggles with the NPS. What relief I felt to finally have what seemed like a willing audience. It appeared Bruce did not get the memo about the "team effort." By the end of the call, Bruce promised to do two things: identify my grandfather as Chief Carver under his photo in the workers' museum, and budget some money to bring me out to Mount Rushmore to perform my show. He ended the call by saying, "Your grandfather is going to get the credit he deserves, Lou. We're going to make this happen."

I hung up the phone and stared at my wife. "I think this guy means business!"

I didn't even know whether he called me on his own, or if Nat Singh had a change of heart and put Bruce in touch with me, but I had a feeling it was the former. I decided to trust Bruse Weissman, hoping that he would become the first National Park Service representative to advocate for Luigi.

A couple weeks went by. Nothing from Bruce. I called, leaving message after message. I knew this was too good to be true. Then I heard from him in February. "I'm so sorry I didn't get back to you."

Bruce told me we were still on track and that he had given my information to the *new* interim chief of interpretation, Blaine Kortemeyer. (What happened to Nat Singh?)

Kortemeyer was interested in having me perform my one-man show at Rushmore on the Fourth of July. What?! This couldn't be happening. I talked to Blaine and he asked me to submit a budget for three shows throughout the day. I furiously wrote one up and sent it in. I made sure Blaine knew I would be happy to negotiate. It wasn't about the money for me. This was way too important an opportunity. Bruce also promised he would do everything he could to have the title of "Chief Carver" placed under my grandfather's photos in the workers' museum by July 4. Bruce Weissman, the angel I had been looking for, had actually found me, not the other way around. It looked like Bruce had succeeded in getting Mount Rushmore to do the right thing. How he did it, I don't know, and I didn't care. It was happening. I penciled in July 4, 2011. I couldn't wait to get confirmation back from Blaine.

February went by with no word from Blaine. I followed up and was told they were "working on it." I chalked it up to the slow wheels of government. March turned into April. I called Bruce Weissman. After waiting weeks for Bruce to get back to me, he called and assured me not to worry—"We are going to make this happen." By May, I was getting nervous. I called Blaine and told him I was anxious to invoice him for the work in July and to discuss all of the details. That's when Blaine said, "It turns out we won't have the budget to bring you out this year."

My stomach dropped. A cold sweat washed over me. Was I really hearing this? Rushmore offers to bring me out to perform, has me submit a proposal, knows I will work with them concerning their budget, leaves me hanging for close to four months, and then casually informs me they don't have the money. It should be noted that I was hearing this while being aware that a $60-million-dollar budget was earmarked to create a digital hologram of the four faces. No money?

In spite of my shock and dread, I knew right away what my answer would be.

"That's okay, Blaine, because I will come on my own dime and do the shows for nothing."

Dead silence on the other end.

I waited.

Blaine, always confident and straightforward, stuttered. "Um, uh, well, let me get back to you and see if we can put you on the schedule."

I could tell Blaine was in a corner. How could he possibly justify turning down three free performances? To my relief, he did get back to me a few days later.

"We would like to put you on the schedule."

Of course, you would; three free shows? Now, in defense of Blaine, he may have just been the messenger. Still, I was pretty annoyed at the unprofessional way this was handled. I was also very confused by the way Rushmore lured me in, made me wait, only to push me away. I was being tested. I think I passed. In the end, the only thing that mattered to me was getting to Rushmore, performing my shows and letting the people out there know about my grandfather. I just knew the tourists were going to react powerfully to his story. How could Rushmore ignore that?

I wanted Camille to come with me. She was my muse, collaborator and the biggest supporter of what I was trying to do for my grandfather. We decided to drive the 1,800 miles Luigi drove 75 years earlier, though we were on much nicer roads with actual hotels. On the way, my face broke out with some sort of contact dermatitis, probably from stress. You'll notice it in some of the photos. The prednisone I was put on made me even more hyper. At least I had Camille to calm me down. I told my family not to worry about making the big effort to come, knowing that even if I lacked their involvement I always had their support, but my sister Maria insisted on making the trip. She was and is very proud of her grandpa. I know my other sisters are, too, but Maria, especially, really wanted to be part of this. We planned to meet her and good friend Rikky Daniels at some point before my shows.

Keystone looked the same as it did during our last trip in 1988. As we got our bags and walked toward our hotel, we overheard a man, wearing a cowboy hat and boots, talking very loudly on his cell phone, "What's that yer gonna have for dinner? Bracciole? Well, that sounds like a real good dago guinea meal!"

Camille and I looked at each other. Whoa. I looked at my new surroundings and all of a sudden, I felt a lot less American and much more Italian. "Dago" and "guinea" are two of the most derogatory words you could use to describe Italian Americans. This guy managed to cram both in the same sentence, and he had absolutely no problem shouting them in public. Was this really the way people in this part of the country viewed us? I tried to chalk it up to an isolated incident. In the back of my mind, I worried that this might be a hint of things to come.

After writing my screenplay in 2010, I felt a connection to the historic part of town, Old Keystone. This is where my grandfather and the family lived in 1935. I wanted to see Battle Creek, where my father and uncles swam as children. I wanted to visit Halley's General store, where my grandmother shopped. I remember visiting Old Keystone back in 1988. My visit during that time was more a mundane walk through with only a vague sense of my family's history here. This time was very different.

The gentleman who owned Halley's was a native of the area and a very friendly guy. I wish I had written down his name. When I told him who I was and why I was here he said, "Del Bianco? Mmmmm. Oh, we're mostly Swedish and Norwegian stock in Keystone. I could tell right away that you weren't from around here."

"You mean that I was Italian American? I asked. "Oh yes," he replied.

Really? It was that obvious? Because of my height and lean build, most people back east peg me for other ethnicities. Maybe it was my Roman nose that I proudly inherited from Luigi that was the giveaway. Who knows. Since he was so aware that I was of another ethnicity and another place, I decided to ask him if he thought my grandfather, an Italian immigrant, would have been treated differently by the natives of Keystone back in the 1930's.

"Oh, people would definitely have had trouble with your grandfather, that's for sure."

I know this was one person's opinion, but this guy was born here and would have remembered the 1930's. He seemed like a shoot from the hip kind of person. Even though I'd always suspected it, I decided not to make a snap judgment and conclude that part of the "sabotage" against my grandfather was racially motivated. After all, I had no hard evidence to support such a claim. But knowing the history of the immigrant in this country and with the "dago guinea" incident fresh in my mind, I wasn't going to ignore it, either.

We chatted further about the Chief Carver of Mount Rushmore, and my new Keystone friend could tell my passion and sincerity was real. When I told him my grandfather taught many of the unemployed miners about pointing and carving, he smiled and said, "Well, everyone who worked on

Rushmore fancied himself a carver. They always used to 'pad their part' if you know what I mean."

Before I left, the owner of Halley's brought me over to a table. There was a piece of granite sitting there. "I sell actual granite pieces from the mountain to the tourists, but you, you can have this one for free."

I was thrilled. I thanked him. I could tell he liked me and was supportive of my mission. He wished me luck, and we posed for a photo that Camille took. As we walked away I kept hearing one thing in my head that he said—"Everyone fancied himself a carver." Did the guys with no experience exaggerate their accomplishments on Rushmore? Did Rushmore accept everything they claimed because it supported their narrative? There was a reason why I met that man that day.

I made sure my next stop in Rushmore was to see my hero, Bruce Weisman. Even though Bruce was unable to get "Chief Carver" inscribed under the photo in the workers' museum, I wanted to thank him personally for his efforts. Bruce's office was in a very remote section of the park, and I could tell he appreciated Camille and I going out of our way to see him. He made no bones about the fact that he was a little out of the norm for a Park Ranger and that he had definitely ruffled a few feathers by championing my grandfather. How ruffled, I really don't know. I told him how much I appreciated his courage and that I couldn't wait for him to see my show on July 3rd so I could thank him publicly. He said he would be there.

Next, we went to the new workers' museum. It was filled with photos, tools and videos of the men who were hired by Borglum after they lost their mining jobs. I saw the photo of my grandpa with his name only and no title. The only title attributed to him was in a daily work record I had sent that listed him as a carver. It felt like a crumb. My family would not be appeased. It just wasn't good enough. Not even close.

I decided to go to the sculptor's studio where I was to perform my shows. Camille and I entered the same room we had visited 23 years ago. The feeling was completely different. I walked up to Borglum's models and remembered the photo Camille took of me posing in front of them back in 1988. I was a young man, flashing a fake smile and lightheartedly pointing to the models for the camera, so unaware of the powerful story my uncle and I were to learn. Today, I was a much older grandson, burdened and a little battle-weary from this mission, yet fully prepared to tell this new story, freshly chiseled out of some very old stone.

Camille and I in front of "the boys."

Camille and I held hands as we gazed out the window and saw the four faces in the distance. Unlike the trip in 1988, I became acutely aware that my grandfather had gazed out this same window to compare the big faces to the small ones. I looked back to the models and imagined him there in his white shirt, striped tie and knickers. Then I turned back to the window. I could see him 500 feet up there on his scaffold, drill in hand, looking down at me and smiling, then nodding with approval for what I was trying to do for him. Oh, how I wished he were there to tell me, *I am Luigi, you are Luigi*. How I longed to feel him hold me in his loving embrace...

I broke down.

Camille, always there to support me, held me close and said, "That's good, you should cry. Let it out. This has been building for a long time." I was feeling the burden and privilege of defending my grandpa's forgotten legacy.

What a rush of relief I experienced. My breath shook from the emotional release. "I'm ready to do this."

Later, I emailed a reminder to Cheryl Shreier, the superintendent, to attend one of my three shows. She responded right away that she was planning on coming and was looking forward to it. I sent a second follow up email to the Friends of Mount Rushmore, formally known as the Mount Rushmore Commission. This was the same board of South Dakota citizens that John Boland headed, the "office at Rapid City" that Borglum complained about in the papers my uncle found. Obviously, 70 years later, the "Friends" was completely different; although, still in charge of raising funds for the mountain. It was the Friends who didn't have the budget to pay me for the performances I was to give. I invited all 35 members and only heard back from one, who responded that this was an "interesting story." It would be interesting to see who attends tomorrow's shows, I thought. Finally, I called Bruce Weissman to remind him to come.

The next day, as Camille and I approached the sculptor's studio to do my performances, I started to feel the impending anxiety of the unknown. How would the people react to this? Will it all come across as sour grapes? Will the staff at Rushmore be resistant? Out of nowhere a young Park Ranger bounded toward me and started shaking my hand.

"Hi, my name is Dustin, and I am so excited to meet you! I read so much about your grandfather, and I can't wait to see the show. What an amazing guy!"

Dusty Baker was like a happy salve that rubbed away my worries. This had to be a good omen. Blaine Kortemeyer introduced himself. He was very formal, but cordial, and helped me set up. Before I knew it, crowds filed in. Show time.

I stood in front of those models, dressed in white shirt, tie and knickers before a crowd of curious tourists from all over the world. I had come full circle, back to that 8-year-old boy who said to his class, "I wanna tell you about my grandpa. He was Luigi Del Bianco, the Chief Carver on Mount Rushmore..."

Bringing my grandpa to life for the tourists in the Sculptor's Studio.

I made the same proclamation to those tourists. The same love and pride was there, just like it was in second grade. That "sense memory" was coursing through my veins. When I transformed into my grandpa, acting out his gregarious, passionate self, I knew I was standing in the same spot, in the same room, where he lived and breathed. It was profound. I'll never forget it. *I am Luigi, you are Luigi*, took on a whole new meaning for me.

At the end, I turned to the audience as Luigi and said, "For me, to be Chief Carver, is a great, great honor. Out of all the artists in America, Mr. Borglum chose only me to do this work. When I was a boy in Italia, I have a dream: To come to America to carve something special. Hey, amici, does my dream come true? Si. This is my passion, to be un artiste." I thank you so much for listening to my story. I am Luigi Del Bianco. Ciao."

I waited for the applause. I had no idea what to expect. The audience wouldn't stop clapping. They got it. I thanked them all and felt a catch in my throat. Now was the crucial moment of the program when I would show the documents that told the rest of the story. Caesar's presence was felt as I read paper after paper, telling the story of my grandpa's vital importance in the eyes of Gutzon Borglum and how he "outclassed everyone on the hill." I read about how my grandfather quit and Borglum hired him back by paying him out of his own pocket; how Luigi was "the only intelligent, efficient carver of the work who understands the language of the sculptor," and how "sabotage was directed against him by influences with the office at Rapid City and the Parks Dept." I read them all. The Q&A lasted as long as the show. I heard:

Wow, I was so moved by this.

Do you think he had trouble because he was Italian?

The most popular response was, *This is amazing. Why don't we know about your grandfather?* I gave the same answer every time—"*That's why I'm here.*"

I added two more shows that day. The demand called for it. I met the nicest people who were transformed by the story. This was proof that it didn't matter where I went: Luigi and Mount Rushmore had universal appeal, *even* at Mount Rushmore. It wasn't just the tourists who were impressed. Park rangers crowded me, "This is fantastic! Can I talk about your grandfather during my walking tours?"

"Are you kidding?" I laughed. "You better!" At that point, it wasn't worth calling attention to the absurd fact that none of the Park Rangers knew anything about Luigi. I was just so happy that, from that day on, they finally did.

My sister and Rikky were so moved by the reactions. I was so happy that Maria got to see the excitement about our grandfather right there at Rushmore.

Cheryl Shreier, superintendent, shook my hand. She couldn't have been more warm and receptive. "It was a wonderful show and I thank you for coming all this way to present it." I, in turn, thanked Cheryl and asked if Camille and I could meet with her the next day to explore some other possible programs regarding my grandfather. She was very amenable to the idea. I felt a slight shift in the earth. Were things warming up at Rushmore?

From left, Superintendent Cheryl Shreier, me as Luigi, and Park Ranger Dusty Baker.

When Camille and I got in the car, I realized that Bruce Weissman never came to any of my shows. He was nowhere to be found. Strange.

That night, Camille and I sat and talked about the amazing day we had. My cell phone rang, but I was too exhausted to answer it. It ended up being a very long message from Bruce Weissman. Unfortunately, I couldn't understand a word he said. It was completely garbled. Bad connection, I guess. I have contacted Bruce many times since and never heard back from him. I gave up. For some strange reason, he doesn't want to talk to me. I'm dying to know what that long message was about and why he didn't attend any of my shows. Maybe someday I'll find out.

The next day, Camille and I visited Cheryl in her office. We had a very pleasant conversation about my performances and how much everyone enjoyed them. Cheryl joked about how she sometimes referred to the carved faces as "the boys" and how she always says, "Good morning, gentleman" when she first eyes them at the start of every day.

I explained to Cheryl how grateful I was for the opportunity to tell my grandfather's story at the mountain. With all the positive feeling in the air, so different from past experiences with NPS officials, I broached the subject of a possible permanent Luigi Del Bianco exhibit at the mountain. To my surprise, Cheryl was open to the idea. Please, somebody pinch me.

While she was open to an exhibit, she made it clear that the mountain was in the middle of what she called a "Long Range Interpretive Plan" and after that was done in the fall, the new Chief of Interpretation Maureen Ballinger would be able to address any kind of exhibit. She also cautioned me about the wheels of government and how "slowly they move." I told her I was very familiar with that fact. Cheryl was excited about Maureen coming on board and wanted me to know that, like me, she was a storyteller.

The ride back to Port Chester was filled with discussions Camille and I had about all the success we encountered. We also talked about the moments that gave us pause. We thought it best to focus on the positive. There had certainly been plenty of that.

CHAPTER FORTY-FOUR:

THE PROPOSAL, A NEW FRIEND, MORE HONORS

I WASTED NO TIME IN getting an exhibit proposal together. My good friend Marshall Toppo, a brilliant musician and teacher who produced and arranged all of my children's storytelling CDs, connected me with Frank Migliorelli. Frank actually specialized in designing exhibit spaces. Like my friends, Alex Fidelibus and Marshall, Frank was a talented Italian-American artist who was all too happy to go above and beyond and help me with this story. Because he had designed exhibits for the National Park Service, Frank already knew that its budgets were tight. He asked me to get a ballpark figure from Cheryl of what Rushmore might be willing to spend on such an exhibit. Frank wanted to make sure we did not "overshoot" our proposal. Below is an email correspondence:

7/29/11

Dear Cheryl,

I hope your summer has been going well. I have been engaged in following up many important connections since I had the pleasure of meeting you.

I had a really wonderful meeting with Frank Migliorelli, who was a senior vice president of design at ESI Design in Manhattan for 11 years. One of ESI's specialties is designing exhibits for museums. Frank has done design work with ESI for several National Park sites: Ellis Island, the American Family History Center and the Eisenhower Memorial, to name a few.

Frank has recently started his own company. He has wonderful ideas and a creative team that he works with. He'll be helping me with a proposal for the Luigi exhibit we talked about.

Frank asked me to find out if you can give us a ball park budgetary range of what the cost of a Luigi Del Bianco exhibit might be. What we're basically asking is what Mount Rushmore would be willing to spend. This will be helpful to Frank as he assists me in putting together a proposal.

I look forward to hearing back from you about this.

Thank you for your time and attention to all things Luigi!

Regards,

Lou Del Bianco

LuigiMountRushmore.com

Hi Lou:

Thank you very much for your message and my summer is going well. It was a pleasure to meet you and I appreciated the opportunity to visit after your presentations on July 3.

In reference to your proposal, we do not have a ball park figure at this time since it would be very preliminary in our exhibit development.

The park will first need to complete our Long-Range Interpretive Plan, and I do not envision the plan being completed until later this fall when our new director of interpretation and education is here officially and she is up to speed on the planning endeavors. The Long-Range Interpretive Plan is our overarching document for managing and planning for new exhibits, waysides and programming.

I believe that a basic proposal would suffice for our needs at this time. Unfortunately, the wheels of progress move slowly and whether the exhibit is temporary or would become part of our permanent exhibits there is a process for us to reach that point.

Hopefully that information will assist you as you develop the proposal, and I apologize for not being able to provide any further guidance at this time.

Thank you very much and I look forward to hearing more about it.

Cheryl

I was a little confused by the fact that we were not given any parameters. Frank decided to offer a two-tier proposal: one larger exhibit and the other more scaled back, just to be on the safe side. We still felt a little funny about having literally no direction, but decided to submit it anyway. Frank did an amazing job telling my grandfather's story through videos, photos, and interactive technology using smart phones. We would just have to wait and see.

I'd also been playing the waiting game with someone I had wanted to talk to for a while, Rex Alan Smith. He was not an easy man to reach. The only way I could communicate with him was emailing him on his website. My emails were very cordial. I praised his book because it deserved praise. My intention was not to pick a fight. I only wanted to know what he knew about my grandfather and to let him know the rest of the story. I never heard back from him. I must have emailed Mr. Smith 10 times over a one-year period.

The rest of 2011 was chock full of surprises. The best one was a phone call from a gentleman named Richard Cerazani. Richard is an actor who wrote a book about his dad, Arthur Cerazani, a talented sculptor who worked at Rushmore for about six months. As I mentioned earlier in the book, Richard discovered wonderful letters that his dad had written to his mom about the trials and tribulations of working on Mount Rushmore. It's a very informative book about Gutzon Borlgum and this iconic stone carving. Just as important, it's a touching love story that Richard tells with great affection. *Love Letters From Rushmore* is a book I highly recommend.

Richard was so excited to talk to me. "My father wrote about your grandfather to my mother. They worked together in 1940!" (You can reference the photo of Luigi and Arthur again on page 160.) After sharing my experiences with Richard, he asked if we could meet so he could share some letters from 1940 where his dad writes, "The only man working on the faces is Bianco." I could tell even though Richard was working on his

Rushmore project, he wanted to help me in any way he could; Richard Cerazani, a good and generous man who sees the big picture.

I met Richard at his office soon after. He was every bit as warm and gracious as he was on the phone. We talked about many things, in particular the plight of the Italian: how my grandfather and his father who worked so hard and gave of their talent remained for the most part anonymous. Richard was so moved by my grandfather's story that he told me he wanted to write a one page bio about Luigi, Chief Carver on Mount Rushmore, and include it in his book. I didn't know what else to do but hug him. The Luigi movement was attracting the best people.

Another pleasant surprise came from Italian Professor Carlo Sclafani, who sponsored my uncle's first lecture back in the 1990's. Carlo invited me to perform my one-man show at Westchester Community College. It was great to see Carlo's face light up when he talked about Casear. Before my show, Carlo gave me the most heartfelt and passionate introduction about Italian-American pride. If only we could clone Carlo Sclafani; we need more people like him.

Carlo Sclafani and Richard Cerazani are two perfect examples of how a movement you start can grow and bring people together, and how people you never pursued will end up finding you. An organization called Storycorp found me and asked if I would do a segment as part of NPR's "Morning Edition." Since my Aunt Gloria was going to visit the family soon, I thought it would be a great opportunity for Luigi's daughter to talk about her father.

My aunt and I had a great time trading memories of Luigi. Since she had many more memories than I did, most of the program was devoted to her, and she was fantastic. Many people heard the segment. It was a hit.

I think this recording session brought my aunt and I even closer. Our long-distance relationship began to intensify. With Caesar gone, I was relying on her more and more for information about her father. We touched base often about the progress I was trying to make. I always looked to her for another perspective on the many frustrating issues I had to deal with.

The year ended with the Westchester Italian Cultural Center in Tuckahoe, New York, wanting to honor my grandfather as part of a larger tribute to the immigrant artisans of our area. Patrizia Calce not only included Luigi in this wonderful exhibit, but also asked me to perform my one-man show at the center, a beautiful building founded by Generoso Pope.

Aunt Gloria and I at NPR's "Morning Edition" studio.
Photo courtesy of NPR.

Throughout this active time period, my wife Camille and I decided to take my screenplay and turn it into an historic novel. Our hope was to get it published in and around the time of the opening of an exhibit. The future was looking bright for Luigi.

CHAPTER FORTY-FIVE:

HIGHS, LOWS, AND HIGHS AGAIN

BY JANUARY, I THOUGHT the new Chief of Interpretation at Mount Rushmore Maureen Ballinger would be settled into her new position. So, I emailed her and introduced myself. I wrote that I looked forward to working with her on the exhibit. I shared the link to my website and encouraged her to go through it. I also sent a specific link to the Borglum/Bianco section so she could read those wonderful papers and learn the significance of my grandfather's role on the mountain. No response. I called her office so we could chat. She was not available. I left a message with the Luigi website address included so the secretary could give it to Maureen. I never heard from her. I sent that information many times with no response.

After those confusing non-interactions, I got the biggest surprise to date. A producer for the "Cake Boss" television show, Nick Briscoe, called me.

"We would love to make a Mount Rushmore Cake in honor of your grandfather," he said. "It will be a very special episode in our upcoming series. We're all excited about it."

I thought for sure my proposal was dead in the water. It had been at least a year since I gave up on this. They finally called back; better late than never.

Camille and I went to the Lackawana Factory in Jersey City to film the consultation.

I decided to come dressed as my grandfather to add a fun flavor to the show. When Buddy Valastro found out that my grandfather was the Chief Carver on Rushmore, you could tell he was really impressed. We decided to have a "Luigi Del Bianco Day" in March at the Port Chester Senior Center. A seven-foot replica of Rushmore in the form of a cake would be presented to the Del Bianco family. The filmed consultation ended with Buddy shaking my hand and saying, "We are going to get your grandfather the credit he deserves."

I thanked Buddy. He was so sincere and down to earth. I knew he would do Luigi proud.

As thrilled as I was with "Cake Boss," I was very anxious to talk to the new Chief of Interpretation Maureen Ballinger about the proposal Frank Migliorelli submitted. I was excited to introduce myself as a fellow storyteller and get to know someone I hoped would finally "interpret" the importance of my grandfather.

After repeatedly emailing Maureen, she finally contacted me and acted as if nothing had been wrong. There was no apology, no explanation as to why she never returned any of my calls or emails. I decided to take the highroad and cooperated patiently as Maureen planned the next steps. First, we scheduled a conference call with Cheryl. Maureen then acknowledged that she had been to the website, but had nothing to say about its contents, in particular those incredible primary source documents. Again, I decided not to press her further. The exhibit proposal was my primary focus right now.

The call started with all the usual niceties. Maureen sounded very friendly and laid back. Before I got to the exhibit proposal, I asked both her and Cheryl if their publisher, the Mount Rushmore Historical Society, might be interested in Camille's and my historical novel based on the screenplay I had written. I also pitched the idea of maybe having the book available by July when I returned to Rushmore to perform my shows again. (This time for pay, I hoped.) Cheryl gave me the info needed to have the manuscript reviewed. Once again, I asked for parameters for their performance budget and could not get an answer. I guess they wanted the ball to be in my court; I would submit a budget again.

Everyone was feeling pretty good until Maureen broached the subject of a Luigi exhibit. In a nutshell, both women felt that Frank's proposal was too ambitious right now, even the second-tier exhibit. Uh-oh. I told them we had nothing to go by and that was why we asked for some parameters.

I offered to have Frank scale back the exhibit even more. I was told that wouldn't be necessary. This exhibit would be part of a long-range plan which, at the minimum, was five years away. What?

According to Maureen and Cheryl, Rushmore was already in the middle of several projects to digitize the faces in various ways. They would have to put the Luigi exhibit on the back burner for now. Those were the last words I wanted to hear. If this was what Cheryl meant by the slow wheels of government, she wasn't kidding. To me, "back burner" was a polite way of saying no. One step forward, two steps back. It felt like a giant carrot had been held out and pulled away. I could not get a handle on the genuine feelings of Rushmore officials. Did they want to honor my grandfather or not? I was disappointed, but at the same time trying to stay positive. I still had the book proposal to send in and the budget proposal for the return performances.

February turned into March. No word from Maureen about my proposal for the performances. The year before, Cheryl told me they would try to make room in the budget for me for the future since the whole day was such a success. I gave the absolute best price I could—$2,000, all expense included, for six shows throughout the weekend.

I sent off the proposal and then had to forget about it. It was "Cake Boss" time!

Family and friends were all coming to the Senior Center for the big day. I wanted people there who had a close connection to Luigi. The producers asked me not to make the event public because it would have been a mad house, due to the show's popularity. The afternoon began with a special Luigi show by yours truly and then the cake delivery. I loved being my grandfather for all these wonderful Port Chester people. There was such emotion in the air. Halfway during my show, the producer kept giving me the finger-slitting-her-throat signal. I was told to cut the show short. Due to the unseasonably hot March weather, the Rushmore cake was starting to melt, and it was making Buddy nervous.

Everyone was told to make their way outside. We all waited in anticipation for the big Carlo's Bakery truck to arrive. Buddy drove into the parking lot and the crowd went wild. They cheered even louder when he stepped out of his truck. Local schoolgirls were crying like Buddy was a Beatle. It was surreal. The cake was so big that it took six guys to roll it out of the van and onto a platform. The four familiar faces looked like a work of art. Buddy and his people out did themselves.

Buddy talking to the crowd.
Photo: Del Bianco Family Collection.

Buddy charmed the crowd and talked about how he and his helpers could step back and inspect the faces as they were being made. He was all too aware that Luigi did not have the same luxury when he carved faces that were 60-feet high.

"After Lou told me the story of his grandfather," Buddy began, "and what he did for Mount Rushmore, I had, like almost a sense of pride. To know that this unsung hero was an Italian immigrant like my grandfathers, to know that he lent a helping hand to something so iconic in America." Then Buddy shouted his signature, "Who wants to eat some cake?" and we all got a piece. It was a great day for Port Chester, a great day for Italian Americans, and a great day for Luigi.

Now, millions of viewers will watch the show and learn a new story in our American history.

Once again, other people were filling the void left by Rushmore and celebrating my grandfather. I could only hope that someday, the park rangers in South Dakota would eventually catch up.

The Del Biancos and extended family with Buddy Valastro.
Photo: Del Bianco Family Collection.

As everything went back to normal, I waited for word about my Rushmore performances as March turned into April. April turned into May with still no word from Maureen. Why does this have to take so long? I emailed Maureen for what felt like the hundredth time. She finally replied:

Mr. Del Bianco,

We do not have the funds to present your program this year. Thank you for your interest in educational programming at Mount Rushmore National Memorial.

Maureen McGee-Ballinger

I immediately wrote to Cheryl Shreier:

To: Mount Rushmore Memorial

May 7, 2012

Fwd: Lou Del Bianco appearance at Mount Rushmore

Dear Cheryl,

As per Maureen's request, I sent her a proposal to perform at Mount Rushmore this season back in February. I never heard back from her so I e-mailed as a follow up today, May 7th. Her response is below.

I have no issue with the fact that you won't be able to have me perform this season, although I did assume from last year's warm reception you wanted me to return and would make funds available. Frankly, I am very surprised to receive this kind of email. The tone is short and dismissive; almost a form letter.

It addresses me as if I had no connection to Mount Rushmore whatsoever.

Is this the way you think this should be handled?

I don't expect to be given special treatment. However, I do expect to be treated like someone who has invested time, energy and love in a story you all embraced, and I hope are proud of.

I look forward to hearing your thoughts on this matter.

Sincerely,

Lou Del Bianco

The latest chapter in this odyssey had started with a breakthrough in relations at Mount Rushmore, a hugely successful visit and great optimism for the future. This quickly devolved in to a failed exhibit proposal and now a routine form letter that treated me like I was contacting Rushmore for the first time. Cheryl never responded to my email.

I was thrust back to square one. It was all very confusing. Camille and I felt so strongly that we had Cheryl on our side. I did not know what to make of Maureen Ballinger. Was she influencing Cheryl? Was she the next chief of interpretation newly indoctrinated to protect the Rushmore narrative? I could spin my wheels forever, analyzing what Rushmore's real intentions were. I decided to move on for now.

Soon after, I got a phone call from a gentleman who was very excited to talk to me.

"My name is Doug Gladstone, and I heard the NPR "Morning Edition" program with you and your aunt. I am a freelance journalist and would love to pitch a story to my local paper about your grandfather."

Doug had fallen in love with Luigi's story. He told me he couldn't stand it when institutions took for granted those who deserved better, like my grandpa. Even though Doug lived outside of Albany, he offered to come to my house to interview me in person. I thought to myself, *This guy is serious.*

Doug and I had a great time during the interview. He would go on to write some really nice articles for *History Magazine*, the *Capital Journal*, Sons of Italy, *USA Today* and many more. Doug became a serious advocate for Luigi.

Camille and I continued to fine-tune the historic novel we adapted from my screenplay. I pursued literary agents in the hope of getting the book published. Because I had included many of the Library of Congress documents, the book could potentially generate a following that would influence the NPS to change its stance on Luigi. I was beginning to feel like that was the only option left at this point. Mount Rushmore appeared to be closing the door on my grandfather. I would have to find ways to force them to open it.

During the summer of 2012, I wrote a children's version of the book Camille and I adapted. It revolved around that day when I was in second grade and said to my class, "I wanna tell you about my grandpa." Because I was a storyteller for children, I loved putting this book together. It was yet another way to get Luigi's story out there. Once again, I pursued literary agents.

I had a lot of irons in the fire. Still, that frustration with Rushmore gnawed at the back of my psyche. Then I had an epiphany: If Rushmore won't give Luigi permanent recognition as Chief Carver, why can't I do it myself, in my own way? How about right here in Port Chester? The idea of a Luigi Del Bianco memorial in my hometown became very appealing to me. I immediately called Michael Keropian, a talented sculptor whom I hired to make plaster copies of the faces on the "Cake Boss" cake. I noticed a memorial plaque in his studio during one of my visits, and I think that's when the seed was planted. Mike loved the idea, and I quickly did a rough design, which he fabricated into a prototype for the final plaque.

I went to family, friends and every civic organization in town soliciting donations to make this memorial happen. Everyone responded the same way—*This is fantastic! It's about time.*

Simultaneously, I was raising funds for the memorial, I decided to sideline the recognition issue with Rushmore and focus on the book Camille and I adapted. I bounced back and forth between Maureen Ballinger and the Rushmore publisher, trying to find out if they would publish our book. I finally got an email from Maureen saying they would have to pass. The reasons why, I won't get into any details, just to say that I thanked her for taking the time to give me the feedback I asked for. It was another disappointment.

I decided to get away from Rushmore and devote my time to other pursuits. Even though the new year had an unlucky number in it, I hoped 2013 would bear sweeter fruit than the years before.

CHAPTER FORTY-SIX:

FIGHTING THE NARRATIVE

I **CONTINUED MY FUNDRAISING EFFORTS** for the Luigi memorial. My goal was to have an unveiling in the fall of 2013 complete with ceremony and media coverage. I was ready to pursue a personal interest story on national media like I wanted to do when my uncle was alive. The time was right. If only I could get Mount Rushmore on my side.

In the meantime, Doug Gladstone had been writing some fine articles and was now working on one for *Westchester Magazine*. To Doug's credit, he found someone I wasn't even aware of. She was Amy Bracewell, the historian for Mount Rushmore. Doug emailed Amy about my grandfather:

> *Ms. Bracewell,*
>
> *Per our conversation earlier today, I am writing about the above for Westchester Magazine. Mr. Del Bianco currently resides in Port Chester, New York, which is in Westchester County.*
>
> *As you know, Mr. Del Bianco's late grandfather, Luigi, worked as the Chief Carver at the Mount Rushmore National Memorial from 1933-1940. Only a little boy when his grandfather passed, Mr. Del Bianco has spent a good part of his life getting the word out about his grandfather, who was regularly credited by Rushmore creator/sculptor Gutzon Borglum as being the glue that held the project together.*
>
> *I believe Mr. Del Bianco's efforts to honor the memory and tout the achievements of his late grandfather are both commendable and worthy of a profile. I hope you agree and can supply me with appropriate quotes for attribution, from either yourself or on behalf of the memorial's superintendent.*

Also, if you have current contact information for that gentleman from Ohio who was part of the Civilian Conservation Corps' work at Mount Rushmore, that would be helpful too. If he's amenable, I want to write about him as well.

Thanks, in advance, for your consideration. I hope to hear from you shortly.

Sincerely,

Doug Gladstone

Here is Amy's response:

Hello Mr. Gladstone,

Thank you for contacting Mount Rushmore National Memorial. I have not done a great deal of research on Mr. Del Bianco and his relationship with Gutzon Borglum, but it sounds like Lou Del Bianco is knowledgeable on his grandfather's life and would be able to speak more to that. Luigi Del Bianco was one of many assistants to Borglum. Gutzon Borglum invited many of his colleagues and co-workers from his home studio in Connecticut to join him on his Mount Rushmore project. Some of them stayed on for a short time and some remained involved in the project for many years. Mr. Del Bianco was one of these artists that joined Borglum from their time in Connecticut. One of the history publications sites at least four or five of these artisans that Borglum invited to the project.

This is all I know of Mr. Del Bianco's involvement with the project. His name is not coming up in my searches of our archives or Borglum's papers.

The gentleman involved in the Civilian Conservation Corps (CCC) is Mr. Elwood Iverson.

Thank you,

Amy Bracewell

This is all I know of Mr. Del Bianco's involvement with the project. Amy Bracewell, historian for the Mount Rushmore National Memorial, doesn't know about the man who was "the only intelligent, efficient stone carver on the work who understands the language of the sculptor." Miss Bracewell doesn't know about the gifted Italian immigrant who stopped all work on the Washington and Jefferson heads when he quit. I could go on. According to her, Luigi was just part of another group, another "team." At least she didn't call him a "worker."

I never sent any documents to Miss Bracewell because I never knew she existed. I did, however, send them time and time again to Maureen Ballinger, Cheryl Shreier and countless officials before them. If you are the chief of interpretation at Mount Rushmore and you receive dramatic papers that tell a new story, wouldn't the *first* thing you do is share them with your historian? If you are the historian for Mount Rushmore, wouldn't you want to go to the Borglum papers in Washington and learn a much fuller history of the "project"? I don't know what actual Borglum papers Amy Bracewell has in her archive. Whatever she has, it isn't much. You can't tell me that the historian for Mount Rushmore doesn't know the entirety of these papers exists at the Library of Congress. As for Miss Ballinger, my guess is that she didn't share those papers with Miss Bracewell because she didn't want to disturb the workers' narrative.

The next day, I sent an email to Maureen Ballinger. As upset as I was, I tried to make it positive. In it was a timeline of all the wonderful things that have happened to celebrate my grandfather. The website, the one man show, the "Cake Boss" episode, the memorial fundraising, and the American organizations nationwide that had shown their support. I wanted her to know there was a growing movement that championed permanent recognition for Luigi as Chief Carver. For this reason alone, I reached out to Maureen to revisit the book Camille and I had written.

I offered to address all of her concerns and make all the changes needed. Here was her response:

> *Good afternoon, Mr. Del Bianco,*
>
> *Thank you for your email delineating the numerous ways you have shared your grandfather's story. You note that your grandfather should be recognized at Mount Rushmore and he is. There is a photograph of Luigi Del Bianco in the Lincoln Borglum Visitor Center, his name is listed on the worker's wall with all the other workers from carvers to*

pointers to powdermen and he is on the worker's site bulletin available for visitors as well as on our web site. We attempt to celebrate equally all those who worked on the mountain.

Thank you for your passionate connection with Mount Rushmore National Memorial.

Maureen McGee-Ballinger

Another polite and patronizing brush off. I'd finally had it. Maureen Ballinger, the storyteller who I thought would embrace this wonderful new story, was proving to be the most evasive and dismissive National Parks Service official to date. I shot out a response hours later:

Dear Maureen,

With all due respect, I found your response very confusing. You didn't address my proposal to modify the book I submitted. That was actually the main reason for my email. The timeline I gave you was merely to keep you up to date on the progress of the excitement being generated by Luigi's story. However, I feel I must address what you wrote because I think it is vitally important at this time that you clearly understand ***my intentions.***

I absolutely agree: There is a photo of my grandfather at the mountain with his name underneath. He is also on the two lists you mentioned. I have never disputed those facts. What I have questioned many times, what I have been very clear about to both you and Cheryl is the fact that Luigi Del Bianco is not acknowledged as the Chief Carver on Mount Rushmore.

After literally 25 years of trying to get Luigi recognition as Chief Carver, I am left with the following questions, which all beg to be answered:

1. *Why won't you acknowledge Luigi Del Bianco as Chief Carver? (I can't even convince you to add the title "Chief Carver" under his photograph.)*
2. *Why do you repeatedly refuse to recognize Luigi's distinct role in comparison to the other men's? (Did you know he trained and taught many of them? Do you realize when Luigi quit several*

times, all work on the heads had to stop? None of the workers affected the carving in this way. Not even close.)

3. *Have you read the Luigi Del Bianco website I have sent you many times? Here it is again: LuigiMountRushmore.com. Have you read the quotes from Gutzon Borglum about how important my grandfather was to the work? Have you read Borglum's testimony as to the harassment and sabotage thrust upon Luigi? If you have, why don't you see that it is only right that he be given special status that befits his contribution? Nothing more, nothing less.*
4. *Who made the policy to celebrate everyone equally on the mountain? Why do you need to do that? The fact is that the 400 men who worked on the mountain did not contribute equally. Luigi Del Bianco is a perfect case in point. Why won't you acknowledge that Luigi was different from the workers as an artist and an immigrant? Aren't you missing a wonderful opportunity to celebrate an immigrant who lived the American Dream on Mount Rushmore?*

I was truly excited and hopeful when I went to Mount Rushmore to perform my one-man show and tell my grandfather's story. I thought I had finally made a communications' breakthrough. Cheryl can tell you the response was extremely positive not just from the tourists but from the staff. Your Park Rangers embraced Luigi's story as something new and exciting. I thought, "Finally, the National Park Service is going to do the right thing and give Luigi the credit he deserves and tell his unique story."

What happened? Why the 180-degree turn? Unfortunately, I often feel there is and has been a deliberate attempt on the part of the National Parks Service to suppress my grandfather's story. Unless you can convince me otherwise, that is the way I still see it today.

I am a very patient man and a gentleman. However, it is time my questions were answered and I can only hope that you will get back to me as soon as possible.

Sincerely,

Lou Del Bianco

I had never been as strong with my language as I was in this email. I thought it was about time I made my feelings clear. What did I have to lose at this point? Like so many times before, Maureen never answered me.

Someone once quoted Albert Einstein's definition of insanity to me: Doing the same thing over and over again and expecting different results. That's the way I was beginning to feel. It was time to ratchet it up to the next level.

The only way to have any chance at a different result was by going over Rushmore's head. I contacted my State Senator George Latimer, an awesome guy and great public servant. He put me in touch with New York Congresswoman Nita Lowey's office. Miss Lowey in turn contacted Elaine Hackett, the Congressional Liaison to the National Park Service. I was eventually put in touch with Mike Reynolds, the director for the whole Midwest of the country. Mike had the power to override Rushmore policy.

I explained to Mike my 20-year dilemma. Knowing that I finally had an audience, I literally read the Library of Congress documents over the phone. At this point, I practically had them memorized. They had become part of me.

Not surprisingly, Mike was impressed. In fact, that's what I remember him saying.

"I'm impressed. It sounds like your grandfather was very important to Borglum."

I was thrilled to hear him say that it didn't make much sense to put my grandfather in the same category as the other workers, especially in light of the very dramatic letters I just read to him.

"Mount Rushmore is probably being a little provincial about this. Let me contact them and see if we can explore changing this oversight."

My heart beat faster. Mike seemed like a very genuine guy who sincerely wanted to help. This was the first time I had ever heard an NPS official even hint at the possibility of a change in their policy. There was no defense this time of the "team effort" that Rushmore kept hammering; no continuation of the narrative that has haunted my family for so long. Why didn't I think of this sooner? I couldn't help but feel optimistic.

One month later, I got this letter in the mail from Mike Reynolds's office.

United States Department of the Interior

National Park Service

Midwest Region
601 Riverfront Drive
Omaha, Nebraska 68102-4226

MAY 7 2013

10.D(MWR-PCL/PAL)

MAY 13 2013

The Honorable Nita M. Lowey
United States House of Representatives
White Plains District Office
222 Mamaroneck Avenue, Suite 312
White Plains, New York 10605

Dear Congresswoman Lowey:

Thank you for your April 10, 2013, letter to Ms. Elaine Hackett on behalf of your constituent Mr. Lou Del Bianco regarding his grandfather's contributions - the late Luigi Del Bianco - to the carving of Mount Rushmore National Memorial (Memorial). As the Midwest Regional Director for the National Park Service (NPS), the region which includes the Memorial, I have been asked to respond to your letter.

Various staff members of the NPS have been in communication with Mr. Del Bianco for several years concerning his grandfather's contributions. As we have discussed with Mr. Del Bianco, the NPS celebrates all who worked on the sculpture. Luigi Del Bianco's name is inscribed on the workers wall; his photograph is in the museum, and his work on the sculpture is referenced in books sold in the Mount Rushmore History Association Bookstore.

Luigi Del Bianco was one of a small set of gifted carvers assisting Gutzon Borglum with his vision, and Borglum's son, Lincoln, discusses these carvers in the book *Mount Rushmore: The Story Behind the Scenery*:

> "Among the few skilled carvers who worked on the project were three who had studied under my father in the East -- Luigi del Bianco, William S. Tallman, and Hugo Villa, and Joseph Bruner, an experienced stonecutter from Indiana."

Although Hugo Villa, William S. Tallman and Lincoln Borglum all supervised the project during periods when Gutzon Borglum was absent, and Lincoln Borglum became the Superintendent of the site and completed the carving after his father's death, none of these men or the other workers are called out for specialized recognition. The expertise of many contributed to the success of the sculpture. If not for the dynamite experts, the carvers would not have had good rock exposed with which to work. If not for the expert blacksmiths fabricating new tools, maintaining drill bits, and keeping equipment in working order, the drillers would not have been able to make the holes for the blasters. All of the workers were essential to achieving the ultimate goal. We do not have the space, budget or staff to develop special exhibits for each of these individuals. All of these men are celebrated in the same way on the worker's wall and in the museum. We recognize and interpret one Master Carver - the artist himself - Gutzon Borglum.

We appreciate Mr. Del Bianco's dedication to his grandfather and hope that he will recognize the value of his grandfather working as part of a team that created an unprecedented masterpiece.

Sincerely,

Patricia S. Trap
for Michael T. Reynolds
Regional Director

TAKE PRIDE IN AMERICA

Do you know the popular scene in the "Peanuts" comic strip, the one where Lucy promises she won't pull the football away when Charlie Brown runs to kick it? The one where she smiles and pulls it away every time and Charlie Brown always falls for it? Well, the NPS was looking like Lucy, the football was Luigi, and I'm Charlie Brown.

The whole letter sounded like Maureen Ballinger wrote it. In fact, one paragraph was almost identical in feeling to a previous email from Maureen.

> *"There is a photograph of Luigi Del Bianco in the Lincoln Borglum Visitor Center, his name is listed on the workers' wall with all the other workers from carvers to pointers to powdermen and he is on the workers' site bulletin available for visitors as well as on our website. We attempt to celebrate equally all those who worked on the mountain."*

I was dying to know the nature of Mike Reynold's conversation with the officials at Rushmore. Did he go to bat at all for Luigi? It didn't feel like it. He must have folded like a cheap suit. All the same catch phrases are used in this letter, especially my favorite, "team."

The only bone they threw my grandfather was placing him in the same class of workers that Lincoln Borglum, in a book he wrote, quoted as "trained men." With all due respect to Lincoln, if I had to choose between him and his father as to who would be a better judge of the workers' abilities, I would go with Gutzon Borglum every time. He put my grandfather head and shoulders above the other carvers. So did Lincoln, in an earlier transcript hidden deep in Rushmore's archives (page 26). It always surprised me that Lincoln never gave my grandfather the same praise in his book that he gave in that interview.

Once again, the people at Rushmore decided to cherry pick their own evidence in order to further their narrative. This pattern of denial was deliberate; I was sure of it now. Mike Reynolds seemed to give in without a fight. If he tried at all, I never knew it, because he never contacted me or returned my follow-up phone call.

I had to get away from all things Rushmore and clear my head for a while. I decided to concentrate on the more positive aspects of this experience, like the fundraising for the Luigi memorial. It was going well. I was getting money from so many caring individuals. Because I performed my one-man show for all the elementary school children in Port Chester, the entire fourth-grade at John F. Kennedy Magnet school offered to raise money on its own for the memorial. How cool is that?

Port Chester is a village of immigrants and has been for generations. At present, the majority of the immigrant population is Hispanic. I was so touched to see this new crop of immigrant children embrace a Port Chester immigrant from another time and place. I think his inspiration moved those children to want to help him. And they did. Those kids presented me with a giant envelope filled with dollar bills and loose change that totaled $250.00.

They gave me a big fake check that read, "Honoring the Great Luigi Del Bianco." Below is a photo of the event. I should have sent it to Maureen Ballinger.

Me with students from John F. Kennedy Magnet School in Port Chester, NY.

In late spring, I got a phone call from Doug Gladstone. He wanted to write a book about my grandfather. Doug was convinced a book could be a great tool to advocate for permanent recognition. He asked for my blessing to pitch a book idea to some publishing companies. I was happy and nervous at the same time. After 20-plus years, my family and I have had little or no success in getting Rushmore to change the historical record. Maybe Rushmore would respond better to someone like Doug rather than Luigi's grandson? I got the feeling Doug wanted to use the power of the pen to put pressure on the NPS to do the right thing. Doug had written some really nice articles about Luigi. I liked his writing style, as did Camille. But a book? That was a huge commitment. What if I didn't like it, or worse, disagreed with his approach? The truth was, Doug could write whatever he wanted, with or without my blessing. The only thing I cared about was getting my grandpa his rightful place in history. I not only gave Doug my blessing, but promised to share all the resources I had to help him in any way I could. Doug was thrilled. Even though he didn't have a publisher, Doug started writing the book.

In the summer of 2013 I decided to take a trip to Barre, VT in July to do some research on my grandfather. I figured since he lived there on and off for at least seven years, maybe I could find some documentation on him. I also thought it would be helpful for the book that Gladstone was writing.

I developed a relationship with Karen Lane, who worked for the Aldrich Public Library. She was a pleasure and really went out of her way to help me. Even with Karen's assistance, I didn't find much. These carvers, not surprisingly, were not written about. Photographed, yes, but usually in large groups. I couldn't find Luigi in any of those photos. Karen gave me copies of the Barre City Directory. I found out he lived in a house owned by the Ellis family on 565 North Main Street. The house no longer exists.

THE LATEST IN NECKWEAR AT HOMER FITTS CO.

78 BARRE CITY DIRECTORY.

Day Harry, emp Smith, Whitcomb & Cook Co., h 100 Seminary
Day James, emp Smith Bros., bds D street cor Batchelder
Day Stella, widow of A. C., h 10 Prospect
Day W. P., draughtsman, bds 84 Merchant
Deaconess Home, Miss Marion Wilson Supt., 83 Berlin
DE BLOIS LOUIS, granite dealer, Goldsbury Meadow, W. Second, h 4 Laurell
DeBrune Jesse C., supt. streets, h 41 Park
DeColaines Don, lineman, h 31 Highland av
Decoteau Henry, emp Canton Bros., h 10 Hillside av
Deeb Monsor, confectionery and fruit, 102 Seminary, h do
DeForge Frank, lumper, h 5 River
DeForge Frank, jr., emp Carroll & McNulty, res 5 River
Degnan James, quarryman, bds Graniteville
Degnan Mark, quarryman, h Graniteville
Delbianco Luigi, stone cutter, bds 565 N. Main

From the Barre City Directory, the last line identifies my grandfather as a stonecutter living at 565 N. Main.

I also discovered he worked for Guidice Brothers and the World Granite Company. Other than that, I found nothing else of any significance. I didn't care. It was great to walk down the same streets as he did and imagine a very young Luigi getting provolone from the local merchant, eyeing the pretty ladies and walking off to work at the quarry with a chisel or two in his hand. I was connecting with my grandfather in ways I never would have imagined. Sense memory again? Not exactly. But I felt bonded to my grandpa in a transcendent way. No task, no amount of sweat equity in search of him was a waste of time. Like my Uncle Caesar, it was something I was meant to do, going back to my grandpa holding me by the shoulders and reminding me that we shared the same name.

Back in Port Chester, I shared the Barre information with Doug. Doug, in turn, shared his writing with me. He had been doing that for a while. It was looking like a fascinating treatise, mixing my grandfather's story with immigrant history, interviews and the hypothesis that Luigi Del Bianco was not being honored on Mount Rushmore because he was Italian. That suspicion of bigotry was the hook of Doug's book.

While I was hopeful this kind of journalism would be effective in shaking things up, I was confused as to why Doug was only using one or two of the incredible documents I had shared with him. Doug's reasoning was that as a journalist, he did not want to come across to the reader as too much in Luigi's favor. He wanted to be as balanced and objective as possible, but don't journalists usually rely on primary sources to make their point? Doug stuck to his guns. I tried to understand his point of view. After all, this was his book, not mine. I would continue to trust his judgment.

In October, I got a phone call from Vinny Sapione, the brother of Jimmy Sapione, my Uncle Caesar's dear friend. "I hear you've been doing a lot of work about your grandfather. I have some of his tools. I think your family should have them back."

Apparently, when my grandfather died, my father and uncles had an estate sale. Caesar approached Vinny, a boilermaker, and offered to give him my grandfather's pneumatic tools. "I don't know what to do with them, Vinny. Do you want them?" Vinny took the drills and chisels and has had them for 44 years. It always bothered me that the family never saved any of my grandpa's tools. Now, I could finally hold them in my hands. I'll always be grateful to Vinny. He gave my family such a great gift.

The first thing I asked myself was, *Did Luigi use these tools to carve Lincoln's eyes on Rushmore?* I immediately contacted Chicago Pneumatic, the manufacturer, and was put in touch with their historian. I was told it was very possible because Chicago Pneumatic supplied Rushmore with most of its pneumatic tools. Still, he didn't have the original receipts to match up the serial numbers. There would never be any way of knowing for sure.

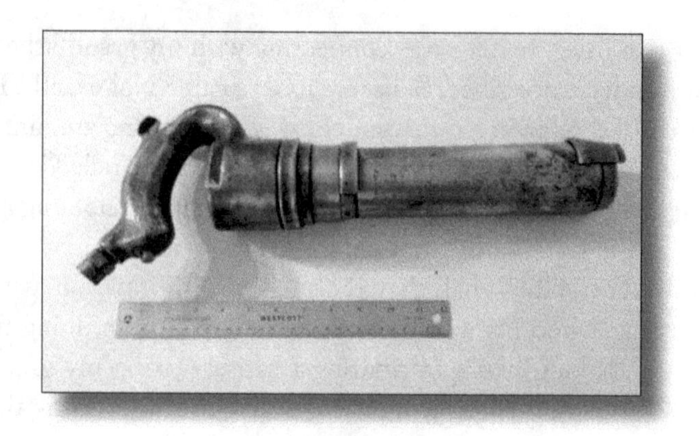

One of Luigi's pneumatic drills.

Luigi's chisels.

The top of Luigi's tool box. I'll treasure it forever.

CHAPTER FORTY-SEVEN:

PUBLISHING, ARGUING, AND UNVEILING

AT 7 AM, STILL half asleep and eating my cereal, I heard the phone ring. It was Doug Gladstone. "I am pleased to announce that *Carving a Niche for Himself* will be published by Bordigherra Press."

Woah…what? I was still groggy but I managed to thank Doug for his efforts in finally landing a publishing deal.

"You know, you could sound a little more excited."

"Sorry, Doug, I just woke up."

Doug must be a morning person. He was pretty fired up. Thinking back, I don't think it had really sunk in: A book was being published about my grandpa.

Bordigherra Press, which operates out of the John J. Calandra Institute in New York City, had decided to take a chance on an unknown stone carver. Doug's book, *Carving a Niche for Himself* is a fascinating read that combines biography, history and investigative journalism. Not only does Doug tell the story of Luigi Del Bianco, but he sheds new light on the history of immigration and bigotry in America with anecdotal evidence, interviews and loads of hard data on the subject. Doug makes a very interesting claim that Luigi's omission from history is based on racism. It would be up to the reader to decide if he proved his case.

For me, I was just so excited to know that I could walk into a book store and see my grandpa's name on the cover of a book. A book that could change the game, because this time Luigi had an advocate that was not a family member. Maybe that would make all the difference? I got on the phone and immediately started calling bookstores. I wanted this book to be the tipping point for Luigi. In the meantime, I would have to juggle this great development with the local projects I had started.

The unveiling for the Luigi memorial in Port Chester was postponed until the spring of 2014. While the plaque was being completed at the foundry, the village asked me to meet with other Port Chester commissions to keep them abreast of what I was doing in town. I sat down one evening with Emily Imbesi, Kathy Rosenfeld and Taryn Grimes-Herbert, all members of the Port Chester Beautification Commission. After a very positive meeting, Taryn asked, "What kind of media coverage are you doing? I ask only because my husband is a producer for the 'CBS Evening News.'"

I have been knocking myself out for years trying to promote this story, and it turns out we have a CBS News producer who lives four blocks away from me. This is just plain good luck! Taryn admitted that she didn't always like to share this info for the obvious reasons. A talented producer and writer herself, Taryn was taken with my grandfather's story as well as my dilemma with the NPS. She wanted to know what she could do to help. Both she and her husband Sean would become two of the most generous and selfless champions for Luigi. I could now move toward the June unveiling knowing that the Herberts would help provide the kind of media attention that could spread this story to the masses.

In April, I got a phone call out of nowhere from Maureen Ballinger. This was the first time she had initiated any kind of contact with me. Maureen was planning an oral history project that would give the descendants of the "workers" on Rushmore an opportunity to record memories, anecdotes and their feelings about the project. The recordings would eventually be accessible on the Mount Rushmore website. I told her I would like to be involved and suggested she email my Aunt Gloria as well. Call me a glutton for punishment, but I took this communication from Maureen as an opportunity to once again broach the subject of simply acknowledging my grandfather as Chief Carver under his photo in the workers' museum. I told her I would go to Staples and make a placard myself. All she would have to do is tack it under the photo. That's when Maureen said in the most patronizing tone, "Your grandfather was not the Chief Carver."

I am sure my face turned ghost white. After years of evading this issue, Miss Ballinger had outdone herself. Countless documents from the Library of Congress identified Luigi Del Bianco as Chief Carver on Mount Rushmore, but she was actually telling me he wasn't. This was truly a surreal moment. I was starting to feel like I was in the middle of some strange government conspiracy against me. I answered back like Maureen was the child and I was the parent, "Oh, Maureen, Maureen, you are so wrong. You have to know what you're saying is just not true."

Her voice did not waver. "Gutzon Borglum was the Chief Carver."

I continued my calm, parental tone. Otherwise I would have lost it.

"Maureen, you know Borglum was the designer. My grandfather, on paper, was the Chief Carver. That is a fact."

We went back and forth a few times. I ended by saying, "I'm sorry. I'm trying to deal with what you are saying here. This is the most bizarre conversation I have had about this. I don't know what else to say to you except go to the website again and read the Borglum papers. Please."

We managed to end the call on an amicable note, probably because I was in a state of shock. She told me a colleague of hers would follow up with me about setting a time to do the oral history recording. A week or so later, I sent an email to Maureen.

Good Morning, Maureen,

I am following up on our conversation a while back regarding oral history recordings. I have not heard from your colleague about that. Can you please let me know the status?

Also, you told me you would look into the possibility of giving Luigi Del Bianco a simple banner under his photo in the workers museum identifying him as the Chief Carver. Can you also let me know the status of that as well?

Lastly, we had a disagreement about Luigi's title on the mountain. You stated that he was not the Chief Carver, but that Gutzon Borglum was. I hope you were able to finally go through the Library of Congress documents on my website. I'm sure you saw that Luigi was the only one on the work that had the title of Chief Carver. Please correct me on this if I am misinformed. It goes without saying that Borglum was the genius and the designer behind the work. If you need more clarification from me on this, please consult the "Borglum/Bianco" link on my website or feel free to contact me.

Best,

Lou Del Bianco

I was convinced that no matter how maddening or exasperating this whole situation was, I would always take the high road and remain a gentleman. For the first time, Maureen responded right away. (In Mount Rushmore time, I consider six days later, "right away.")

> *Good Afternoon,*
>
> *I have been waiting for information from staff on the potential dates for an oral history recording. Now that we have some of our summer volunteers returning we have sufficient staff to work on the oral history recording. Are you available either Friday, May 2 or Thursday, May 8 after 11:30 AM your time to do the recording via telephone?*
>
> *We discussed that I would check the museum to make sure that your grandfather Luigi Del Bianco has his name under his photograph. Yes, Luigi Del Bianco is identified in the photograph.*
>
> *When I stated that Gutzon Borglum was the Chief Carver, I was not stating that was his formal title. Gutzon Borglum was the artisan behind the sculpture and as far as we know was not referred to by a formal position title.*
>
> *I look forward to hearing from you to finalize the time and date on your oral history recording.*
>
> *Maureen McGee-Ballinger*
>
> *Chief of Interpretation and Education*
>
> *Mount Rushmore National Memorial*

We discussed that I would check the museum to make sure that your Grandfather Luigi Del Bianco has his name under his photograph. Yes, Luigi Del Bianco is identified in the photograph. Unbelievable.

I never wondered if my grandfather's name was under that photograph. I *never* asked her that. I could wallpaper my living room with all the emails I have sent to Maureen over the years begging her to add "Chief Carver" under his name. How could she hear my crystal-clear plea over and over again and then *completely* ignore it? Of course, I knew why.

When I stated that Gutzon Borglum was the Chief Carver, I was not stating that was his formal title. Gutzon Borglum was the artisan behind the sculpture and as far as we know was not referred to by a formal position title.

This, my friends, is called back peddling.

For the record (again) I sent one more response, clarifying what had already been clarified:

Hello Maureen,

Thank you for the quick response. I was hoping you would be able to speak to me and my aunt as well. She is the only surviving child of Luigi. I am available on May 2 at 11:30 AM my time. I am giving you my Aunt Gloria's email so you can coordinate with her as well. Thank you so much.

I know that my grandfather's name is under the photograph in the workers museum. My simple request is that under the photograph would appear not only his name, but his title of "Chief Carver."

Let me be clear so there is no misunderstanding. This is what I would like it to say under the photo:

Luigi Del Bianco
Chief Carver
1933-1940

"He is worth more than any 3 men in America
for this particular type of work." - Gutzon Borglum

Let me know how we both can proceed to make this happen.

Again, thank you for the opportunity to be part of your oral history program.

Best,

Lou Del Bianco

She never responded.

The oral history went well. Maureen asked the questions, and I answered. I read every document written by Borglum that I felt was relevant. I felt like Rushmore was throwing me another bone to further appease me. Who knew how much play these recording would get and whether they would be made available anytime soon. In spite of how I felt, I read those documents like my life depended on it. I made sure I read

"Chief Carver" loud and clear every time it appeared, which was often. While I was reading, I couldn't help but wonder what in God's name was going through Maureen's mind? She had to be hearing all of this incredible proof. Did she just compartmentalize what she heard and turn it into what she wanted to hear? I'm not a therapist. I won't go there.

At the end of the oral history recording, Maureen politely thanked me for participating. I asked her if she had gone to my website and read the documents once and for all. She very politely told me there wasn't any time to discuss that. I couldn't help but laugh and say, "Okay!"

My Aunt Gloria had an even more disconcerting experience at the end of her oral history interview:

> *"I waited until the interview was over before I asked Maureen, 'Aren't you ever going to acknowledge my father as Chief Carver?' She replied, 'There is a photo of your father in the workers' museum. He is listed in a daily record. Several books in our store mention him.' I told her I knew all that and reminded her that nowhere is he recognized as Chief Carver. There was dead silence. Then Maureen said, 'That will never happen.'*

Today, in 2017, I occasionally go to the Mount Rushmore website to see if the oral history recordings have been posted. As someone who worked in the recording business, I know how easy it is to upload recordings to a website. If the recordings are there, I can't find them.

The day of the Port Chester memorial unveiling, June 21, 2014, turned out to be very much like putting on a show; the plaque and stone provided the set, the speakers were the actors and the audience stood in the street, which was blocked off by the police. When I was scouting locations, my sister Andrea suggested the traffic island right up the street from the house where we grew up. I was focused on putting it in our biggest local park. When that fell through, I revisited her idea and realized it would be the perfect location. The street got a lot of foot traffic from hundreds of local high school kids coming home every day. They would walk right by the memorial. Generations of school kids would come to know about my grandpa.

It was a great day for Port Chester. So many people contributed money to make the memorial a reality. Others donated by providing materials and labor. Lou Larizza and Nick Gonzalas provided the base. John Zicca planted the beautiful landscaping. Ron and Mike Luiso provided the bluestone, and Jerry La Bella made sure the memorial was lit at night.

Below is the program for the ceremony.

SPONSORED BY THE PORT CHESTER COUNCIL FOR THE ARTS

LUIGI DEL BIANCO MEMORIAL DEDICATION
SATURDAY JUNE 21, 2014
1:30PM

Welcome:
Denise Colangelo, Port Chester Council for the Arts
Michael Keropian, Sculptor of Memorial Plaque
Anthony Tamburri, Dean of the John D. Calandra Italian American Institute
Andre' DiMino, Executive Director of UNICO National
Gloria Del Bianco, Daughter of Luigi Del Bianco
Port Chester Mayor Neil J. Pagano
Rye Town Supervisor Joseph Carvin
New York State Senator George Latimer
Lou Del Bianco, Grandson of Luigi Del Bianco
Memorial Unveiling

Special Thanks:
The Port Chester Council for the Arts, Port Chester Mayor Neil J. Pagano
Port Chester Board of Trustees: Gregory K. Adams, Gene Ceccarelli, Daniel Brakewood, Joseph D. Kenner, Luis A. Marino, Saverio L. Terenzi
Port Chester Village Attorney Anthony M. Cereto, Port Chester Village Manager Christopher Steers
Port Chester DPW: Rocco Morabito, Chris Summa
Port Chester Beautification Commission
Port Chester Parks Commission
Andrea Daur, Maria Del Bianco, Amy Del Bianco, Reception
Camille Linen
Lou Larizza and Nick Gonzalas, Lazz Development
Ronnie Loizzo of Byram Mason, Building, Stone and Landscape Supply
John Zicca Landscaping, Inc.
Jerry LaBella, LaBella Electric
Nicholas Melendez, Wells Fargo

MANY THANKS TO ALL THE GENEROUS CONTRIBUTORS
WHO MADE THIS MEMORIAL POSSIBLE.
For a detailed list of contributors, go to WWW.LUIGIMOUNTRUSHMORE.COM

My Aunt Gloria was the featured speaker. She came all the way from California to be there. After sharing a touching anecdote about Luigi's battle with silicosis, her voice broke with emotion as she spoke about her father.

"He was a man who lived with his own set of rules, no matter the danger. This is the same man who took his life in his hands to carve Mount Rushmore, to carve the refinement of the figures right alongside his master, Gutzon Borglum, as Chief Carver, and all the other brave men who helped create the national monument for the United States of America. He was an immigrant who fulfilled his dream."

I was the last to speak, and I shared the realization I'd had several years back.

"I've been telling stories for 27 years. This is the story I was meant to tell."

I asked my Aunt Gloria and the rest of my family to take hold of the rope for the unveiling. The crowd gasped when Michael Keropian's beautiful bas-relief plaque was revealed.

Photo by Dawn Talia.

As everyone gazed at the plaque, Aaron Copland's "Fanfare for the Common Man" played. The words of all the wonderful speakers still rang in everyone's ears. One underlying theme echoed throughout the afternoon: that we live in a great country and all of its citizens, no matter what their backgrounds, have a right to be recognized for their achievements and contributions. Luigi was slowly becoming a symbol for the immigrant and the American Dream.

A proud Del Bianco family. Photo by Dawn Talia.

Soon after, "CBS Evening News" contacted me. Reporters there wanted to do a story about Luigi and my family's quest to get him recognition. The segment would be produced by CBS News Producer T. Sean Herbert. Ann Marie Green, a CBS News correspondent, was deeply touched by what she saw and heard.

Millions of people nationwide saw the story. I received many emails and phone calls from people who encouraged me to *Keep going! Don't give up!* Thousands of Italians and non-Italians signed a petition I created calling for the Department of the Interior to change its 73-year-old stance on Luigi Del Bianco. Doug Gladstone continued his vigorous letter writing campaign to shake things up. In addition, he aggressively pursued politicians to enlist their support. Finally, Doug started communicating with Maureen Ballinger about getting Mount Rushmore to carry his book.

Because of the great response to the CBS News story, Taryn and Sean Herbert sat me down and told me they wanted to produce a documentary about Luigi and my family's fight. They didn't care about profiting from it in any way; they just wanted to help. These are the kind of people who have kept me going all these years. Just when I felt like giving up, someone would come along and say, *I want to help.* It would always buoy my spirits. Taryn and Sean would not only provide high level expertise in TV and the media, but as friends they were an emotional support.

An interview with Anne Marie Green with CBS News camera operator Michele Worst in my living room.

After I got done hugging and kissing them both, we all got to work. After all, we needed to raise money for this. An Indigogo account was set up. I got on the phone and started calling every organization I had been in touch with in the past 10 years to solicit donations. Even though we hadn't raised any money yet, we started shooting some scenes. Matt Wachsman, a talented cameraman, generously offered his skill and equipment pro-bono. Matt loved the Herberts and was also inspired by this story.

By 2016, a stunning mini-documentary would be completed and seen by so many. "Through Lincoln's Eyes" is a heartwarming testimony to a grandson's love, a grandfather's legacy, and a family's perseverance in advocating for their immigrant father and grandfather. In this time of the tweet, Facebook page and smart phone, the Herberts succeeded in communicating an important message: We become better, fuller, richer people when we connect with the stories of our ancestors. I will always be grateful to Taryn, Sean and Matt for giving so much of their time, talent and friendship.

Taryn Grimes-Herbert, Sean Herbert, myself, and Matt Wachsman.

Italy has also discovered Luigi. A popular Italian program, "Voyager," filmed an entire episode about my grandpa that eventually aired in 2016. The Luigi movement was now spreading outside America back to my grandfather's homeland. Five million proud Italians were able to learn his story.

Lou with the Italian production crew from "Voyager."

Back to 2014. In the fall, Karen Lane and Patty Meriam with the Vermont History Museum collaborated to bring me out to Barre to perform my Luigi show at the Barre Opera House, managed by Dan Casey. The idea was to do "Luigi," but also add a component of Barre Granite history to the show for the schoolchildren during the day and then families at night.

In November, I made a special trip to Barre to do the Luigi show at Aldrich Library. Doug Gladstone would also be there to talk about his book. After my show, Doug got up to speak. Before he addressed the crowd, Doug made a clear comparison between the two of us.

"Lou is a really nice guy. He gives everyone the warm fuzzies. I'm not so nice."

It felt like a good cop/bad cop scenario. Doug was right, in a way. I was a nice guy and while hard working and determined, always tried to be a gentleman in my approach. Doug approached getting Luigi recognition with the hard-edge of a journalist who will stop at nothing to get to the truth. I was impressed with Doug's dogged persistence and hoped his approach would be a game changer.

The shows at Barre Opera House were a success. I met some really great people who loved learning about Luigi and his time in the adopted city of his youth. It was a great way to end 2014.

CHAPTER FORTY-EIGHT:

THE FINISH LINE

MOUNT RUSHMORE CHIEF OF Interpretation Maureen Ballinger kicked off my 2015 by drawing a line in the sand. In a commentary by Doug Gladstone in Vtdigger.org on January 23, 2015, Miss Ballinger was quoted as saying, "I have seen the letter in which Borglum refers to Del Bianco as Chief Carver, but I consider Gutzon Borglum the Chief Carver."

After three-and-a-half years of dodging and evading, Maureen Ballinger *finally* admits she read a document where Gutzon Borglum himself names Luigi Del Bianco the Chief Carver. So, what does she do? She interprets Borglum to be the actual Chief Carver. Her completely lopsided and unbelievable stand on this issue is *now* public. I felt like we were losing more and more ground. I was feeling depressed and angry. My instinct was to email Maureen. I convinced myself not to and concentrated on more productive things.

In the spring, Doug Gladstone emailed me that he had connected with the new Midwest Director of the National Parks, Cam Sholly. Apparently, Mike Reynolds left the position. I wasn't aware of this because I had turned the reins over to Doug a while ago hoping he might have more success with the NPS than I had. Doug scheduled a phone conversation with Cam Sholly. The Herberts, who were working on the documentary, offered to go to Albany where Doug worked and film the conversation.

According to Doug, the conversation went well. After Cam shared Mount Rushmore's tired dogma with Doug, he made his case for Luigi and told Sholly what the Del Bianco family's wishes were: permanent recognition as Chief Carver for Luigi Del Bianco. Doug was happy to tell me that Cam seemed sympathetic to the cause and open to possibly changing the historical record. I was happy to hear that, too, but I remembered that Mike Reynolds had given me the exact same hopeful rhetoric.

All in all, I was content with this development, with one big exception. Cam did not know about my website and those amazing historic documents. You can be sure the people at Mount Rushmore didn't tell him about them. With all due respect to Doug, he made a strong choice not to include them in any of his arguments, with the exception of one letter naming Luigi Chief Carver. Knowing in my heart that Mount Rushmore rejected these papers all these years because of the power they possessed, I could not let this opportunity pass. Cam had a right to know about these documents so he could make the best-informed decision.

The Herberts filmed me one Friday afternoon in my office. The cameras were on me as I dialed Cam Sholly's office number. We were gambling that he would be available to talk and as fate would have it, he was. I introduced myself and felt my heart beating against my chest. For some reason, I was more nervous than usual. All of a sudden, the stakes felt extremely high.

The conversation started with Cam reiterating everything that the Rushmore people had told him: There was a photo of Luigi in the workers' museum, everyone contributed equally... I thought to myself, *Oh, God, here we go again.* I had to change the subject and fast.

"I was happy to hear that you had a conversation with the author, Doug Gladstone. I wanted to talk to you as well, because I have some vital information you should know about."

I sat there and read each relevant document like it was the Gettysburg Address. I didn't stop until I went through every one, word for word. Cam didn't make a sound. I could tell he was listening intently. When I was done, he said, "Wow. Those are really impressive."

I said, "Thank you. I helped my Uncle Caesar research them from the Library of Congress. These papers have been on my grandfather's website for years, and they've also been shared with a slew of officials at Mount Rushmore since the early 90's."

"Really?" Cam, incredulous, blurted out. "And you say you have a website about your grandfather?" He didn't know about my website; thank God I called him.

He ended the call by saying, "You've got some compelling stuff here. Let me talk to the people at Mount Rushmore, and I'll get back to you."

Just like Mike Reynolds, Cam Sholly was a gentleman. Just like Mike Reynolds, he was impressed and would talk to Rushmore officials. Just like Mike Reynolds, he seemed optimistic. For me, optimism was not exactly coursing through my veins. If anything, I felt like the protagonist in some Hollywood thriller. *Don't talk to Rushmore!* I panicked. *They'll get to you like they've gotten to everyone else!*

I calmed myself down. What will be will be.

Knowing Cam would not get back to me for at least another week, I tried to concentrate on fundraising for the documentary and my very full-time career as an actor-singer-storyteller. No matter what I was doing, whether it was working at my computer or performing in front of an audience of 300 school kids, Cam Sholly and his ultimate decision hung over my head like the sword of Damocles, wondering if this journey would ever end with my head intact.

One week later, the phone awakened me from a late afternoon nap.

It was Cam Sholly. He sounded upbeat. "I have a proposition for you. Based on all the documentation you read to me, I would like to send two of my top historians to your house to go through every document you have on your grandfather. What do you think?"

You'd think I would have cheered or shouted with joy.

"What do you mean, two historians? What does that mean?"

Cam was taken aback. I don't blame him. He very patiently explained the proposition again. I suddenly became aware of my strange reaction. I apologized and blamed it on the nap. I was a little groggy from sleep, which was partially true.

"Not a problem," Cam assured me. "You know, up until our conversation last week, I honestly did not know what to do with this story. After hearing those documents, now I do. I will really be looking to the historians for their help and expertise with this."

The conversation ended on a very positive note. He told me he wanted to arrange a meeting with me and the historians in the next few weeks, hopefully sometime in October. I told him I looked forward to it and thanked him. I could hear the words coming out of my mouth, but wasn't sure how I was able to make them. I must have still been in shock.

When I got off the phone, I felt horrible about the way I had reacted. I then realized why I had acted that way. I got my bearings and immediately shot off an email to Cam.

Dear Cam,

I want to thank you again from the bottom of my heart for reaching out to me with your offer to bring two reputable historians to review my documentation from the Library of Congress. I'm sorry if I might have come across as slightly suspicious at the beginning of the call. I blamed it on a nap. Looking back, I think I was just stunned and didn't know how to react. Please understand I have spent the past 25 years going back and forth with a minimum of 15 different NPS officials with no result in the end. Even though I have persevered, I think I've been programmed to always expect another brick wall. You changed all that, and boy did it throw me! Now that the dust has settled I am so excited at this new prospect and very grateful to you for doing what so many others (with all due respect) were unwilling to do. I just felt I owed you an explanation.

I look forward to hearing from you soon about the details of the meeting.

Best,

Lou Del Bianco

It felt so good to do that. I promised myself I wouldn't grouse about the fact that Cam's proposal should have been made 25 years ago by one of his predecessors. The fact is, he stepped up to the plate and had the guts to do what so many before him were unwilling to do: disturb the Rushmore workers' narrative. Cam Sholly was now officially Luigi's hero.

Cam Sholly, the guy who changed the game.

I began putting together a presentation book filled with all the documents arranged chronologically in a way that would tell the story of Luigi's time at Rushmore. The beginning of the book had bullet points listing what these primary source documents prove, once and for all.

LUIGI DEL BIANCO DOCUMENTATION

THE BORGLUM PAPERS

MANUSCRIPT DIVISION

LIBRARY OF CONGRESS, WASHINGTON, DC.

THE ENCLOSED DOCUMENTS WILL SHOW THE FOLLOWING:

- Luigi Del Bianco, an Italian immigrant and classically trained stone carver, was the Chief Carver on Mount Rushmore between the years 1933 to1940.
- Luigi Del Bianco's talents and abilities were vital to the work.

- Luigi Del Bianco was Gutzon Borglum's right-hand man and the only artist charged with carving the "refinement of expression" on the four faces.
- Luigi Del Bianco not only performed the duties of Chief Carver, but also instructed and mentored many of the untrained and trained men on the work.
- Luigi Del Bianco, in spite of the harassment directed at him by the offices at Rapid City, persevered with strength, dignity and artistic acumen unparalleled on Mount Rushmore.
- Luigi Del Bianco was much more than one of the 400 "workers" on the mountain and deserves special recognition for his great contribution.

Two weeks went by without a word. I had to keep reminding myself that Cam was the director for all the National Parks for the entire Midwest. I mean, the guy had other things on his mind, not just Luigi. I emailed him anyway. He responded that afternoon.

Dear Lou,

As you and I discussed on the phone last month, we have assembled a great team to evaluate available historical information relating to your grandfather, and his role at Mt. Rushmore NM [National Monument].

Bob Sutton is the National Park Service Historian, located in our headquarters in Washington, DC. Bob has worked in a variety of capacities during his career, including as Superintendent of Manassas National Battlefield Site in Virginia. Tim Good, is currently the Superintendent of Ulysses S. Grant National Historic Site and has an extensive background in history and education. Both are cc'd on this email.

I chose them both because of their extensive and diverse backgrounds, and I trust them to look objectively at the totality of information; both as presented by you, by the park, and others if necessary. They will reach out to you directly to work on scheduling a visit. As we discussed, their scope will include:

- *An evaluation of all available information relating to Luigi Del Bianco and his role at Mt. Rushmore NM; including review of documentation provided by the family, park, and others;*
- *Interviews with Lou Del Bianco and any other persons identified as having pertinent information relating to this topic;*
- *An assessment of current recognition of Luigi Del Bianco at Mt. Rushmore;*
- *Based on evaluation of all available information, develop recommendation(s) for me regarding whether Luigi Del Bianco should be recognized at levels beyond current;*
- *Secondarily, they may evaluate book authored by Doug Gladstone on Luigi Del Bianco.*

Both Bob and Tim will be a pleasure to work with. Thanks Lou, and Bob or Tim may ask you for a phone number to connect with for scheduling purposes.

Cam

This was getting better and better. I looked up Bob Sutton and Tim Good on the Internet, and they were everything Cam said they were: historians of the highest caliber. In spite of this promising development, I couldn't keep those neurotic thoughts out of my head; all of those "what ifs." What if Mount Rushmore starts talking to the historians and sways them to their way of thinking? What if some surprise character appears out of nowhere and sabotages the meeting Cam was organizing? Camille kept assuring me that unlike all the other times, this was a *real* breakthrough. She encouraged me to stay positive. I did my best and had some good moments of optimism. Still, after 25 years of being let down again and again, in the back of my mind recurred one thought: *This is too good to be true.*

Soon after, I received a very cordial email from Tim Good.

Dear Lou,

Bob and I are both honored to have the opportunity to work with you on this project. There are three dates that work well for Bob and I: Tuesday, October 20th; Wednesday, October 21st; and Thursday, October 22nd.

Would any one of those days work well for your schedule?

Also, we are prepared to meet you in New York. What place/address would work best for you?

Thank you.

Tim

Okay, I'm really hearing from one of the historians. This is actually going to happen!

No anxiety with this email. That's a switch.

The day of the meeting, I made our dining room into the meeting area and placed the presentation booklets I created for the meeting on the table. I crossed my fingers looking at them, hoping to God they would be the game changer I always hoped they would be.

Our meeting was scheduled for 10 AM, and I was ready by 9:30 AM. The worst thing I could do was give myself extra time to just wait. Bad idea. I thought, *I'll move my car out of my driveway so one of the historians can park there.* I got in my van and noticed the floors were a little messy. I panicked. Oh, no! What if I have to take the historians in my van, and they see the dirty floor and car mats? The dashboard is dusty! I immediately drove into town. Twenty minutes before my meeting with two National Park Historians, I was on my knees at the local carwash vacuuming the floors of my minivan. Let's just say this was my way of getting nervous energy out of my system.

Camille came home from teaching, and the historians arrived. I wanted her there for this. Both men immediately put me at ease. They were warm, personable and looking forward to our meeting. When I sat them down and showed them the booklets, I could tell they were impressed with how comprehensive they were. All the research was laid out before them. They simply had to listen to me and read along.

I started from the beginning, in 1933, when Luigi was first hired by Borglum and read the documents in chronological order. Because the documents, mostly in Borglum's own words, were so detailed and well written, they actually told a story that the two gentlemen listened to intently. As I read from Borglum letter to official record to telegram to memorandum, my voice started to crack with emotion. I was not ready for that. I got to Borglum's letter, where he defends "Bianco" to the "Office at Rapid City." I started to read the line, which was Uncle Caesar's favorite— "He is worth any three men in America for this particular kind of work...."—when a flash of memory hit me.

I suddenly recalled those days at Grant Street in my grandfather's tiny bedroom. As I started to read the words in that quote, my 52-year-old self became 5 years old again. I could see him sitting on the edge of his bed, calling out to me. *Come, give your grandpa a hug.* I could feel him looming over me, holding me by the shoulders...

He is worth any three men in America...

I am Luigi, you are Luigi.

My words became infused with the tight, straining sounds we make when we are choking back, trying not to cry. My throat ached as I struggled to read the excerpt without breaking down. Half embarrassed, half relieved, I could feel the historians near me, silent and respectful of this 25-year, full-circle catharsis playing out before them.

The flood of tears passed. I thought, *I've got this.* I read the rest of the book with more conviction than ever. Occasionally, Bob or Tim would inject a question or comment, but for the most part they were like the school children I held in rapt attention during one of my assembly programs. After I was done, I felt so relieved. What a weight lifted. Tim was the first to speak.

"So, you have been sharing these documents with Mount Rushmore for how many years?"

"Twenty-five," I answered.

After I said the number I realized that meant a quarter of a century. I had never looked at it that way until now.

Tim leaned toward me.

"Lou, this must have been a very frustrating 25 years for you and your family. I commend you for always being a gentleman with Mount Rushmore no matter how exasperated you must have been. Other people would have lashed out and undermined their mission. You didn't."

Wow, I thought. Being a nice guy has paid off.

Bob and Tim both applauded me for the incredible papers that my uncle found all those years ago. I said that I was convinced he knew about this day and somewhere, he was wrinkling his twisted nose and smiling.

Tim chimed in. "Lou, this is the ideal situation for us as historians, not to have to deal with hearsay or even circumstantial evidence, but primary source documents. Bob held up the booklet.

National Park Historians Bob Sutton and Tim Good.

"That's what you've presented to us today, and I can tell you right now we plan to recommend further recognition for your grandfather. I think a plaque at Mount Rushmore would be appropriate."

Camille squeezed my hand. This was *not* too good to be true. It was good, it was true and it was happening. I blurted out, "Really?! I had no idea you would be deciding today!"

"The evidence was too compelling. You made this very easy for us."

Then Bob smiled and said, "I'm satisfied. How about lunch?"

After a great meal at Camille's and my favorite Italian restaurant, we all sat and chatted a bit.

Tim turned to me and said, "Before we leave, I need to tell you that you have an incredible story here. Nothing has been written about your grandfather using these historic documents."

I told Tim that my Uncle Caesar wanted to write the story years ago, but was too overwhelmed with the task.

"It will take a lot of work, but I know you can do it. After all, you are a storyteller. Make sure you use the documents to tell his story and chronicle your family's journey in getting him recognized."

I was inspired. I thanked Tim for his support. There was one thing still left on my mind.

"Tim and Bob," I began. "I know you will make a recommendation to Cam for permanent recognition. I guess it's all in his hands now."

Tim said, "Well, you have to know, for the Midwest director of the National Parks to fly us here on his dime, he must be very serious."

Bob added, "We know Cam is looking to us to guide him in making a decision."

That's all I needed to hear.

The day ended with a special trip in my freshly vacuumed van to the Luigi Del Bianco memorial. I wanted them to see it because I told them this would be a great model to use for the plaque at Rushmore. The mold was already cast; only some of the text would need to be changed. They loved the idea. They also loved the plaque when they saw it.

This all happened on October 21, 2015. Weeks went by without a word from Cam. I lived my life, trying to stay positive. I was at the end of a long odyssey. I had done this standing on the shoulders of so many who came before me. I could feel them all lifting me up: Silvio, patiently caressing my tender ego; my grandmother, sensitive to my every move; my father challenging me; Caesar passing the baton while still holding onto it. Finally, my grandpa, who didn't need to push the grandson who bore his name. All the struggle, all the heartache, all the years fighting, hoping and praying led to this one final moment…

Hi Lou,

I hope you're doing well. We have made a decision to further recognize your grandfather's contributions at Mount Rushmore based on Tim and Bob's meeting with you and their discussion with the park. I think I mentioned to you that even if we decide to increase the recognition, it would be a while, and another process, to determine what that might be.

We will definitely be in touch with you as we move along and develop some potential options.

Thanks, and we hope you have great holidays.

Cameron Sholly

EPILOGUE

"I am Luigi, you are Luigi."

AS I WRITE THIS, my publisher and friend, Anthony Fasano, Host of The Italian American Podcast is working tirelessly to get this book to print on time as we wait anxiously for the big day: September 16, 2017. After nine months of deliberation, the National Park Service determined that a plaque honoring my grandfather will be unveiled at the mountain; the icing on a many layered cake of ups and downs over a 25 year period. It's almost here, and I feel like a little kid standing in front of the Christmas Tree at three in the morning, antsy in my pajamas, waiting for the sun to rise…

Even in the waiting there has been a lot of planning, a lot of doing and, yes, more waiting. Although Cam Sholly and his colleagues decided on further recognition in December 2015, a "memorial packet" had to be assembled and put through the grinders of Washington Bureaucracy for final approval. (Oh, boy. I have no more nails to bite.)

As the months crawled by, I finally received an email from Cam telling me that the memorial packet had just been signed. My heart soared. And then sunk with Cam's reminder that this was just the first in a series of signatures needed for final approval. What if we don't get all the signatures we need? What if during this little packet's journey through Washington, someone in the chain of command, in an office somewhere, refused to sign? Would all be lost? Would we have to start all over again? Cam cautiously assured me he was confident it would go through.

With each signed approval, we inched closer. The date tapped for the ceremony was June 24, 2017, providing our little packet received approval. This mysterious folder, traversing a bureaucratic obstacle course, had become like a new member of the family we all cheered for. I nervously waited on the sidelines, ready to call my family so they could book flights and hotels, only to be told by Cam that the NPS needed more time. This was far from Cam's fault; it was all part of the process. The ceremony had to be moved to the fall.

Sometime during the winter months of 2016, I got an email stating that our little packet got the final signature and made it to the finish line. It broke through the tape that was put up all those years ago. I remember jumping up and down in front of my computer like a little kid. As my grandfather would have said, *Finalmente!*

In a long telephone call with Cam, he revealed that he, too, was relieved that the process was over. It suddenly occurred to me that this National Park Service Administrator, out of Omaha, Nebraska not only believed in this story but had become emotionally involved. Cam Sholly will always be like a brother to me, and an honorary grandson of Luigi's.

So here we are. After going back and forth about the content on the plaque, the ceremony and myriad other details with Cam's wonderful assistant, Lauren Blacik, we wait for September 16th. The flights and hotels have been booked. Speakers and dignitaries are lining up. Notes of support from celebrities like Lidia Bastianich and Tony Bennett will be read throughout the ceremony. It's all coming together.

In just a few weeks, my big, bright and loud Italian family will descend upon Mount Rushmore. Camille will be by my side with my sisters and Gloria. Caesar will be there, too, I'm sure. And Luigi? He's been there all along. His spirit never left the mountain. I'm sure as Cam and I unveil that plaque, those long, sinewy arms will become young and strong again, helping us pull the sheet away as we change the historical record for good. For that "great, big Italian." For Grandpa.

Luigi's plaque as it will appear at Mount Rushmore.

GLORIA DEL BIANCO

MEMORIES OF MY FATHER...

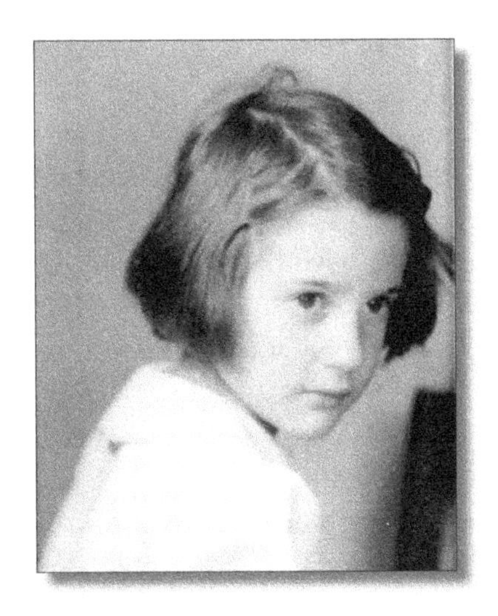

Gloria Del Bianco, the last surviving child of Luigi Del Bianco, at age 5.

MY PARENTS, LUIGI AND Nicoletta (Cardarelli) Del Bianco welcomed me into this world in March of 1946 in Port Chester, New York. I joined my three much older brothers, Silvio, Vincent and Caesar. I was named Gloria Theresa, my middle name after my sister who had passed at 4 years old from spinal meningitis. My mother was 44 and my father 54 when I was born at eight months, weighing only 5 pounds. I was nicknamed "Peanut" by the nurses at the hospital. Because I was so much younger than my brothers, my brother Caesar liked to say, "You weren't even a thought when Pa was working on the Mountain," as they referred to Mount Rushmore. My father had finished his work on Mount Rushmore years before I was born.

As I grew older, I would periodically hear about Mount Rushmore but never realized my father's significant contribution until I was in my 20s. As the years passed, and I learned more and more about my father, I could actually envision him high on the mountain carving and refining the figures. Even though many years have passed since then, I still have fond memories of my father and will try to recount as many as I can.

Let me start off by saying that I was the apple of my father's eye, and he was mine. My mother told me that when I was around 3 years old, my father would leave the house for an appointment for his stone carving business, and I would stand at the screen door crying and kicking the door after he left. She tried to explain that he had left on business and couldn't take me along. This didn't matter to me; I still cried and kicked, sometimes until he came home. When I was older, I was able to go with him a few times, and I was able to see how truly happy everyone was to have my father carve their relative's tomb stones as a remembrance of them. Many times, they would offer us traditional Italian food and wine for my father. Sometimes my father would give me a little glass of port wine, and I felt like a real grown-up!

When I was 3 or 4, I remember my father building the house we lived in on Clinton Street. I was not in school yet, so I got to hang out with him. He would ride me in the wheel barrel full of cement, and I loved it. After the house was finished, he had his studio in the garage in the back of the house. I used to go in there to see him doing his work. There was a long and very thick rubber belt, which gave his drill power to break up the stone he needed to carve. It was very loud and very scary to me. The studio had many of my father's sculpted works hanging and arranged on high benches. Busts of Teddy Roosevelt, Lindbergh, a mosaic of Lincoln and others filled the studio. There was a black potbelly stove with a pot on top where he would sometimes cook us breakfast or lunch. It was always a treat, and I can still see him stoking the fire and can smell the food cooking on that old stove. I loved being with my father during the times he was carving. In fact, my mother told me later on that my father wanted to sculpt a bust of me when I was young. Needless to say, I was a rambunctious kid and too impatient to sit for any length of time. I certainly regret that today.

My father helped me build a pigeon coop. It looked like a little house standing on legs with windows, a door and an opening on the top of the roof for the black and white pigeons. It was during this time I spent with my father and the pigeons that I noticed he had a scar on his right hand just above his pinky. He told me that there was still a bullet in his hand from when he was in the Italian Army and that an enemy soldier had shot him, but that he had fired back and shot the enemy. I'm not sure if he had made that story up, but I never questioned him again about the scar.

My father was always very caring, and I remember two times in particular when he was there for me. First, when I was about 4, I darted out in front of traffic and almost got hit by a car. My father scooped me up in his arms, and I cried until a police officer came over to us. My father put the policeman's hat on my head, and I stopped crying. Then, at around 10 years of age, I was climbing a tree in our yard when the trunk of the tree broke and down I came, hitting the ground hard. My father was there again for me, picking me up to make sure I was okay.

When I was around 11 or 12, my father caught me smoking. I didn't want anyone in the house to smell the smoke so I blew it out the upstairs window. It just so happened that my father, who had been in his studio working, walked into the back yard. He looked up just as I blew a big puff of smoke out the window. I heard this loud exclamation in Italian, and I knew I was in *big* trouble. He took me to the family doctor, who questioned me about smoking, and with my father sitting right there, I had to confess. Needless to say, I never smoked in the house again until I was much older. Then there were the boys who would come to the house to pick me up for a date. My father would stand there when the door opened, and then the boy would get the third degree.

"So, you like my daughter," my father would say very sternly in his broken English accent. "What time will you bring her home?"

Not waiting for my date to answer, he would add, "Be home by 11 PM, you understand?"

"Yes, sir, Mr. Del Bianco," and off we would go. I was embarrassed, but I knew he was protective of me because he loved me.

My father made me a ring from a stone, a beautiful agate, he had gotten from the Black Hills when he was at Mount Rushmore. He carved it into an opal shape, smoothed it to a glossy black and gray, and then set it in 18K gold. When I held it up to the sun, it appeared translucent. I wanted it for my 16th birthday to wear to my Sweet Sixteen party my parents were throwing for me at the YMCA, but he said I was too young and that I would have to wait. I remember that party like it was yesterday, my father in his handsome brown suit, my mother in a beautiful dress and all my friends, and of course, great food. When I later asked for the ring again, he said he couldn't find it and that one of my brothers must have found it and sold it. I was furious and had a big argument with all my brothers, who denied everything. When I finally reached 18, and my father thought I was old enough, he gave me the ring. It was stunning, and I was so proud to wear something so beautiful that my father had made. The stone came loose many years later, and I put it in a drawer in a little green basket with a top until I could get it repaired. I went to get the box from my drawer a few days later and it was gone. I looked everywhere but never found it.

There are many adjectives that describe my father: handsome, strong, intelligent, funny, creative, charismatic and kind, to name a few. But above all he was humble. He was very protective of me, and I believe this partly came from losing my sister, Teresa, when she was 4. He was a respected resident of Port Chester and walked through the town with his fedora on, tipping his hat to the people he met. Being from Northern Italy, he spoke beautiful Italian. My father was a charmer with the ladies, and he would tell them they were very pretty. They all loved that. I can remember a few of them giggling when he said it, especially my mother's friends who would come over to the house for coffee and whatever dessert my mother had to serve that day. Most of the time there were four to six women chatting away, and my father would come into the room to see who was there and what they were talking about. He had to put his two cents worth in, and they loved it.

My father was also very nurturing. I remember one time when I was sick with the flu; I had this terrible headache that went on for days. I would cry out to my parents and ask when the headache was going to go away. Every day when asked he would say, *No worry, very soon you feel better.* When I was little and it was very cold outside, my father would bring my mother and me coffee with a little whiskey in it to warm us up.

My father wasn't always perfect that's for sure. He could have a bad temper, and you certainly didn't want to be the cause of that anger. When my mother and him would have verbal fights, it was scary, but my mother, at 4'11", was never afraid of him and always stood up to him. When the fight had ended, they would talk and within a couple of hours, it was like nothing had ever happened. When I was bad, I remember both my parents chasing me through the house, and I would hide under the bed. Then the broom came out to shoo me from under the bed, my mother on one side and my father on the other. I knew at that point there was no way to escape.

Gloria and a bust of her Daddy.

Sundays at the Del Bianco's meant macaroni and meatballs. I remember my mother cooking the macaroni and making the meatballs, and my father helping her fry them. He would walk around whistling a tune from an opera, with a dishtowel tucked in his pants, stirring the gravy. I would grab a few raw seasoned meatballs to taste. My mother would yell at me not to take anymore, but they were so good. I can still smell those meatballs and gravy cooking. Everyone would gather in the kitchen after church on Sunday, talking and laughing and waiting for dinner. Once the food was prepared, we would all sit down at the kitchen table. There was laughter, discussions about one thing or another, Sinatra playing in the background, and great food. My father would always put grated cheese on his gravy and I would ask, "Daddy, why so much cheese?" He would answer, "Because I'm a rat." This would bring laughter from my three brothers, my mother and me.

It was at one of these Sunday dinners when I was around 10 that I learned my father was Chief Carver of Mount Rushmore. I remember my brother Caesar at the table holding up a photo of Rushmore and telling me, "Papa did this."

My father used to love to tease me by kissing my ear, which would make it ring, and I would yell at him to stop. He would just laugh. As I got older, he would sit at the dinner table, and I would get behind him and kiss his bald head and that would make him laugh. We were always teasing each other.

My father was also a great cook. He made the best risotto, stracciatella soup, and lentil soup. I think one of his favorite things he would make for himself was a raw egg that he would beat with warm milk and cornflakes in the morning. If he hadn't gotten silicosis, he would have probably lived a long time because he ate so healthy.

My father had a friend named Alfonso, who had a dog named Tiny. Alfonso would send me to the bungalow bar man, who came around selling ice cream from a truck, with enough money to get an ice cream for myself and one for Tiny. I loved it and so did Tiny. I remember Alfonso used to hunt, and I remember one time he came into our kitchen and threw a plastic bag on the floor. Inside was a skinned rabbit, and he announced he had brought it for "Lueeg." My mother promptly gave it to my father who cooked it and was the only one who ate it. My mother didn't want anything to do with it.

Alfonso was a stone mason. When he got sick and was on his deathbed, my father took me to his house and asked me to say hello and give him a hug. I did what my father asked me to but it was kind of scary for a kid because we knew he was dying. I knew it was important to my father, so I did as he asked to be respectful to his dying friend. It was a sad moment for me and one I have never forgotten. I am glad that my father taught me about this kind of compassion and respect.

He worked very hard as a carver. He had his own business carving grave stones and other statues in order to support his family. The weekends would roll around, and my father had a ritual. He and his friends would gather on the front porch and drink that good ole Gallo Wine! They would drink, talk and laugh until late into the night. I can still hear them if I close my eyes and listen carefully.

I remember my father sitting in a high back chair with the rest of us nearby, watching television. If an actor or a comedian came on that he didn't care for, he would abruptly stand up, say some choice words and leave the room. My father usually watched comedians; his favorites were Sid Caesar and Jackie Gleason. I once saw Sid Caesar when he was much older at a local restaurant here in Los Angeles, and I told him about how much my father enjoyed his work. He smiled and winked at me. My father went to bed early, and my mother and I would stay up with our snacks of pistachio nuts or candy bars and watch television together. Then my father would come back into the room after about an hour and want to know when we were going to bed. He couldn't sleep unless he knew everyone was in bed. My mother and I would put away our goodies and head to bed also.

I remember our family was watching "To Tell the Truth" in the 50's and one of the contestants was Lincoln Borglum, Gutzon Borglum's son. When the show was over, the phone started ringing off the hook. Family and friends were asking if we saw the show. My brother Caesar called New York City to talk to the station. He told them about my father and Lincoln and sure enough they got Lincoln on the line to speak to my father. They spoke for some time, and we all listened to my father's end of the conversation. They hadn't spoken for years, and I was always grateful to my brother Caesar for making that possible.

When I was around 16, my father had trouble breathing and was diagnosed with silicosis from the dust produced during his carvings. As it became harder for him to breathe, the doctor admitted him to the hospital. When he felt better, he would just dress and leave the hospital on his own. The administration department at the hospital would always know when he was admitted, but never knew when he left. The clerk would say, *Mr. Del Bianco just decided to leave. We're really not sure when he left but his bed is empty*, adding, *Mr. Del Bianco is such a nice man and very handsome.* The doctor was surprised that my father lived so long with his silicosis, but my brother Vincent said it was wine, women and song. He had a great spirit for life! The last job my father did before he sold the house was for a Mrs. Nighe from Rye, New York. She had a clay bust of her daughter that she had made and wanted my father to cast it for her and to tutor her. They worked together in the studio for a few months in the summer. My daddy did complete the work, but it ended up being his last.

Because of my daddy's influence in my life, I became stronger in dealing with life's challenges. He was a brave man. He faced many dangers in carving Mount Rushmore. This says a lot about how he dealt with other challenges in his life as well. From the loss of his daughter, Teresa, at such an early age through his health issues, he never complained. This has made me stronger and more disciplined in my life both in my artistic endeavors and my outlook on life in general. He is always here with me, and I am so proud of his accomplishment on Mount Rushmore. When I see the mountain and the beauty of the carvings, I say, *That was the work of Luigi Del Bianco, and Luigi Del Bianco is my daddy!*

LUIGI'S GRANDDAUGHTERS CHIME IN

"From the eyes of a child, my grandpa was an overpowering presence. He had chiseled majestic features and a distinctive twinkle in his eyes. I remember having lunch with him and my nana and going into the garage to look at all those statues. Of course, it was years before I understood how talented he truly was. Through my own Dad, I heard many stories in regard to Mount Rushmore. I could not be prouder of the long daunting task my Uncle Caesar and my brother Lou pursued to bring recognition to you, Grandpa! Oh, and what a smile he had."

—ANDREA DAUR

"As a child, I was always fascinated and afraid of Grandpa at the same time. His size was intimidating, but his soft spirit overpowered his stature. I spent many days in his garage just watching him do his handiwork, whether on a statue or the marble tile portrait of Abraham Lincoln. I remember walking around with a news article about him; none of my friends believed he was the Chief Carver so I had to show them proof! Who knew he was destined for greatness? I don't think he ever thought about being recognized for his talent, as he was busy just doing what he loved."

—LINDA DEL BIANCO

"As a young child, I remember going to his house for meals and remember the black and white mosaic portrait of Lincoln. Being so young, I didn't have the appreciation at that time for what he had accomplished in his life as a sculptor. Throughout my adult life, I was always proud to talk about his role on Mount Rushmore and enjoyed the reactions of others when they heard about it. My biggest thrill was to finally see the mountain when I met my family out there in 2005! I will always remember the feeling when I first saw it… indescribable!"

—NANCY HUDSON

"The weekly visits to my grandparents' house on Grant Street are my only memory of him. My grandmother was always at the kitchen counter or stove, and my grandfather sat on a mustard colored velour chair in the living room. I remember sitting on his lap one day and looking up at him while he spoke in broken English. The work my brother and uncle did to uncover the truth regarding his incredible talent, work ethic, and leadership has made us all very proud. We were always proud, but this recognition will establish the credibility and success he really deserves. This memory is the best memory in the world!"

—AMY DEL BIANCO

"I was 11 when my grandpa passed. I remember going there every Sunday for dinner, looking for the Mayfair cookie box on the washing machine and my Nana with her crystal blue eyes cooking at the stove. I was intimidated by my grandpa because of his height and strong roman features. He had a hole in his hand like Jesus Christ. Was my grandpa Jesus Christ, I thought? In his final months, we visited him in his bed. He would reach out with his huge hand and tap on the bed. Whenever I was going on vacation, my Dad would say, "When are you going to the mountain?" If I only knew then what I know now. Proud to be his granddaughter."

—MARIA DEL BIANCO

PROMINENT AMERICANS CONGRATULATE

LUIGI DEL BIANCO!

At the September 16, 2017 plaque unveiling at Mount Rushmore, famous Americans contributed some thoughts that were read at the ceremony. Below are some of our favorites:

"I loved discovering this immigrant story of Luigi Del Bianco, a master carver who brought Mount Rushmore to life with his artistry to make it one of the most recognizable man-made wonders of the world. There are so many immigrant stories of the men and women who built this great country and its fitting that artisans such as Luigi Del Bianco are recognized for their contributions."

— TONY BENNETT

"One of my grandsons and I recently drove from Texas to Mt. Rushmore so that he could see the monument for the first time. As he looked up to the shrine, his first words were 'what a tremendous amount of work.' Indeed. For too long, Luigi Del Bianco, the chief carver of Mt. Rushmore, was unheralded for his work. Now, we recognize him for the talent, dedication and hard work that he contributed to the making of what has become one of our national treasures."

— DAN RATHER

"Luigi Del Bianco. This extraordinary artist and meticulous craftsman was a Master stone carver...an Italian immigrant. We celebrate this long overdue recognition of his remarkable achievement of bringing stone faces to life on Mt. Rushmore."

— ALAN AND ARLENE ALDA

"As an Italian American, I feel immense pride in knowing that Luigi Del Bianco was chief carver of Mount Rushmore and that he will at long last be recognized. God bless his family for fighting so long and hard for his honor, it means so much to all Italian Americans!"

—LENA PRIMA
Daughter of Singer Louie Prima

Note: These quotes are not endorsements of this book, but of the story of Luigi Del Bianco and his work on Mount Rushmore.

ACKNOWLEDGMENTS

BECAUSE OF THE VERY nature of this story and the way I've written it, I have already had the opportunity to thank so many people who have helped me along the way. There are, however, some very key players that I want to acknowledge.

First, and foremost, I want to thank my publisher, Anthony Fasano, of Niche Content Corp., for reaching out to partner with me and help make this book a reality. I am forever grateful to Anthony for his vision, commitment and friendship. He is fast becoming a strong, positive voice in the Italian-American community, and we are lucky to have him leading the way.

I would like to thank my editor, Dolores Alfieri, for coming in at the last minute to steer the ship in the right direction. When I was feeling the crunch, Dolores lightly guided me with her expertise and did it with grace, enthusiasm and an infectious laugh that can make anyone smile.

Lastly, I want to thank my book designer James Woosley of Free Agent Press for his talent, expertise, and commitment to this project. He took my homemade manuscript and turned it into a work of art. Luigi would be impressed!

On a separate note, I want to thank Gloria Del Bianco for sharing such wonderful memories of her father. My aunt would like to thank her spouse, Kathi Del Bianco, for love, support and assistance in writing those memories.

Here are some wonderful people not mentioned in the book who gave selflessly to help me to tell this story:

> Lou Gallo, Matilda Cuomo, Sandra Gallo, Silvia and Marshall Toppo, Francis Polizio, Henry Varriano, Vinny Bell, Donna Cribari, Dana Rutson, Denise Colangelo, Mario Toglia, Michael Genovese, Toni Salvatore, Lou Truini, Richie Scafa, Gennaro Cardarelli, Gina Truini, Robin Borglum-Kennedy, Len Charney, Lou Magnan, Joe Stagneta, Marshall Toppo, Kathy and Paul Zaccagnino, Andrea Daur, Linda Del Bianco, Nancy Hudson, Maria Del Bianco, Amy Del Bianco, Sean Herbert, Taryn Grimes-Herbert, Lauren Blacik, Matt Wachsman, Jim Anderson, Carla Scacchi, Margherita Ganeri, Mauro Belvedere, Valentina Loreto, Roberto Giacobbo and the crew of RAI TV's "Voyager."

And all the people out there, too numerous to mention, who came to my lectures, cried for my Grandpa, hugged me and encouraged me to never give up. You impacted this story more than you'll ever know.

I would like to thank the following prominent Americans for their praise of Luigi and/or this book:

> Tony Bennett and his publicist Sylvia Weiner
> Dan Rather and his producer Phil Kim
> Alan and Arlene Alda
> Lidia Bastianich
> Douglas Brinkley
> T. Sean Herbert
> Daniel J. Longo of OSIA
> Lena Prima
> John Viola of NIAF

I would like to end by again thanking my wife and collaborator, Camille Linen. To say she is a big contributor to the success of this book would be an understatement. As Editorial Consultant, Camille helped me to shape the tone and structure of this special story in a way no one else could have. She has been my sounding board for many of the creative decisions I've had to make throughout this whole process. When the love of your life is also your artistic partner, you thank the great spirit for such a gift. I love you, Camille. I know Luigi does, too.

ABOUT THE AUTHOR

Photo by Mike Pierro of Vita Studios.

LOU DEL BIANCO HAS been an actor, singer and storyteller for 30 years. His children's recordings, which include original stories and songs of his childhood, have garnered five Parents Choice Awards.

Lou's latest one-man shows feature dramatic portraits of Abraham Lincoln, and Lou's grandfather, Luigi Del Bianco, Chief Carver on Mount Rushmore. "Abraham Lincoln: From Railsplitter to President" was endorsed by the Lincoln Bicentennial Commission, and "In the Shadow of the Mountain" has been performed at Mount Rushmore.

Out of Rushmore's Shadow was written at the bequest of National Park historians and is Lou's first non-fiction book. He has also co-authored a young readers' historical novel and a screenplay about the carving of Mount Rushmore. He and his wife, Camille Linen, live in Port Chester, N.Y.

LEARN MORE AT

LuigiMountRushmore.com

CPSIA information can be obtained
at www.ICGtesting.com
Printed in the USA
BVHW072118281220
596592BV00009B/163